"Skillfully written and expertly explained, yet practical every step of the way. A must for businesses, healthcare workers, recruiters, and anyone seeking a truly fresh perspective on cognitive diversity and the singular value proposition of authentic neuroinclusion."

—Denise Brodey
Senior Contributor, Forbes

"*The Neurodiversity Edge* is an absolutely transformative work, especially timely given the seismic shifts confronting today's organizations. As a serial entrepreneur and educator, I have witnessed firsthand the power of Dr. Dunne's pioneering frameworks in action within enterprises. Deeply rooted in rigorous research and enriched by practical insights from real-world implementations, this guide offers invaluable strategies for fostering inclusive environments that leverage the unique strengths of all individuals."

—Shailu Tipparaju
Co-Founder, Examity, 4x Exits,
Venture Fund Partner, Emerge Education

"If you're looking to enhance and leverage the diversity within your organization, then Dr. Maureen Dunne's groundbreaking guide is the book for you! *The Neurodiversity Edge* clearly and concisely explains how to cultivate an organizational culture that embraces the full spectrum of neuro-diversity, and it does so using state-of-the-art cognitive science research, real-life anecdotes, and in-depth case studies. The practical and easily understandable tools it provides will help you ensure the inclusion and prosperity of people with cognitive differences, which will benefit both them and your organization. Innovative and accessible, the guide offers a comprehensive strategy for tapping into the vital resource that is cognitive diversity and building an organizational future where every mind is recognized as a valuable asset."

—Erin Britton
San Francisco Book Review

"This is the right book at precisely the right time. Our business, social, political, and environmental problems are increasingly complex. The traditional solutions, linear thinking, and consensual decision making that landed us here are woefully insufficient to create successful, socially responsible, and profitable social systems and organizations for the future. This text should be considered required reading for business management, human resource, and social science courses."

—Therese Fitzpatrick, PhD
Senior Vice President, Kaufman Hall

"Maureen Dunne dismantles the stereotypes that surround neurodivergent people and makes a powerful business case for true inclusion. *The Neurodiversity Edge* is an eye-opening read. It is also a practical manual for change."

—Caroline Grossman
Executive Director, Rustandy Center for Social Sector Innovation, the University of Chicago Booth School of Business

"An original and inspiring game-changer for neurodiversity employment today. In this book, Dr. Dunne makes a thoroughly compelling case for neurodiversity as a competitive advantage and does so with rare depth and insight. She also provides practical advice to companies for utilizing this competitive advantage. It is a book that speaks both to members of the neurodiverse community and to employers who will hire them."

—Michael Bernick
Former Director, California State Labor Department.

"An epiphany. It will open your eyes to the most underappreciated human resources opportunity of our time. A tour de force bursting with wit, humor, and rare insight while establishing a coherent framework of actionable strategies. An indispensable resource for businesses, government agencies, and other organizations eager to get ahead of the curve and the competition by proactively embracing cognitive diversity."

—Christopher Kennedy, PhD
Senior Economist, U.S. Department of State

THE
NEURODIVERSITY
EDGE

MAUREEN DUNNE

THE
NEURODIVERSITY
EDGE

THE **ESSENTIAL GUIDE** TO
EMBRACING **AUTISM, ADHD, DYSLEXIA,**
AND **OTHER NEUROLOGICAL DIFFERENCES**
FOR ANY ORGANIZATION

WILEY

For general information on our other products and services or for technical support, please contact our Customer Care Department within the United States at (800) 762-2974, outside the United States at (317) 572-3993 or fax (317) 572-4002.

Wiley also publishes its books in a variety of electronic formats. Some content that appears in print may not be available in electronic formats. For more information about Wiley products, visit our web site at www.wiley.com.

Library of Congress Cataloging-in-Publication Data is Available:

ISBN: 9781394199280 (cloth)
ISBN: 9781394199297 (ePub)
ISBN: 9781394199303 (ePDF)

Cover Design: Wiley
Cover Images: © Lucky Team Studio/Shutterstock; © Arlenta Apostrophe /Adobe Stock

SKY10064710_011524

*for the pathfinders and those who empower them to discover the
space where we each can belong*

Contents

Introduction

"Not at all silly," said I, losing my temper; "here for example, I take this Square," and, at the word, I grasped a moveable Square, which was lying at hand—"and I move it, you see, not Northward but—yes, I move it Upward—that is to say, not Northward, but I move it somewhere—not exactly like this, but somehow—" Here I brought my sentence to an inane conclusion, shaking the Square about in a purposeless manner, much to the amusement of my Grandson, who burst out laughing louder than ever, and declared that I was not teaching him, but joking with him; and so saying he unlocked the door and ran out of the room. Thus ended my first attempt to convert a pupil to the Gospel of Three Dimensions.

—Edwin A. Abbott, from *Flatland*, 1884[1]

The genius of Edwin Abbott's classic, *Flatland: A Romance of Many Dimensions* (1884), lies in how it constructs a universe that allows the reader to effortlessly awaken to the sense that we are constantly surrounded by solution pathways we are unable to perceive—or capitalize on—without access to new concepts outside our comfort zone or sphere of awareness.

Flatland injects the reader into the everyday household, economic, social, and political life of beings inhabiting a world bounded by just two spatial dimensions. We witness their trials, tribulations, and triumphs in entirely familiar terms and recognizable scenarios.

But all of it happens in a world with only length and width—the Z-axis is every bit as alien to them as a fourth spatial dimension would be to us.

Abbott transports us across dimensional layers, first visiting the claustrophobic reality of one-dimensional life before being swept up into the mind-bending expanse of three-dimensional space. This is a great narrative trick, and it hits home.

As three-dimensional readers, we frown in bewilderment at the hapless Flatlanders and their failure to spot the N+1 spatial axis. If only they could see that new direction, we think as readers, they would have access to so many new possibilities. In the same breath, we are left with an almost urgent revelation that we might be in the same boat—surrounded by new directions and opportunities if only we could see perpendicularly to our familiar frame of reference.

Why are we starting with a Flatland metaphor? The short answer is that one of the defining premises of this book is that cognitive diversity is an N+1 axis for organizational culture. The long answer is the rest of this book.

This isn't a low-stakes game, either. To meddle with society's underlying neurodiversity zeitgeist is to meddle with the lives of perhaps about one of every five people on the planet. In fact, the numbers may even be much greater than that and growing at an unprecedented rate.

The results of a recent study by ZenBusiness showed that about half of the members of Generation Z (born between 1997 and 2012) identify with the neurodivergent umbrella. Twenty-two percent said they were "definitely neurodivergent" and 31% reported they were "somewhat neurodivergent." The study was based on a survey that collected responses from 1,000 young adults between the ages of 18–25.[2] Another study by Tallo reported that the vast majority of Gen Z job seekers (80%) would prefer to work for a company that supports neurodivergent people.[3]

This book is not your standard guidebook. There are plenty of practical tips, strategies, and actionable frameworks. But this is also a guide in a broader sense. Foreign travel often helps to foster respect, appreciation, and empathy for different customs and unfamiliar ways of tackling the mundane demands of everyday life. In that spirit, through first-hand accounts, anecdotes, thought experiments, unique explanatory devices, and case studies, this book endeavors to foster respect, appreciation, and empathy for the rich tapestry of human neurodiversity.

My hope is that, by the end of this book, you will not only be armed with valuable new tools but also feel that you have traveled on a journey that leaves you with a deep appreciation for all kinds of minds.

Ground Rules

The concept of "neurodiversity" has many different interpretations, definitions, and manifestations. But all of them roughly overlap around the central premise that neurodivergent people—such as the autistic, ADHDers, the dyslexic, the dyspraxic, synesthetes, the hyperlexic, the dyscalculic, and those identifying with other cognitive differences—deserve to be valued and seen as members of the natural spectrum of human cognitive diversity. A strengths-based lens helps manifest this value and guide others to see that neurodivergent people are just people with unique strengths and challenges.

I use "neurodivergent" in a manner that reflects the current best-supported scientific framework, which means that the degree of neurodivergence in any one individual is independent of any ideas about cognitive ability, intelligence, knowledge, or aptitude.

In other words, if I told you I planned to introduce you to someone tomorrow, and I further informed you that this person has been diagnosed with ADHD, or identifies with an emerging term called VAST (variable attention stimulus trait), you would have no basis to extrapolate that fact into any preconceptions about that person's intellectual capabilities, general knowledge, or capacity to success- fully perform any given task or role.

Put another way, intellectual capability is entirely independent of the presence or absence of a neurodivergent cognitive profile. An autistic person may, for example, be either highly intellectually gifted or have an intellectual disability, or fall anywhere in between, just like any person. The same can be said of ADHDers or the dyslexic, or, for that matter, those with blue eyes or left-handedness or perfect pitch or dark hair or an anxiety disorder or a cleft palate.

This is a very important point to acknowledge at the outset.

In addition, as I use the terms here throughout, an individual can be either neurodivergent or neurotypical but not neurodiverse. Only a group of multiple individuals can be neurodiverse and only if it is populated by both neurodivergent and neurotypical members. I use the terms "neuroinclusion" and authentic neurodiversity inclu- sion interchangeably. A terminology resource guide appears in the Appendix for easy access to definitions and explanations of con- cepts, cognitive typologies, and terms used throughout this book.

The legacy framework for understanding neurodivergent people is generally known as the deficit-based perspective, or the medical- deficit model, which still dominates how most people view neurodi- vergence at all levels of culture today. According to this model, any given person is either neurotypical or dysfunctional. For decades, this framework has formed the basis for how we evaluate students, employees, parents, children, active community members, artists, public intellectuals, next-door neighbors, and everyone else.

The deficit-based perspective is a colored lens through which most of us have viewed cognitive differences all our lives, and the collective experience of that reality has sown hidden, deep-seated biases that are not only counterproductive to organizational outcomes but also run contrary to a growing body of research, as we will cover in the chapters ahead.

Levels of support needs are as varied and diverse as neurodi-vergent people themselves. Some people identify as disabled while others identify as simply being wired differently. I believe that a strength-based approach empowers everyone to reach their full potential but does not imply that support and accommodations are not needed or important. Nor does a strength-based perspective change any legal obligations such as those defined by the Ameri-cans with Disabilities Act (ADA). As emphasized in the Pyramid of Neuroinclusion introduced in chapter 5, a culture of psychological safety, trust, transparent communication, support, work adaptations, and empathy is essential for all to thrive.

Possibly, the most important shortcoming of the pure medical-deficit perspective is that it orients us, by default, toward a set of standards inextricably tied to seeing neurotypical cognitive profiles as inherently more valuable or more acceptable than neurodivergent profiles without an appreciation of the rich diversity of gifts and talents that often go hand in hand with neurodivergent cognition.

It's a bit like the hidden, deep-seated bias we all share about understanding the Earth from a north-is-up assumption. There's no fundamental reason to place north as the central orienting direction when viewing a map or globe. More to the point, there are plenty of times when seeing the world "upside down" can offer important insights about the layout of the planet. Yet we all end up feeling a bit uncomfortable looking at a map until we turn it so that north points up.

The net result is the habitual pattern, in most of the business world, to define workplace rules, performance assessments, and hir-ing practices by a set of standards that, at root, are ultimately just about turning our perception map until neurotypical "points up."

From this perspective, "different" equals "deficient." That puts neurodivergent people at an instant and unfair disadvantage: unfair to neurodivergent employees who are cast aside despite having applicable skills and motivation, and unfair to the organization's other employees—as well as to customers, partners, and shareholders.

In short, it's a lose-lose framework for two reasons: first, it blinds us to the untapped substantive value to be reaped from hardworking, motivated, skilled and possibly uniquely talented people traveling through life with a cognitive profile compass that doesn't orient toward neurotypical; and second, because that mentality fosters a game-theoretic landscape that incentivizes everyone to try to appear neurotypical, forcing millions of talented people to literally waste their lives away in a likely futile acting audition when they could just be themselves instead and possibly help us solve real problems.

To return to the Flatland metaphor, the pure deficit-based perspective forces us to live trapped in two dimensions, oblivious to the N+1 axis of cognitive diversity—invisible, yet all around us, ready to be tapped to help us escape an unnecessarily bounded and limiting way of understanding people, teams, and skills.

The Crux of the Matter

One in every five people you see each day may be living in a world defined by systematic and counterproductive exclusion from the opportunity to productively contribute to society. In terms of human capital potential, this is a devastating failure. Morally, it's a plague of injustice.

Countless contributions are being forsaken that might otherwise add value to all our lives and, in the same breath, offer millions of talented but sidelined people—our siblings, parents, children, and spouses—a path toward genuine actualization.

Through a social infrastructure of customs, linguistic conventions, habits, assumptions, rules, social scripts, traditions, institutional protocols, technology, and cultural legacy effects, we produce "society" every day—in our schools, at our workplaces, at social events, and in our households.

Occasionally, we become collectively aware of something amiss in the fabric of that process. And sometimes such an awareness crystallizes enough to force a paradigm shift—the revelation that we have been looking at some specific and important dynamic all wrong and to our distinct collective practical and moral detriment. Hopefully, the strength of such a crystallization of awareness will be strong enough to propel us collectively on to a different path aligned with an alternative framework.

In essence, there's a vast gulf between (1) being willing to hire token neurodivergent people and provide them access to cosmetic accommodations as part of a PR agenda and (2) genuinely understanding and embracing authentic neurodiversity inclusion as a powerful long-term strategy for organizational success.

Neurodivergent people perceive the world differently when compared to their neurotypical peers, but we also diverge from each other. We each take in unique details, hold distinct assumptions, create new patterns and frameworks to view a problem, and, ultimately, offer different solutions.

One key axis of reasoning in this book is that these types of differences are inherently valuable. Different perceptual tendencies and different ways of forming conclusions add to the diversity of thought available to any group of people, whether it's a community, an organization, a small company, or any other social context where a bunch of people have come together to make things work for each other.

The ideas and methods considered when making important decisions within an organization are narrowed when everyone on a team is highly cognitively correlated. That narrow band of cognitive and experiential tendencies can present risks and undermine the upside. Under such conditions, creativity and innovation can be stunted, and potentially catastrophic risks and vulnerabilities are more likely to go undetected.

In addition, divergent thinking broadly correlates with increased innovation. We will cover the research as we go, but the basic premise shouldn't be all that controversial: most instances of innovation involve thinking about something in a new or unconventional way.

While I will be clear from the start that this book does not purport to speak for all neurodivergent people, I have found that many neurodivergent people across typologies are gifted lateral and nonlinear thinkers in some form. Yet, most of our shared everyday communal world is linear—built by linear thinkers for linear thinkers—creating a natural friction.

As a result, there are many examples of neurodivergent trailblazers who have put an indelible stamp on our shared history. We can say for certain with some, such as Sir Richard Branson, Elon Musk, Tori Amos, and Dan Akroyd, to name a few, because they have publicly disclosed their neurodivergence. Many historical figures have also been widely speculated about in terms of potential neurodivergence due to recorded observations of behavior patterns that fit with this notion, including Benjamin Franklin, Albert Einstein, Winston Churchill, Thomas Edison, Leonardo da Vinci, Andy Warhol, Woodrow Wilson, and Thomas Jefferson. Naturally, we will never know for certain.

However, and this really gets to the crux of the matter, neurodivergence aligns with other outlier lists as well—lists that are hard to reconcile with each other: it turns out that neurodivergent people may be reflected disproportionately on the "Nobel Prize winners" list while also being disproportionately present on the "currently or formerly incarcerated" list, the "unemployed or underemployed" list, and the "suicide risk" list.

One of the central questions I will explore in this book is the following: How can neurodivergent people be responsible for a disproportionate share of our important innovations while most are so strikingly left out of the economy or on the margins of society?

The answer, as we will see, has a great deal to do with built-in biases. For example, a 2020 survey of UK employers revealed that a shocking 50% openly admitted that they would not hire a neurodivergent job seeker.[4]

Society has institutionalized standards for elements such as job interviews, evaluations, and everyday office politics. And this averaging dynamic for social scripts imposes clearly identifiable biases that work against people with minds that don't sync up well with standard expectations for how people "ought" to think, act, and strategize. The chapters to follow will target and expose these unproductive biases.

I'll also explain why the neurodiversity paradigm, and its mission, can and should be couched within an actionable framework for diversity, equity, and inclusion (DEI). A culture of appreciation and belonging for cognitive diversity—a diversity of thought and of ways of thinking—is just as valuable to organizational and societal success as are other forms of diversity typically included in the continuously evolving DEI context.

At the end of the day, we face a critical choice about the type of world we want to live in.

We can live in a world where millions of uniquely talented but quirky people are left to suffer massive underemployment and ostracism, while masking who they really are, and perhaps getting by through government assistance. Or we can proactively support the actualization of human potential for everyone, reaping the benefits of a wellspring of creativity and new perspectives that could open the door to untold future innovations, better hedging against groupthink, and the knowledge that millions of would-be outcasts have been accepted into the fold, finding a productive and self-affirming place in the fabric of our culture and economy.

This book argues for the latter case.

It also argues that authentic neurodiversity inclusion is an ascendant concept in our culture, meaning that most organizations will likely adopt some version of this principle over coming years—whether by proactive choice for maximum value or through reactive and grudging late-adopter acquiescence to some form of social or regulatory pressure.

These two arguments for embracing authentic neurodiversity inclusion are both important and compelling. Authentic neurodiversity inclusion is (1) an unambiguous moral and ethical social value and (2) probably inevitable for most organizations in the long run in any case, whether by choice on your terms or by pressure on someone else's.

However, this book will concern itself most with arguing the point from yet another direction: authentic neurodiversity inclusion is a critical organizational value. If properly implemented, it offers a competitive advantage for any business by expanding the breadth of cognitive resources available for innovation, creativity, group decision-making, strategy, motivation, and loyalty, as well as massively increasing the pool of available talent by connecting innovative organizations with skilled people eager for a chance to contribute.

A Mystery Story

How is it possible that an identifiable and definable group could be both obviously valuable and undeniably excluded? Part II dives deeper into this mystery and offers a framework to reverse course and strengthen organizational culture from the bottom-up. But there's an important point to be made at the outset: deepening the mystery—because it will become relevant for how firms react to awareness of the first mystery and its origins—how is this group not currently an explicit part of diversity, equity, and inclusion (DEI) organizational frameworks?

This question, in turn, raises other questions as well: What do we really mean by "DEI"? Is the goal to put our finger on the scale enough to weigh simultaneously and materially in favor of moral justice and economic functionality? If so, how are we not including in DEI organizational goals a specific and identifiable contingent of society that has clearly been discriminated against in terms of appropriate employment opportunities despite mounting evidence of its potential to offer productivity and workforce value?

Make no mistake, a culture of belonging is an important part of this story, especially given the crucial importance of intersectionality among the neurodivergent.

It has been well established in prior research—as we will see along the way—that firms genuinely invested in improved inclusivity metrics, more broadly defined, have been shown to increase financial returns and productivity while also serving a valuable public moral imperative and reaping rewards in reputational value (especially those first into the breach).

Companies with more diverse management teams demonstrate, on average, 19% higher revenues due to increased innovation and 9% higher margins.[5]

The mechanism behind that data appears to be linked to the relationship between diversity in background and diversity in perspective. In other words, groups with a wider range of lived experiences tend to bring to the table a wider range of available ideas. That expands the menu of available ideas in discussion during problem solving, planning, and other strategic activities.

Traditional diversity theory argues that diversity among those involved in corporate strategy discussions provides a hedge against the perils of groupthink. Neurodiversity may be just as powerful an asset. Neurodiversity represents a different way of thinking, and there is an inherent value to being different. A team of neurotypical people, no matter how smart or well-educated, is subject to the twin risks of missing new opportunities and ignoring unrecognized threats.

The scales have tipped: the future is likely going to belong to organizations that manage to accommodate cognitive diversity proactively rather than those that fail to confront the issue, hiding behind claims of a lack of expertise. We need unique problem solvers more than ever, especially considering that we are at an inflection point of accelerating change due to the integration of artificial intelligence into nearly every aspect of our daily lives. Skills of the future, such as lateral thinking, systems thinking, visual-spatial thinking, creativity, and hyperfocus, can often be found in neurodivergent populations where employers have not been looking—or where standardized hiring processes have historically sidelined such talent from consideration. The path from here, with respect to including neurodiversity at all levels of the business economy, is about *how*, rather than *if, why*, or *whether*.

The winners will be organizations that manage to weed out implicit biases from interviews and hiring practices and effectively integrate and retain a talent pool made up of all kinds of minds. Many corporate giants such as Ernst & Young, Google, Ford, JPMorgan, Microsoft, SAP, and Wells Fargo have been underscoring the numerous gifts that neurodivergent workers offer employers in recent years.

This perspective carries with it an implicit moral imperative driven by the simple fact that the neurodiversity community represents a huge piece of our society; according to some estimates, 50 to 60 million Americans identify as neurodivergent, and the percentage is even higher in many countries around the world.[6]

If we have the choice to take a step that stands to offer more opportunities to more people and at the same time drive greater innovation and productivity throughout the economy, is that a difficult choice?

Do we prefer a world where a fifth or more of our population is left out of the equation, relegated to an artificial second-tier status, structurally unable to actualize their potential? Or one that values all individuals fairly for the skills and talents each of us uniquely possesses? Wouldn't we all prefer to live in a world where the seeming misfit segments of our collective whole find a suitable home in the evolving twenty-first-century economy?

In the marketplace for labor, the neurodivergent and our many talents have been historically undervalued—and, due to unprecedented changes in the role technology stands to play in our economy over coming years and likely decades, we appear destined to need unique minds more than ever.

The Organizing Premise

This book is the result of more than 20 years of research, interviews, in-depth discussions, and organization client relationships, as well as my own lived experiences as an entrepreneur, board director, social impact investor, researcher, executive, and consultant.

My aim here is to convince you that authentic neurodiversity inclusion is not only an essential ideal for every organization, and a strong competitive advantage for first movers for very specific, compelling, and evidence-based reasons but also that it is an ideal only accessible to organizations willing to commit to deep work at the very foundations of organizational culture.

There are neurodiversity-at-work-type guides and playbooks out there full of useful tips for managing neurodivergent employees. These are important, but without working on organizational culture at the DNA level, I have found over many years of close observation that such approaches are akin to a fad diet plan—you will lose 10 pounds in two months, but fast-forward another six months, and you're right back where you started. Improving an unhealthy weight situation on a sustained basis is about much more than being told too many carbs are a problem. It's about relationships, family life, deeply ingrained habits, financial stress, sleep disorders, feeling valued, and potentially many more variables that are all part of a deeper overall problem where unhealthy and unwanted weight gain is just one superficial symptom. You aren't going to catalyze lasting change with only a new fad diet handbook filled with tricks for losing pounds fast. It may drive short-term gains toward a desired outcome but nothing more.

In much the same way, organizations aren't going to gain access on a sustained basis to the fruits of authentic neurodiversity inclusion—a significantly wider pool of talent, a massive expansion in diversity of thought and lived experience, creativity, loyalty, and groupthink immunity, among other dynamics—without embedding a deeper values-driven approach.

In other words, the path I am offering here is not a superficial makeover or even cosmetic surgery. This is gene therapy. To work, this must be a change at the DNA level of an organization's culture because, as a core value, it permeates every facet of every department at every organizational level, from the mail room to the boardroom.

Luckily, that doesn't make it any harder as a path. It just implies a different focus—a focus not on maintaining a list of accommodative practices for the quirky people at the office but, instead, a focus on transporting the entire organization from one world where there are quirky people with special needs and normal people without them to a different world, where there exists a wide range of types of people and a system of universal accommodation that works for everyone—a world where the broadest possible range of cognitive diversity is celebrated as an asset.

Part I will answer the question: *Why* should an organization be interested in authentic neuroinclusion and belonging? This will span technology, innovation, cognitive diversity, labor supply, and public brand and reputation factors, which are all significant and well established in this field. We examine cognitive strengths with a more in-depth focus on embracing autism, ADHD, dyslexia, synesthesia and other cognitive profiles.

Now armed with the sense that authentic neurodiversity inclusion is a crucial value to embrace, Part II focuses on answering the question: *What* should an organization do to manifest that value? We will cover the goal of a durable and authentic culture of neurodiversity inclusion among all tiers of an organization by introducing The Pyramid of Neuroinclusion, which forms the conceptual basis for an actionable framework to help formulate and achieve objectives aligned with this core value. Psychological safety and trust is introduced as the bedrock of an inclusive, thriving organizational culture. From there, teams can benefit from diversity and flourish with a focus on inspiring transparent intraorganizational communication, accessible workplace supports, universal design principles, and an empathy infrastructure to bridge gaps in shared experiences.

Finally, Part III will answer the question: *How* can an organization set about achieving the objectives implied by the Pyramid of Neuroinclusion in terms of strategies and tactics? This is where we drill down further, adding nuance to our discussion of universal design, recruitment processes, hiring decisions, workplace support, and employee retention to build a thriving organizational culture with inclusivity as a core value. This will also be augmented by exclusive access to indispensable tools and resources found in the Appendix and on the book's companion website (www.TheNeurodiversityEdge.com), which has been designed to aid in implementation and management of the process.

Part I

Why

Chapter 1

A Tale of Two Worlds

"Change the way you look at things and the things you look at change."

—Wayne W. Dyer

As a very simple visual metaphor, imagine a performance line representing an individual's skillset across a variety of domains. It goes wildly up and down, representing powerful skills in math, poor performance in debate, all-star status in statistics and logic, and abysmal proficiency at retention of historical models. Now add another individual with a performance line that's mostly a mirror image of the first. It peaks where the other troughs and vice versa. Finally, let's add two more individuals to this group, each with performance lines that peak and trough at still different points. Together, the four individuals make up a diversified portfolio of cognitive profiles with very different strengths and weaknesses.

Now, let's imagine four new candidates. In this second group, all members have very similar performance lines: they all score "pretty good," "average," or "slightly below or above average" at every skill—none extraordinarily good or terribly bad at anything.

Which group of four should you hire?

The painfully obvious answer is both! Just as painfully obvious is the notion that either one, without the other, would contain the seeds of its own destruction in the context of a competitive market

economy facing rapid evolutionary and revolutionary transformations ahead. It is through the complementarity of different cognitive
profiles, working together, that we arrive at the optimal configuration. And, naturally, evolution got there before us.

It turns out that some researchers now believe certain beehives
have a minority cohort that behaviorally diverges from the rest of
the hive in terms of responding to honeybees' most important social
phenomenon: the waggle dance—a figure-eight dance performed to
share information with other members of the colony about the direction and distance to patches of flowers yielding nectar and pollen, to
water sources, or to new nest-site locations.

Some researchers believe that about one-fifth of the bees in a
honeybee hive ignore waggle dance instructions, instead flying off
in apparently random directions, while the other 80% of the bees
in the hive follow instructions effectively and pursue the endorsed
objective.[1]

I am not in any way suggesting that neurodivergent individuals are comparable to non-waggle-dance-following bees. However,
the example points out something important about the difference
between thinking about individual-level traits versus thinking about
community-level traits.

Through the lens of a deficit-based perspective, those divergent
bees are failures because they won't or can't behave according to the
standard expectations for proper bee behavior. However, it turns out
that divergent bees appear to be a significant strategic asset for honeybee hives. The divergent cohort of the hive bucks the norms, charts
a new course, and widens the scope of the hive's territorial reconnais-
sance operations and its behavioral matrix. At the end of the day, this
divergent minority appears to account for a disproportionate share of
new pollen discoveries, helping the whole community thrive.

In other words, the whole of the hive community is a complex system. Analyzing each member with only an appreciation for

differences according to individual-level standards obscures value at the system level.

The deficit-based perspective sees a group of five bees. It recognizes four of them with gold stars for successfully fitting in. And it bemoans the other one—the misfit—who has totally failed according to established protocols and standards of bee conduct.

But the strength-based perspective sees a completely different picture: "divergent-inclusive hives," at some point in the evolutionary past, decisively outperformed "divergent-unfriendly hives" in a Darwinian scramble for dominance. And this victory came not despite, but precisely because of, the behavior of the divergent cohort in the hive.

In other words, at the community level (or at the organizational level), including individuals with divergent traits produces powerful value that would be unattainable through any other configuration. The challenge is being able to implement that community-level realization in the course of individual-level relationships and management within the fabric of a thriving organizational culture.

What I have couched as a "community-level dynamic" can, in fact, be discussed in more rigorous evolutionary terms.

Many of the neurodivergent cognitive typologies we discuss in this book are believed to have a hereditary basis in genetics. Given that, there's plenty of room to build a theoretical foundation for explaining the universality, persistence, and pervasiveness of neurodivergence displayed in human populations across both geography and time in terms of community-level fitness.

One theoretical framework that has been developed toward precisely this objective is the theory of "complementary cognition," which asserts that successful adaptation in humans arises from collaboration between individual members who are specialized in different but complementary neurocognitive search strategies.[2]

Essentially, the theory proposes that human cognition evolved to be in-group complementary in order to promote cooperation and improve group performance.

Complementary cognition proposes that humans evolved to specialize in different, but complementary, cognitive strategies, or "ways of thinking." This specialization is thought to have arisen as a way of coping with the challenges of living in a complex and ever-changing environment.

There is evidence to support the theory of complementary cognition from a number of different sources. For example, studies have shown that humans have different cognitive strengths and weaknesses. Some people are better at spatial reasoning, while others are better at verbal reasoning. Some people are better at thinking outside the box, while others are better at following rules.

These different cognitive strengths and weaknesses are thought to be the result of natural selection. Over time, individuals who were better at thinking in certain ways that were complementary with the distribution of cognitive strengths across the community were more likely to survive and reproduce. This led to the evolution of a population of humans with a wide range of cognitive abilities.

Complimentary cognition holds important implications for our understanding of the factors involved in organizational success. For example, it suggests that we should not expect everyone to think the same way and that this diversity in cognitive strategies presents advantages capable of supporting the success of the wider community. We should also be aware that our own cognitive strengths and weaknesses may lead us to have different perspectives on the world.

Once again, this view returns us to the pitfalls we face when considering our appraisal of individual-level cognitive strengths and weaknesses and how that appraisal may be in conflict with the reality of team dynamics and what drives the performance of any given group of humans when viewed at a community level.

Complimentary cognition is still a relatively new idea, but it has the potential to revolutionize our understanding of human behavior. This theory was developed to help explain cognitive differences associated with developmental dyslexia by providing the theoretical understanding of why "search specialization" is likely to have evolved as well as its significance for understanding human adaptation and cultural evolution.

But such a framework could just as easily be applied to autism or ADHD, which present potential complementarity implications for the performance of human groups at a community level.

The big takeaway from a complementary cognition interpretation of neurodiversity is the idea that, in our environment of evolutionary adaptation (roughly, sub-Saharan Africa, tens of thousands of years ago), not everyone could find a meaningful route to social—and thus, reproductive—success by being a perfect neurotypical subject: great at toeing the line, acting within the boundaries of social scripts, and quickly picking up commonly needed skills.

There would have been a small but not insignificant route to social and reproductive success for people built to buck the main road and march to the beat of their own drums, exploring different ideas and different ways of living, perhaps being impulsive or constantly finding new and different ways of solving problems.

Some percentage of these neurodivergent members of the community would strike gold in some way, providing some outsized value to the community and gaining status and social capital as a result. Not only would this dynamic maintain the genotypic and phenotypic pervasiveness of neurodivergent traits within a given community, but it would also confer an advantage to communities that accepted and included such individuals over communities that shunned and excluded them. Over time, extrapolation of this evolutionary game-theoretic landscape results in the world we see around us today in terms of population genetics and community-level distributions of cognitive strategies.

Sadly, the same cannot be said of the corporate landscape, where we see a heavy skew toward neurotypicals when compared to the broad population.

At its core, complementary cognition strongly suggests that human cognition evolved to be complementary in order to promote cooperation and improve group performance. The theory points to the potential that, by recognizing and leveraging complementary cognitive abilities, groups can enhance their problem-solving and decision-making capabilities, leading to better outcomes. After all, communities with a stable abundance of neurodiversity are more effective over time than communities that exclude neurodivergent individuals.

There is even a line of reasoning that suggests this complementarity extends to communities that will likely soon come to include artificial intelligence. As large language models such as Google's Bard or OpenAI's ChatGPT have demonstrated, an incredible amount of extrapolation, analysis, and linguistic modeling can be automated. But the gap in their conceptual coverage map is likely to be found in the territory of nonlinear thinking—in what we might call "intuitive leaps of insight"—that might otherwise go unexplored.

Yet, employers are still, by and large, reluctant to embrace authentic neuroinclusion. This is a central paradox motivating this book.

As a final note, this argument is not meant to suggest that only forms of neurodiversity with some genetic basis can play a productive role as complementary pieces augmenting the functionality of a community. There is every reason to believe that the evolutionary data simply demonstrate that cognitive diversity in all forms is a value-added dynamic at the community level.

Neurodiversity World 2.0

Today, we live in Neurodiversity World 1.0. But the future belongs to Neurodiversity World 2.0.

In 1.0, the vast majority of neurodivergent people—more than a fifth of the global population—are either excluded entirely or included in some nominal sense where our gifts and talents are rarely tapped. This disproportionality between the potential to contribute, on the one hand, and the lack of opportunity, on the other, is a moral and practical crisis for society. In 1.0, the neurodivergent are spectators choosing between complete exclusion or inauthentic inclusion.

Inauthentic inclusion is a critical idea in establishing the context for neurodiversity inclusion in the business world and something, at the start, to become aware of. This is when someone with an atypical cognitive profile is "technically included" in the process, but that inclusion is predicated on the tacit guideline that the neurodivergent person will work to maintain a neurotypical façade. In other words, the price of inclusion is fitting in.

In cases of inauthentic inclusion, social position, workplace rules, methods of working, and job performance are all explicitly and implicitly determined by neurotypical standards and assumptions. In such cases, neurodivergent people often engage in an arduous process of fitting in, also known as "masking," where enormous energy is expended through superficial impression management and deeply felt stress to hide neurodivergent traits.

Sam, a late-diagnosed male with a master's degree in history who has been largely unemployed over recent decades, describes his experience:

> *I need a job really badly. And I really want to feel included. It's just that there is always this giant price I end up paying in terms of my mental health for forcing myself too hard to fit in rather than be me, quirks and all.*

As shown in Figure 1.1, the covered divergent gold balls symbolize the all-too-common phenomenon of masking.

As we will explore in the chapters ahead, there are many advantages to being a first mover in the transition from World 1.0 to World 2.0,

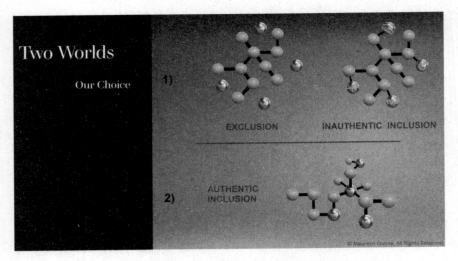

Figure 1.1 Technical inclusion vs. authentic inclusion.

including reduced groupthink risk, heightened innovation, reduced brand risk, and access to a wider pool of available workers.

World 2.0 is a superior configuration. For everyone. It represents a world that works better, both morally and functionally.

In World 2.0, businesses have discovered that it takes very little investment of time, money, and mindshare to embrace and implement authentic neuroinclusion and that the associated benefits far exceed those minimal costs, with a large collateral payoff for those in the neurodivergent community as well as everyone else living in this world.

World 2.0 is also a superior configuration in providing organizations access to a wider field of people, as well as far more per capita innovation, perspective, and motivation, as we will cover below.

Authentic inclusion is at the core of the transition to World 2.0, so we need to explore what we mean when we use this term—what *authentic* neurodiversity inclusion means, why it is so rare, what its advantages are, and how organizational cultures can evolve to tap this powerful resource.

Authentic inclusion is fundamentally about maximizing what any given individual can contribute within an organization and doing so in a way that appreciates and values diversity. To create alignment with this ideal, every organization should start with an honest examination of its core values—not the core values written in the emails or on the bulletin board, but the core values exposed by a brutally honest analysis of the allocation of time, money, habitual practices, implicit rules, and mindshare over a sufficient sample period.

Those are your only resources. Where they are being spent is what you value. There is no escaping that fundamental truth.

Often, the values that companies and organizations espouse in diversity statements are not fully backed up by genuine efforts to foster true inclusion, as suggested in a recent report by *MIT Sloan Management Review*.[3]

My aim is to convince you how and why your organization should include cognitive diversity as a fundamental value. World 1.0 versus World 2.0 is a choice hiring managers, administrators, and leaders make every day—whether they are consciously aware of it or not. The good news is that, even if your team has been making the wrong choice yesterday and every day before that, we can all make a different choice tomorrow.

As noted in the introduction, the neurodiversity paradigm frames cognitive types such as autism, ADHD, dyslexia, synesthesia, and dyspraxia as simply different ways of processing information within the expected range of variation for humans. Wherever you, your coworker, employee, or boss happen to fit into this range—neurotypical or neurodivergent—there are pros and cons.

We may never fully understand why this cognitive variation, with all its richness and complexity, is the norm, with neurodivergent

A Tale of Two Worlds

people exhibiting uniquely spikey profiles of strengths and challenges. But one might speculate that the answer should incorporate a community-level analytic framework—how it works at the level of the group as a functioning entity—rather than merely an individual-level framework.

Accordingly, a systems theory approach is one alternative framework to better understand how and why we are collectively stronger as organizations, companies, and communities when we can embrace rather than subvert differences.

The Strength-Based Framework

Divergent thinking drives innovation and creativity as it invokes methods of solving problems that defy standard approaches. The term "divergent thinking" encapsulates specific kinds of hidden strengths that have historically been underappreciated by employers but that are significant assets.

While profiles both within and between different cognitive typologies are unique, evidence supports the idea that particular strengths often, although not always, go hand-in-hand with ADHD, dyslexia, autism, synesthesia, and other types of neurodiversity.

Following are examples of just some of the cognitive advantages that can go hand in hand with neurodivergent cognition. There are many others. As we will see in the chapters ahead, the minimal cost and investment in developing or deepening a culture that fully supports cognitive diversity stands to more than pay off through the addition of diverse viewpoints, habits aligned with values, enhanced innovation and productivity, and improved well-being among all employees, not just neurodivergent people.

Strengths That Often Go Hand-in-Hand with ADHD/ADD. ADHD/ADD is characterized by challenges with attention, as well as hyperactivity and impulsive behavior. However, seeing ADHD only through this lens would miss the N+1 axis of high energy, 'out of the box' thinking. Cognitive psychologists Holly White and Priti Shah have demonstrated that ADHDers are particularly creative with novel ideas that are not derived from existing concepts. One study demonstrated how ADHD students performed significantly better in novelty, originality, and flexibility in creative tasks. The researchers suggested that this may be due to increased cognitive access to a wide range of semantic concepts.[4]

Another study found that ADHD participants showed less "design fixation" and relied less on existing knowledge, which allowed for more original and flexible thinking. College students with ADHD were compared to neurotypical peers on two creative generation tasks. One of the tasks required participants to imagine types of fruits that could exist on another planet. The ADHD students created alien fruits that were original and deviated to a greater degree from standard earthly fruits when compared to the neurotypical students (see Figure 1.2).[5]

Additional studies have highlighted a positive correlation between self-reported experiences of ADHD and creative achievements, indicating that individuals with ADHD might excel in creative tasks in daily life. Divergent thinking, creativity, and ADHD are also interconnected in terms of underlying brain science with further supportive evidence from neuroimaging studies.

Strengths That Often Go Hand-in-Hand with Dyslexia. Many dyslexic individuals recognize connections between seemingly disparate concepts, objects, or perspectives. Looking at Dyslexia through this lens, the difficulties with reading and writing tasks in dyslexic individuals are compensated by enhanced creativity.

In a 2021 meta-analysis of 14 studies, dyslexic adults showed greater creativity than neurotypical adults across various measures. A study of European dyslexic children and adolescents found them to be significantly more original in the drawing tasks of the Torrance

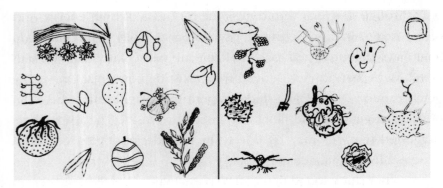

Figure 1.2 Invention of alien fruits by neurotypicals (left) and ADHDers (right).

Test of Creativity than their neurotypical peers.[6] In a separate study, dyslexic junior high school students outperformed neurotypical peers in connecting disparate concepts in original ways.[7]

There is compelling evidence to suggest that original thinking, combinatorial thinking, and divergent thinking are part of the hidden profile of dyslexia. These skills may become increasingly important in the context of the transformative technological changes we face in coming years.

Strengths That Often Go Hand-in-Hand with Autism. Autism spectrum disorders are generally characterized by difficulties with social interaction and communication, as well as repetitive behaviors. A strength-based lens allows autistic people to be seen more fully. Uncommon skills that autistic people bring to the table may include attention to details, pattern thinking, authenticity, and original solutions to problems. Autistic individuals demonstrate more consistently objective and rational decision-making and are less susceptible to cognitive biases, social pressure, and visual illusions. They also exhibit superior performance on visual-spatial and pattern thinking tasks.

Autistic individuals, irrespective of age and cognitive ability, out-perform neurotypical individuals on the block design test, indicating their enhanced ability to detect visual patterns and segment a gestalt with less expenditure of mental resources.[8] Autistic individuals also exhibit extraordinary attention to detail and superior skills on the Embedded Figures Test.[9]

Neuroimaging studies have indicated differences in brain activation and functional connectivity between autistic and neurotypical individuals. The unique information processing and brain connectivity of autistic individuals underpin unique talents and hidden cognitive profiles.

Recent research, including my own, supports the hypothesis that autistic strengths also include increased creativity and original thinking. A study found that those with strong autistic traits were more likely to produce exceptionally original or creative ideas. Participants were asked to come up with alternative uses for common objects. Those who generated more unusual responses were associated with higher degrees of autistic traits. Interestingly, autistic participants produced fewer interpretations for abstract drawings but scored higher in creativity and originality.[10]

The findings suggest that people with autistic traits may approach problems that demand creative solutions in a different way, possibly leading directly to less common, but more original, ideas.

Strengths That Often Go Hand-in-Hand with Synesthesia. Synesthesia, which occurs in about 4% of the population, is a neuro-divergent cognitive typology where the various senses (sight, hearing, taste, smell, and touch) get crossed up.

Synesthetes generally experience one sense through the lens of another. Some people taste shapes while others perceive the alphabet or numbers as particular colors. It tends to be overrepresented in the creative professions, such as art and music. Musician synesthetes, such as Tori Amos, report seeing music as colors, visual shapes, or streaks of light. Chromesthesia is a type of synesthesia that evokes an involuntary inner experience where sound or music is automatically translated into visual-spatial shapes, color, or movement.

As with other neurodivergent typologies, this access to an alternative way of processing reality often confers advantages expressed in the form of creativity, heightened pattern detection, or skills in design, visual arts, and music. There is substantial research that suggests that heightened creativity and artistic work may be associated with synesthesia because of strong and meaningful associations across modalities.

Psychologists Katrin Lunke and Beat Meier examined creativity and involvement in the arts among people with varying types of synesthesia. Participants were administered psychometric tests and then asked to report on time engaged with the creative arts. Synesthetes were significantly more likely to engage in creative arts, especially when factoring in the type of synesthesia. Synesthetes who see colors or visual experiences from music were the most likely to play a musical instrument. Overall, synesthetes outperformed neurotypical peers on one version of the psychometric measures. Researchers concluded that synesthetes were more likely to be linked to the creative arts but that underlying processes may be distinct from those captured on psychometric tests.[11]

Thinking from Thirty Thousand Feet

When taken together, there is a plethora of compelling research demonstrating a correlation between neurodivergence and uncommon skillsets, including unique problem-solving abilities, increased creativity, and original thinking. However, the last thing I want to do is imply that the only value to neurodiversity inclusion is the search matrix population density for creative genius.

In fact, I would strongly contend that the most important asset all neurodivergent people bring to the equation is a divergent perspective: a way of seeing the world and approaching tasks and problems that will almost certainly be uncorrelated to the dominant vibe permeating any organization; a whole personal life history of traveling an unconventional path with new and rare insights to contribute.

That alone is inherently valuable.

At the same time, the neurodiversity framework characterized in this book does not make the case that 20% of humans are oddball misfit fountainheads of creativity and innovation, while the other 80% are indistinguishable cognitive drones plodding along in clockwork unison, doing only as told.

This isn't Macs versus PCs in a twentieth-century TV ad.

If you identify as neurotypical, you may well be on the cusp of revolutionizing the frozen breakfast market through narrative dance. If you're neurodivergent, you may be on a path toward achieving perfect predictable and efficient conformity. Any attempt to generalize among humans is ultimately futile upon granular scrutiny. Exceptions are the rule, and all the lines are fuzzy. Nothing can be counted on to hold up in small-sample examination.

That said, research suggests that, from 30,000 feet, neurotypicals make up roughly four in five, and the neurodivergent—the other one in five—are a comparatively more heterogenous cognitive set.

To sum it up: the spectrum of *normal* human cognitive variation *includes* a subset (about 1 in 5) that can be differentiated as "neurodivergent" relative to the rest of the population. And this subset contains people with different strengths and challenges who learn differently, perform differently, and think differently—not only differently from neurotypical people but also differently from each other.

The legacy perspective on this variation has been defined solely by the medical-deficit model.

Rapidly gaining traction is a new perspective that reframes this picture through behavioral, observational, evolutionary, and cognitive data and research to suggest that this divergent 20% plays a crucial role in advancing the interests of the whole community.

As we will see, this has powerful implications for business strategy, team management, human resources, workplace management, and executive leadership in the twenty-first century.

Key Takeaways

- It is through the complementarity of different cognitive profiles, working together, that we arrive at the optimal configuration.

- We can best explain the universality, persistence, and pervasiveness of neurodivergence displayed in human populations across both geography and time in terms of complementary cognition and its implications for community-level fitness.

- Communities with a stable abundance of neurodiversity are more effective over time than communities that exclude neurodivergent individuals.

- Yet, employers remain reluctant to embrace neurodiversity inclusion due largely to erroneous beliefs and fear of the unknown. This is a central theme motivating this book.

- Neurodiversity World 1.0 is a world where the neurodivergent are either excluded or included inauthentically. It is a world of checklist solutions to inclusion, a world of neurodivergent "masking," and a world of wasted talent.

- Neurodiversity World 2.0 is a world of authentic neuroinclusion, psychological safety, innovation, employee satisfaction, and actualized talent.

- While profiles both within and between different cognitive typologies are unique, evidence supports the idea that particular strengths often, although not always, go hand-in-hand with ADHD, dyslexia, autism, and other types of neurodiversity.

- ADHD: Recent studies have shown that ADHDers are more likely to think originally and flexibly, often creating completely new concepts in creative tasks. Hyperactivity and impulsivity are seen as drivers of these achievements.

- Dyslexia: Dyslexic individuals are often better at recognizing connections between disparate concepts, objects, or perspectives, suggesting compensation for difficulties in reading and writing through enhanced creativity. They often perform better in tasks requiring original and combinatorial thinking.

- Autism: Autistic individuals typically demonstrate objective and rational decision-making, less susceptibility to cognitive biases, and superior visual-spatial and pattern thinking skills. Other strengths include attention to detail and original thinking.

- Synesthesia: Synesthesia is a neurodivergent cognitive typology where the various senses (sight, hearing, taste, smell, and touch) get crossed up. Synesthesia has been found to be overrepresented in the creative arts and music professions.

(continued)

(continued)

- The most important asset all neurodivergent people bring to the equation is a divergent perspective: a way of seeing the world and approaching tasks and problems that will almost certainly be uncorrelated to the dominant vibe permeating any organization; a whole personal life history of traveling an unconventional path with new and rare insights to contribute.

- The strengths-based model leverages behavioral, observational, evolutionary, and cognitive data and research to reframe neurodivergence as a community-level asset contributing cognitive diversity, creativity, originality, and a wider menu of search strategies and perspectives—all critical factors for organizational success. Yet, most organizations continue to exclude the neurodivergent and the value they have to offer.

Chapter 2

The Perils of Groupthink

"In the long run my observations have convinced me that some men, reasoning preposterously, first establish some conclusion in their minds which, either because of its being their own or because of their having received it from some person who has their entire confidence, impresses them so deeply that one finds it impossible ever to get it out of their heads. Such arguments in support of their fixed idea as they hit upon themselves or hear set forth by others, no matter how simple and stupid these may be, gain their instant acceptance and applause."

—Galileo Galilei, *Dialogue Concerning the Two Chief World Systems* (1632)[1]

As a board director involved in governance for many nonprofit and for-profit organizations, I have been struck by how often I witness the power of the herd overtake the independent reason, will, and courage of fiduciaries precisely when those qualities are most needed.

At one nonprofit organization, the CEO's salary and other perks grew to more than 10% of the operating budget of the organization even as that budget was sliding due to declining revenues. He seemed to have a circle of friends on board in key decision-making posts.

I was one of the few truly independent voices on the board. On one occasion, bylaws were interpreted inaccurately and in a way that could have spurred a costly mistake. The conversation shifted when I spoke up. But just before I pointed out the problem, a director stood up, emphatically praising the CEO and the performance of the organization. The majority of the heads in the room nodded along like mice following the pied piper.

As with many such situations, a complex system of factors contributed to the process that had eroded the power of the guardrails, checks, and balances at this organization over time. But, also as is usually the case, all of those factors could be boiled down to people subordinating their own hearts and minds to the power of the group.

The standard definition of "groupthink" is "a phenomenon that occurs when a group of individuals reaches a consensus without critical reasoning or evaluation of the consequences or alternatives."[2]

Another I have seen can be approximated as "a phenomenon that occurs when a group of people make decisions or take actions without fully considering all options or alternatives."

Both of these definitions get at the consequences of groupthink but speak little of the dynamics involved in bringing about those consequences. Instead, I would submit the following as a more effective way to understand and define groupthink:

A level of homogeneity of thought that crosses some theoretical threshold where individual reasoning becomes subordinate to some emerging consensus within a group, resulting in a decision-making outcome that is driven by factors, including social dynamics, unrelated to an objective and rational evaluation of information relevant to making the most effective decision.

That definition captures both the danger and its causal roots.

While similarity of cognitive profile plays a big role in group-think, it isn't the only factor. Researchers have found other important factors as well, including a reliance on social transmission of ideas to gain information and a preoccupation with social status and perception to a degree that hinders the willingness to contradict the tide of group opinion.

This dynamic is often tied to certain social dynamics: faith in the credibility or knowledge of other outspoken members of the group; pressure to conform to the opinions of others; pressure to get behind the will of the group leader or the majority of the group; or faith in the group as having some special ability to make the right decision.

Groupthink can be disastrous. Many of the most spectacular failures in business and government can be tied to this dynamic. Important information or potential problems are overlooked. Creativity is abandoned. New ideas or alternatives are kept hidden and given no voice.

Symptoms of groupthink include a high and unbalanced level of cohesion among group members, a lack of critical evaluation of ideas and alternatives, an illusion of invulnerability, an illusion of morality, stereotyped views of out-groups, direct pressure on dissenters, self-censorship, and a shared illusion of unanimity.

Reducing the risk of groupthink in strategic decision-making *must* be a primary goal of managers, executives, and board members in any organization that plans on being viable and competitive for the long term.

The established playbook to stave off this risk includes actively encouraging dissenting opinions, considering multiple options and alternatives prior to any final decision, fostering transparency and diversity in the decision-making process, and training leaders to be aware of the groupthink risk.

While these may represent valuable steps in the right direction, the risk will remain whenever key decisions are made by groups composed entirely of people with a strong inclination to succumb to group dynamics and peer pressure and a strong intrinsic resistance to skepticism about the information they are receiving through social transmission within the group.

As we will attempt to show here, authentic neurodiversity inclusion is a bulwark against this risk that is hard to replicate through any other strategy.

Groupthink Is a Breakdown in Community-Level Efficacy

In their 2014 book, *Wiser: Getting Beyond Groupthink to Make Groups Smarter*, Harvard's Cass Sunstein and Reid Hastie examine why group decision-making so frequently fails.[3]

A theme that repeatedly emerges throughout Sunstein and Hastie's book is reminiscent of our beehive allegory from Chapter 1—the sum of the intelligence, wisdom, courage, analytic acumen, insight, and diligence of each individual in the group, added together across the group, is not the same as the intelligence, wisdom, courage, analytic acumen, insight, and diligence of the group as a whole.

In other words, the quality of the individual-level dynamics involved in the group provides no real estimate of the quality of the group-level dynamic.

In the beehive example, perfect bee behavior, on the individual level, is about precision in following the instructions passed along through the waggle dance. But a hive made entirely of similarly perfectly behaved bees drastically underperforms a hive that also includes a divergent cohort with a nonstandard behavioral profile.

Similarly, Sunstein and Hastie consistently point to the group-level dynamic as the most important frame of reference for group performance on any task.

A popular example is the familiar notion that an NBA team made up of all the best players in the league can rarely beat a team with few stars but great team chemistry and plenty of unselfish players willing to do the thankless grunt work that really wins games.

One might call this a "systems theory" perspective.

One of Sunstein and Hastie's big findings is that, compared to individual decision-making, decisions made through a group process tend to increase individual-level confidence among group members while decreasing the variance of individual-level opinions without increasing the accuracy of the end result. In other words, take a bunch of individuals and place them in a group to make an important decision, and you end up with a unified, overconfident group that, by and large, gets it wrong.

And yet, this process is a primary engine for almost every business. The vision, the strategy, the minor objectives, how to react to unexpected challenges—for most businesses, all these elements are, at least in part, subject to this pitfall.

The goal of any such process is to make the group more accurate than the individual. It stands to reason that this should be possible. After all, the sum of the knowledge and experience of all members of a group is always going to be greater than the knowledge and experience of any one member of that same group.

But it doesn't end up working out that way. Another common pitfall in group decision-making is a bias to shift toward a more extreme position than that which defined each member's pre-deliberation position.

And yet, on some level, you will need effective group decision-making in order for your business to grow and succeed. Crucially, there are many examples of companies that get this dynamic right.

The Perils of Groupthink

So it can be done. But to formulate a better understanding of why and how, we need to dig a little deeper and excavate the factors that seem to be at the heart of this common failure.

There are a few clear culprits here. But one of the most important is highlighted by a Colorado study where people living in a politically left-of-center community (Boulder) and people living in a politically right-of-center community (Colorado Springs) were both polled about a series of issues: affirmative action, same-sex unions, and climate change.[4]

People in each area were first asked for their views on these issues individually, privately, and anonymously. At this stage, respondents in both communities were very diverse in their views, with more differences among respondents in each area than between areas, on average.

Next, focus groups in each area were asked to address these same issues as a group, deliberating together and returning individual responses, but as a group, with no anonymity. You can probably guess what happened—the responses unified within each group and became more extreme in alignment with political orientation. In other words, all of the richness of the knowledge, experience, and personal judgment present in the individual-level anonymous responses disappeared. In its place, extremism and conformity emerged to shape the outcome.

Thinking Right and Wrong

Behavioral economics may evolve into one of the most important and revolutionary fields of this era. It is the science of human decision making and largely grew out of the work of Amos Tversky and Daniel Kahneman beginning in the 1970s.

Behavioral economics has unearthed several reliably present heuristic biases that plague human decision making and frequently play a large role in driving performance failures in the business world.

Common examples of persistent biases in human decision making include:

- The planning fallacy: We tend to chronically underestimate the amount of time it will take to complete a task, as well as the costs and risks associated with that task—even if we should know better directly from past personal experiences.

- The availability bias: We overemphasize the importance of whatever piece of evidence is easiest for us to recall. The more psychologically available examples or data points end up being those we believe should provide the best context for future predictions.

- The optimism bias: Most people tend to think they are above average in every context.

- The self-serving bias: We generally tend to think our side of any given competition framework is right or morally superior or destined for victory.

- The loss aversion bias: We tend to place greater importance on avoiding loss than on gaining advantage.

- The anchoring bias: We tend to frame valuation around whatever anchoring value has arisen to define a negotiation, rather than reverting to our own ground-up assessment of value based on analysis.

- The overconfidence effect: We tend to inaccurately overestimate our own judgments or knowledge.

These tendencies present barriers to optimal decision-making because they divert reasoning away from a rational appreciation of reality in service of satisfying some built-in psychological need. Research on group decision-making reveals the scary conclusion that although we suffer from all of these biases as individuals, they seem to have an outsized impact on the decision-making capabilities of groups.[5]

Let's examine why.

One of the most important causal factors driving this failure is pressure for people with dissenting views to stay quiet or to conform to the viewpoint that emerges first as the most popular framework among the group. Pressure can come in many forms. It doesn't have to be in the form of direct verbal command. It can be self-inflicted social reasoning. Perhaps the classic experiment demonstrating this dynamic was conducted by Polish American Gestalt psychologist Solomon Asch in the early 1950s.[6]

Asch had 50 male students from Swarthmore College take a "vision test." Each subject was put in a room with seven other people who were working with Asch. But the subject didn't know these other seven participants were confederates aiding the experiment. He assumed he was simply one of eight people taking the vision test.

The group was then shown two images side by side. One was an image of a line of a certain length that was labeled the target line. The other was an image of three lines of different lengths that were labeled line A, line B, and line C. They were then asked which of the three lines (A, B, or C) was most similar in length to the target line. The answer was always obvious and unambiguous.

Answers were given out loud starting with each of the seven confederates going one by one, with the real subject going last. As you may have guessed, the confederates all gave an obviously wrong answer. And about three quarters of the time, subjects ended up conforming to the group pressure and giving an obviously incorrect answer as well.

The experiment also included a control group where different subjects took the same test with no confederates in the room. Control group participants failed to get the right answer less than 1% of the time.

Thus, group pressure skewed accuracy by more than 74% under conditions where incorrect reasoning emerged as a front-running view among a group. In other words, people in groups tend to endorse obviously wrong ideas if the alternative means going against the dominant shared view of the group, even when it is extremely obvious that the dominant perspective is highly flawed.

By contrast, individuals addressing problems by themselves have no reason to conceal their real views, experiences, judgments, or ideas because they aren't being presented with a social context that might contain other views, experiences, judgments, or ideas at odds with their own. In other words, as a separate individual, your views can be expressed as you address some problem or decision without the act of that expression implying dissent to a superior in a hierarchy or potential social stigma or any of a range of other possible concerns that have nothing to do with the problem being discussed.

To be successful, organizations must manage to harvest decisions and work products from teams and groups. Yet, humans tend toward exacerbating negative outcome potential when acting in groups.

This dilemma is fundamental and must be faced and overcome. Cognitive diversity can play a major role in resolving this dilemma and unlocking optimal group performance. While it is always dangerous to generalize, and applying general conclusions to any given individual is usually a mistake, patterns can be derived from the data.

As future chapters will elaborate upon, while each neurodivergent person is unique, neurodivergent people have been found to more easily maintain their ability to form independent conclusions even when confronting peer pressure to conform to an established view from the rest of the group.

This is because neurodivergent people—with distinct traits across the neurodiversity umbrella—are often processing information and attending to environmental stimuli differently, noticing different details and drawing conclusions based on different base assumptions. And, at the same time, they also often have identities less reliant on peer social acceptance than their neurotypical peers.

While neurotypical people are wired to arrive at and communicate knowledge via a sociocultural transmission process, many neurodivergent individuals may become particularly adept at problem-solving by consistently finding creative workarounds, especially when we may have missed something either in the flow of conversation or due to different attentional or self-regulatory mechanisms.

While it is crucial to appreciate that no two neurodivergent people are alike, my own research over the years suggests that some neurodivergent thinkers appear to be less likely to rely on or fully trust outside sources for answers to complex problems and may instead display a tendency to rely on a first-principles approach, employing pattern thinking, multifaceted visual-spatial skills, systems thinking, or reverse engineering to arrive at new conclusions. ADHDers, for instance, tend to require strong intrinsic motivation in completing tasks and are less influenced by the kinds of external rewards that motivate many neurotypical people.

Additionally, while this may not be everyone's experience, many neurodivergent individuals also appear to be generally less concerned with social status, which makes them less vulnerable to implicit or explicit peer pressure. The evidence thus far suggests that autistic people, as a group, are perhaps the most immune to concerns with social reputation and instead make consistent decisions regardless of social pressure.

In one intriguing study, for instance, researchers Keise Izuma and colleagues asked autistic and neurotypical participants to donate money to UNICEF on two separate occasions. The first donation request occurred without any social pressure and without other people knowing the outcome. By contrast, on the second occasion, participants were asked to donate as a researcher was watching by standing right over their shoulders during the donation decision process.[7]

The findings were illuminating: Autistic participants were not influenced by social pressure and donated the same amount regardless of how it might affect their social reputations. In contrast, neurotypical participants donated considerably more when there was an observer, presumably more concerned with their own social status than what the increased sum could achieve for UNICEF programs.

According to traditional decision science models, a rational agent carefully considers all relevant factors when making important decisions. However, as discussed above, various cognitive biases can impact that process. Several research studies further suggest autistic people are less prone to those same biases, especially the framing heuristic and marketing gimmicks that tend to strongly influence decision-making among neurotypical individuals. In other words, the data suggest autistic people make more consistently rational decisions when the calculus centers on something other than social positioning.

For example, in a 2017 study published in the journal *Psychological Science*, George D. Farmer and colleagues examined the choices of autistic and neurotypical participants when presented with consumer products, including an objectively less desirable "decoy" option.[8] When choices were framed in a particular way, and the order of presentation switched accordingly, neurotypical participants made rational decisions less consistently when compared to autistic participants, who were less influenced by framing techniques.

In another study published in 2019, Kuzmanovic and colleagues showed an irrational asymmetry by neurotypical (but not in autistic) participants in belief updating: neurotypicals disproportionately and inaccurately focused on good news while neglecting bad news during self-referential judgments. By contrast, autistic participants in the study demonstrated significantly lower bias in updating beliefs when making similar self-referential judgments.[9]

Yafai and colleagues published further evidence that autistic children are more likely to resist social pressure in a study highly reminiscent of the classic 1956 Asch study covered above. Autistic children were compared to neurotypical children on a task where each child was asked to report which line out of three available options matched another line in length. In a test of social conformity, child participants were sometimes misled as to what other people thought in terms of the correct response. The autistic children were significantly less likely to go along with the misleading incorrect option.[10]

Sometimes, all it takes in a group decision-making process is one or two people either noticing an alternate path to progress or failing to be influenced by a popular but irrational choice and then speaking up against a dominant view to introduce new angles or perspectives into the group decision-making process.

That can be enough to both expand the range of possibilities under consideration and to give others in the room the confidence to speak up, which unearths what Sunstein and Hastie call "hidden profiles"—experience or information or perspective that gets locked away inside of people who don't feel comfortable taking a vocal minority view in the discussion. It is precisely this process that strengthens the group's ability for thoughtful deliberation that ultimately improves the likelihood of a successful outcome.

As we will illustrate in more detail in the chapters that follow, many neurodivergent people representing different cognitive typologies demonstrate spiky profiles with unique perceptual, analytical, and problem-solving abilities. As already argued, by adding cognitive diversity into the mix of the group, the dynamics change and details that would previously go unnoticed emerge into the conversation.

Additionally, even when the individuals within the group recognize a risk or shortcoming, the social pressures of conformity can be so strong that no one is willing to speak up about the issue. Again, while no two neurodivergent individuals are alike, research suggests that neurodivergent individuals are less susceptible to concerns about social status and, by implication, more likely to risk that status to the benefit of group decision-making outcomes.

The *Challenger* space shuttle may have made it safely into orbit if hidden profiles had been unlocked in group discussions when it was decided to not worry about the temperature being a few degrees colder than the specs for the O-ring.[11] Swissair may have avoided bankruptcy in 2002, Coca-Cola may have saved billions by avoiding the New Coke disaster in 1985, and the US may have avoided the Bay of Pigs calamity in 1961 that nearly spurred nuclear war a year later.

History is full of disaster post-mortems that find groupthink holding the smoking gun. Cognitive diversity is the vaccine that may have prevented all of them.

The Groupthink Recipe

Another way to approach this argument is to imagine, based on all available research, a group that might be seen as maximally susceptible to the perils of groupthink.

Such a group would be made up of individuals with very similar backgrounds, cognitive profiles, and values. It would also be made up mostly of people who are particularly vulnerable to peer pressure, such as those most concerned about social status, and who are used to gaining information about the world by way of social transmission rather than independent research or analysis. Finally, such a group would have strong social cohesion—members of this hypothetical group would get along well with each other and have strong social bonds.

Note, in this example, these traits are all shared by the same people. It may be unrealistic, but the goal here is to imagine the extreme scenario—the ultimate groupthink risk.

This, then, is our group: 10 men, close in age, of similar ethnicity from similar socioeconomic and educational backgrounds and similar overall temperaments that care a lot about how they are seen by others, especially others in this group. None are neurodivergent. All are very social and place disproportionate weight on gathering information from peer social transmission. Finally, these guys take genuine pride in their membership in this group and respect the group's capacity to achieve strong results.

While some organizations would celebrate this type of chemistry, the reality is that such a group would be a ticking time bomb.

They would have countless blind spots and no means of correcting course. They wouldn't know what they don't know, and they would have no built-in tendency to explore the space of ideas outside of their individual comfort zones. An organization relying on such a group to make strategic decisions would be pregnant with its own inevitable failure.

Obviously, this is an extreme example. But extreme examples help highlight principles.

My own research and experience strongly suggest that the risk of groupthink disasters may be mitigated, even in such a compositionally stricken group as our "ultimate groupthink risk" group, by adding a small number of neurodivergent individuals into the mix. That would likely be enough to break up opinion cascades and force reconsideration of bad ideas.

To return to our Flatland theme, the two-dimensional Flatlanders have no means of seeing that third-dimensional axis. But what if the only path forward to success is perpendicular to known reality?

Groupthink is an essential risk for most organizations—one that is made more insidious by the simple fact that those organizations most susceptible to it are also those most blind to the risk it poses, by definition.

One of my clients is a top-tier global brand with award-winning in-house designers and marketing experts. I was brought in to help do damage control within the neurodiversity community after a well-intentioned ad was released—targeting neurodivergent consumers—containing ideas and designs that turned out to be highly offensive to neurodivergent people. In this case, an overconfidence bias was to blame as the award-winning neurotypical team presumed to know everything necessary to understand how to build a winning campaign about neurodiversity without actually consulting any neurodivergent people in the process.

In short, they failed to include neurodivergent lived experience in the process and the result immediately tarnished their multi-billion-dollar brand. As the event unfolded, executives at the company quickly recognized their team had gaps in knowledge and expertise and immediately withdrew the marketing ad, committing to involving neurodivergent people as teammates in the future when addressing similar messaging themes.

It was only through preexisting access channels to allies in the neurodiversity community, including myself and my team, that they were able to react quickly and prevent a far more expensive lesson in the importance of including lived experience.

Everything we have discussed in this chapter lends itself most naturally to imagining some huge strategic decision—a fork in the road where an organization has to either go left or right. One way spells disaster while the other leads to the promised land.

While this type of all-or-nothing archetypal scenario is an easy lens through which to think about this topic—groupthink is too subtle and pervasive a risk to be truly captured by such a simplistic analytic approach. Every day, organizations go about their operations, relying on a status quo of assumptions. Over time, without someone to stand up and risk their own social status to point out what the emperor isn't wearing, organizational risks pile up. But history is clear: the risk of ostracization is just too great for most people, no matter how well intentioned.

Not only will it put your organization at risk when confronting some huge strategic fork in the road or in the course of simply dealing with the subtle evolution of an organization's culture on a day-to-day basis, but, by the same token, it also fosters the type of routine complacency that can metastasize into a collective subconscious risk aversion when faced with new opportunities to innovate.

After all, someone usually has to speak up and point out that there may be a better way to do things when the group has become entrenched in self-satisfied acceptance of an inefficient status quo.

Embracing authentic neuroinclusion as a strategic choice in steering organizational culture is a powerful vaccination against these risks. In fact, I would take the argument one step further and speculate that neurodiversity inclusion may be the *only* reliable solution to groupthink risk. No system of guidelines or protocols will be guaranteed to prevent succumbing to conformity pressure when the people involved tend in that direction in a fundamental sense.

In other words, a group made up entirely of neurotypical members is *fundamentally* susceptible to groupthink risk.

It's also important to note that it isn't just the operational team in focus here. In my experience, boards are just as vulnerable to this risk. Board directors have broad fiduciary responsibilities to make decisions in the best interest of the organization and to provide oversight for executive performance. Cognitive diversity is every bit as critical in fulfilling those responsibilities as it is across other areas of an organization.

In sum, there are recommended strategies to reduce groupthink risk. For example, several authors recommend encouraging dissenting opinions, encouraging newer group members to speak up, questioning assumptions, and explicitly stating that no one will be looked down on for raising concerns at any stage. However, my supposition is that these steps, in the absence of robust cognitive diversity, will merely create a fragile and temporary shield against groupthink. While there are always exceptions, the group will still generally be composed of people used to prioritizing social status in group hierarchies and social transmission of information over directness, radical honesty, and independent thought.

In other words, in my experience, a purely neurotypical group will be far more likely to eventually settle back into an equilibrium state of vulnerability to groupthink.

Key Takeaways

- Groupthink occurs when factors unrelated to a rational evaluation of the facts involved in making decisions take over and individual perspectives become subordinated to some emerging group consensus. Homogeneity in cognitive profile can be an enabling factor. Neurodiversification is the cure.

- The sum of the intelligence, wisdom, courage, analytic acumen, insight, and diligence of each individual in the group, added together across the group, is not the same as the intelligence, wisdom, courage, analytic acumen, insight, and diligence of the group as a whole.

(continued)

(continued)

- Compared to individual decision-making, decisions made through a group process tend to increase individual-level confidence among group members while decreasing the variance of individual-level opinions without increasing the accuracy of the end result.

- Persistent biases in human decision-making present barriers to optimal outcomes by diverting reasoning away from a rational appreciation of reality in service of satisfying some built-in psychological need. Research on group decision-making reveals the scary conclusion that, although we suffer from all of these biases as individuals, their impact seems to be even more pronounced and harmful in the context of group decision-making.

- One of the most important causal factors driving groupthink failures is pressure for people with dissenting views to stay quiet or to conform to the viewpoint that emerges first as the most popular framework among the group.

- Research suggests that neurodivergent members involved in group processes tend to maintain their ability to form independent conclusions even when confronting peer pressure to conform to an established view from the rest of the group.

- Sometimes, all it takes to eradicate the risk of groupthink in a group decision-making process is one or two people either noticing an alternate path to progress or failing to be influenced by a popular but irrational choice and then speaking up against a dominant view to introduce new angles or perspectives into the group decision-making process.

- History is full of disaster post-mortems that find group-think holding the smoking gun. Cognitive diversity is the vaccine that may have prevented all of them.

- What organizations may celebrate as culture-fit chemistry is a groupthink ticking time bomb. Disproportionate cognitive and experiential cohesion leads to countless blind spots with no built-in tendency to correct course on the basis of rational thought and an honest appraisal of the facts at hand. Such groups don't know what they don't know and fail to proactively explore the space of ideas outside of their individual comfort zones. An organization relying on such a group to make strategic decisions would be pregnant with its own inevitable failure.

- The groupthink risk is not just about avoiding disaster. It also fosters routinized complacency that can metastasize into a collective subconscious risk aversion when faced with new opportunities to innovate.

- Boards are also vulnerable to this risk. Board directors have broad fiduciary responsibilities to make decisions in the best interest of the organization and to provide over-sight for executive performance. Cognitive diversity is every bit as critical in fulfilling those responsibilities as it is across other areas of an organization.

- A purely neurotypical group will eventually settle back into an equilibrium state of vulnerability to groupthink because they are used to prioritizing social status in group hierarchies and social transmission of information over radical honesty and independent thought.

- Neurodiversification may be the only sure path to eradicating these risks.

Chapter 3

The Economics of Neurodiversity Inclusion

"Before all masters, necessity is the one most listened to, and who teaches the best."
— Jules Verne, *The Mysterious Island*, 1875[1]

One of the most powerful arguments for embracing authentic neurodiversity inclusion is rooted in recent developments in the evolution of the supply of labor in developed world economies. In short, most businesses have started to struggle to find enough qualified workers to meet demand. And that's likely to continue for years to come and to worsen over time for reasons we will cover below.

There are two questions that employers will be asking themselves as they wrestle with this dynamic:

1. How will this translate to the bottom line?

2. Is there anything organizations can do about it?

To work through these questions and see where they lead, we need to start by dusting off that old Econ 101 textbook from freshman year.

Imagine you sell apple pies at an apple pie stand. Every day customers stop by on their way home from work to purchase apple pies. If you are the only one on the block selling apple pies, then you have cornered the market and you have a lot of pricing power. But the very fact of your wide profit margins ensures you won't be alone in that market for very long.

Once someone else sees the big profits you are making, a competing apple pie stand opens next to yours offering the same product for less, and you are forced to lower your price to remain competitive.

But what about the apples? You need plenty of them. So does your new competitor.

You make all your pies from Red Delicious apples because that's what you're used to. That's what everyone is used to. You know how to evaluate Red Delicious apples for quality. Your equipment is set up to handle their size and shape easily. You know where to go to get Red Delicious apples when you need more.

Naturally, your competitor uses only Red Delicious apples as well. The increase in demand for Red Delicious apples paired with the increase in supply of apple pies on the block—both due to the presence of your new competitor in the marketplace—have made it tougher to stay in business. Input costs are rising. Output prices are falling. It's a squeeze.

Now, the bad news: recently, you have started to learn that many of the apple trees at the local orchard are aging. Apparently, there has been a wave of early retirements among the trees due to the apple-tree-bug epidemic. We have also begun to weather the tragic loss of hundreds of productive apple trees due to premature death in the apple-tree-bug epidemic. And the historic recent drop in apple tree imports due to rising nationalism has further weighed on the supply situation.

In other words, you are now facing a full-blown structural apple shortage. Do you give up? Do you simply pack it in? New competition appearing on the scene was a major blow. Now you have this whole apple-tree-bug epidemic on your hands. And this sudden drop in apple tree imports! It's as if everything is going wrong at the same time. It's hopeless.

Or is it?

Imagine what it might mean for you to start making some of your pies with Granny Smith, Fuji, Honeycrisp, or McIntosh apples, instead of simply hammering out nothing but Red Delicious apple pies at every turn, eating higher costs and getting pinched.

Diversifying your supply equation could be the difference between prosperous long-term success and outright failure.

However, to make that strategy work, you would need to invest in "authentic apple-diversity inclusion." You can't expect your in-house de-seeders and slicers and skinners and seasoners to work just as well for Granny Smith, Fuji, Honeycrisp, or McIntosh apples as they do for Red Delicious apples (just to be clear, yes, I know those pieces of equipment don't exist, and that there's no such thing as an apple pie factory supporting a single-location food stand—bear with me: it's an extended allegory).

After all, your entire production system has been designed from the ground up in a universe built on the unexamined assumption that "Red Delicious" equals "North" on the strategic compass in your industry. The solution is to question the foundational assumptions and start fresh with everything set toward "universal design" in the apple-pie processing space.

In other words, force-fitting Granny Smith, Fuji, Honeycrisp, or McIntosh apples into the production process optimized for Red Delicious apples isn't going to work. However, as you can imagine, that's exactly what most companies try first. But what do you suppose the ultimate upshot of that tendency has been?

To keep within the confines of our allegory, apple pie stands that try to become more inclusive of other types of apples while maintaining a production system clearly biased toward one particular legacy type of apple end up in bad shape. Operational performance

59

The Economics of Neurodiversity Inclusion

deteriorates along with end-product quality. And, wrongly, they tie these results to the imagined "error" of incorporating a more diverse field of apple types in the first place.

Perhaps the most important point to make at this juncture is this: any decrease in efficiency or output quality that results from jamming Granny Smith apples into a Red Delicious apple processing system is *not* the result of some form of fundamental flaw in Granny Smith apples. It is simply the fundamental problem that arises when you start with a built-in systemic bias and then attempt to exploit the level of optionality that can only be accessed by systems designed from the ground up according to a universal design principle.

In other words, the best long-term path forward in this case is to question initial design and management assumptions and to reset to a universal design standard. Do it early and comprehensively. That's where the edge is.

It shouldn't be surprising to learn that all of this applies to people, too.

The labor market is susceptible to the forces of supply and demand every bit as much as any other part of the economy. The main dynamic we are discussing in this chapter is a growing and persistent shortage of the supply of workers in the labor market for reasons we explore below. Given that the demand for workers is relatively steady over time, a structural shortage in the supply of workers is bound to lead to structural upward pressures on labor costs and a margin squeeze.

To sum it up, the labor shortage will put upward pressure on unit labor costs throughout the supply chain. So not only will you have to pay more for your own workers, but your input costs for materials from suppliers will also rise as those suppliers pass along their increased labor costs to you to the extent they can in the form of price hikes.

That gives us the most basic answer to question #1 above—How will this translate to the bottom line? Increased costs, tighter margins, and a generally tougher operating environment. That brings us to question #2: What can businesses do about it other than swallow the bitter pill?

The Structural Labor Shortage

Consider that, in the US alone, there are approximately 60 million people that fall into the neurodivergent category—about one in every five Americans.

This group is chronically unemployed and underemployed despite having the skills necessary to succeed if given the chance, if equipped with the right accommodations and supports, and if embraced within a strength-based framework in an organizational culture built from a universal design perspective.

Researchers from Chapman University cite 2016 National Autistic Society data contending that 85% of autistic adults are unemployed or underemployed. At the same time, in a recent study by JPMorgan, autistic employees were found to be 48% faster and up to 140% more productive at a range of tasks when compared to their neurotypical peers employed in the same position.

The story is similar for other categories of neurodiversity, with estimates for unemployment among neurodivergent adults estimated to be approximately 30–40%.

At the same time, for the sake of comparison, the unemployment rate across the general population as of December 2023 is well below 4% for all people pursuing employment in the United States.

In other words, prospective neurodivergent workers seeking gainful employment that provides a level of responsibility and compensation commensurate with their experience and skill level have been chronically excluded from the economy. And yet, in a labor shortage context, they represent an enormous undervalued and untapped resource that can be unlocked through the principles of authentic inclusion and universal design.

Businesses that shy away from this challenge—from taking the proper steps to hire, retain, and authentically include neurodivergent workers—are actively choosing to paddle upstream in a flood against the wind.

According to researchers from the United States Federal Reserve, the labor shortage hinges on a combination of factors including an aging population, a wave of early retirements due to the pandemic, the tragic loss of hundreds of thousands of potential workers due to Covid deaths, and a historic drop in immigration that has been based, in part, on rising nationalism and Trump-era policy changes that have a base of popular support among US voters.

In other words, none of these factors are likely to go away any time soon.

In the December 14, 2022, Federal Open Market Committee meeting, Fed Chair Jerome Powell noted in his remarks, "I mean, I think we've—it feels like we have a structural labor shortage out there where there are, you know, four million fewer people, a little more than four million who were in the workforce available to work than there's demand for workforce."[2]

One way to think about what we are facing is to consider how wealth is distributed across the population of a country such as the United States. Most of it is in accounts owned by the oldest quintile of the population. It's the nest eggs of the country.

But, as people continue to live longer and longer lives, the number of retired people living off accumulated savings and passive fixed income such as pensions and social security, as a percentage of the total population, is growing. Since that retired contingent is still consuming goods and services but is not available for employment, and since the entire rest of the population is both consuming and producing according to roughly normal historical per capita rates, there is a growing percentage of demand that is not balanced by production.

Lives lost to Covid and the immigrant deficit are both idiosyncratic situational factors that are certainly part of the equation. They account for a big part of the current labor shortage we have been seeing. But the persistent, structural factor that economists see dominating our future is demographic.[3]

We saw something of the opposite situation take hold in the early 1980s. Back then, economists used the term "demographic dividend"—referring to a situation where the proportion of the total population actively in the working population was relatively high historically.

You can think about it like a group of people carrying a tree trunk across a field. In this scenario, let's imagine that every person in the group has to either shoulder some of the weight or ride on top of the tree.

Imagine a scenario where there are 20 people and all 20 of them are young healthy adults, so all of them can shoulder some of the burden. Contrast this with a scenario where only 10 are young healthy adults and the other 10 are infants, toddlers, and very elderly people, all of whom have to sit up on top of the tree trunk, making it heavier.

The difference between the two scenarios is stark.

The baby boomer generation was the biggest in history, comprised of people born as part of the post-WWII boom in births from 1946 to 1964. In the early 1980s, they were anywhere from 17 to 34 years of age—just coming into their prime working years as productive members of the economy.[4]

Now, this same generation is about 60 to 80 years of age, with the median boomer somewhere around 70 years of age with about

$200K–250K in savings. There are about 76 million baby boomers, which adds up to about $16 trillion in total wealth in the US alone. Forty-four percent of baby boomers also have pension income. Given that pension income is gradually becoming a relic of times past, this is another significant factor when considering the distribution of buying power and the incentive to work in the economy ahead of us.[5]

In other words, we are increasingly moving into a world where the vast majority of spending power is in the hands of people who are past their prime productive years and have both the savings and the passive income to stay out of the labor market altogether.

It all compounds the issue for businesses hoping to stay competitive. In other words, the world ahead is one in which demand stays high, but workers are increasingly missing from the equation on a relative basis.

Note that none of these dynamics are cyclical. In other words, they won't be solved by the normal ebbs and flows of the business cycle. Instead, they are structural, suggesting that we will be living in a labor shortage context for many years to come.

The Game-Theoretic Exacerbation

If you think that already sounds bad enough, don't worry, it gets worse. There's more to the problem for employers than just the number of workers available versus the distribution of savings in the economy.

As with most economic issues, there's a game-theoretic layer that comes along with the deal when a major dynamic shifts relative to historical standards. By shifting the "who needs whom more" balance, all sorts of power relationships are transformed. And that has consequences.

Namely, there are knock-on effects as workers become increasingly aware of the power they have in a world where employers need employees much more than employees need any given employer. That shift in balance of power is evidenced by the rising pricing power employees can wield for their services. That value can be conveyed most simply through rising wages. But it can also be conveyed by other dynamics.

Some recent examples include "quiet quitting," "loud quitting," and "rage applying"—all of which are directly related to the sense, at this stage in history, that employers need employees far more than employees need employers.

Quiet quitting has become code for the increasing number of employees who have simply checked out in their jobs over the past two years. The term captures the concept of an employee who simply does the bare minimum each day to skate by. They can get away with this because their employer isn't willing to terminate their employment and risk having to find someone new to fill their role.

Loud quitting is the process of letting your employer know that you are dissatisfied and may be heading to greener pastures unless something shifts in your direction—such as a raise, better benefits, a promotion, etc. It's a threat that carries increasing weight in a labor shortage environment.

Rage applying refers to the process among disgruntled employees of mass applying to new opportunities with little concern for appearances. You are fed up, and you want every one of your employer's competitors to know about it—or at least, that's a productive sentiment to demonstrate in the course of negotiating better terms on a current job.

Some researchers and media influencers have made the case that these are all separate and distinct new phenomena in the landscape of the business economy. But my sincere belief is that it's always a better bet that we are seeing fundamental changes to the context around human psychology than fundamental changes to human psychology, itself.

At the end of the day, all these dynamics are rooted in the economics of a labor shortage imbalance.

And employers who want to gain an edge under these conditions will need to open up new avenues of employee accessibility. Under these conditions, businesses able to harvest and capitalize on talent from the ranks of the 60-million-plus that fall into the neurodivergent category in the US will have a clear edge. And, as discussed above, those same businesses will stand to benefit from increased innovation and reduced groupthink risk.

However, these advantages—access to a larger pool of potential workers as well as a boost to pound-for-pound innovation potential along with reduced groupthink risk—will only be available to organizations committed to authentic neurodiversity inclusion.

The Winds of Change

Along with structural factors impacting access to labor, there are other structural factors that make it easier to be more inclusive, which is a key dynamic offsetting the obstacle.

For example, the flexibility of adding a work-from-home option to employee arrangements has enormous implications for neurodiversity inclusion.

Recent research analysis from Global Workplace Analytics suggests that 56% of the US workforce is employed in a job that has some component of remote work, while only 3.6% of the employee workforce was working remotely at least half-time prior to the pandemic. That number is projected to rise seven to nine times over, which would result in 25%–30% of the entire workforce working remotely over the long term.[6]

This shouldn't be too surprising. Several likely long-term trends were born in the pandemic. And all of them share a basic philosophical kinship: they are all shifts that likely would have happened without the pandemic, but they simply would have taken longer to mature into mainstream trends.

In essence, the pandemic forced the expediting of inevitable transformations. There are many examples of this phenomenon, including ecommerce, food delivery, remote education, and tele-health—in short, anything where we have the technological capability to do something that reduces human contact while still serving the basic function, but a significant proportion of the population had yet to join the demand side of the equation.

And then the pandemic hit.

Work from home falls right dead center into this category: many jobs can be done from home, and there are many platforms that facilitate this capability, and many more that took off during the pandemic (such as Zoom). The only missing piece was the motivation to shift workplace habits.

Now that it has become more common and more accepted—not to mention more technologically feasible—to operate with work-from-home optionality, the door is open to provide more operational flexibility in implementing an authentic neurodiversity inclusion strategy.

As we will discuss in a subsequent chapter, offering greater flexibility around working from home for neurodivergent employees can have an enormous payoff in terms of productivity, loyalty, motivation, and innovation.

One ADHDer I know very well works in the finance field as a capital markets analyst. He was given the freedom to work from home several years ago, and his productivity and performance skyrocketed as a result. He shares:

> *I set up my ideal environment—I actually redesigned my garage as a market analysis hub. I built a giant workstation. I could move around freely. Jump around. Talk out*

loud. Sing. Whatever. The feeling of having no constraints on my hyperactivity is so freeing. Not having to spend half of my mental energy just working on fitting in. Being able to express myself in designing my workspace. Optimizing my workflow according to how I know I work best. My level of investment in my role with the company increased dramatically. And my output and performance noticeably jumped. So did my attachment to my team, manager, and the company. They gave me the freedom to be myself and to create a situation that really worked for me. That means a lot. It's a form of compensation. The difference, in terms of tapping into my potential to contribute, has been huge.

This is not an uncommon story for neurodivergent individuals freed from the shackles of what they perceive as the "limitations of neurotypical standards of office comportment." But there's more in that testimony than just the functional value of flexibility for the people who peculiarly thrive on it. There is an explicit expression of very real gratitude.

I love this quote because it resonates so clearly with that intangible factor. And, while that factor is difficult to quantify, it shouldn't be overlooked: Just because something is difficult to quantify doesn't mean it's unimportant. In fact, it is often the case that the most important things are hard to quantify. And some organizations become obsessed with optimizing around only those ideas they can easily quantify, gravitating toward the security of a spreadsheet mentality, a kind of epistemic fetish—if you can't observe it, it isn't real; and if you can't quantify it, you can't observe it.

Of course, that kind of analysis is an illusion.

Clearly, you can imagine some advanced civilization that has perfected some mechanism for measuring brain states, including emotions, leading to the ability to perfectly quantify concepts such as loyalty, frustration, and motivation.

Just because we haven't developed such a hypothetical technology yet doesn't mean those data points don't exist. They are very real. To disregard them because precise measurement and quantification is beyond our current technology horizon is unproductive. If you were operating a courier business in ancient Rome that involved running messengers, you wouldn't disregard running speed just because the stopwatch had yet to be invented.

If you need to find some way to score attributes that are difficult to perfectly quantify, you can do that on a relative basis. For example, you can probably confidently state which of two employees at your organization is more motivated to help drive the organization's success just as you could run one-on-one races in the ancient Rome courier business to see who is the fastest.

In the case of the employee captured in the above quote, the key factor that is highlighted is *loyalty*.

In a world defined by how hard it is to find and retain qualified workers, there may be no greater asset in the relationships that most centrally define organizations than that kind of loyalty. By investing in your employees and authentically supporting their ability to succeed, which necessarily involves respecting them enough to take their own self-assessment seriously, you earn that asset, and your investment gains value.

Note, this isn't confined to just neurodivergent workers. It happens anytime you give an opportunity to someone who desperately wants one but has had to navigate an upward climb through life toward finding an opportunity even close to consistent with their capacity to contribute. Show such an individual trust, respect, and a clearly demonstrated expression of their value to you, and the payoff is loyalty. In other words, your authentic commitment to them leads to their authentic loyalty to you.

In my experience, that payoff is probably more attainable with neurodivergent employees because they are more likely to have taken a hard road laced with past rejections to get to where they are.

In summary, the economics of neurodiversity inclusion is inextricably tied to how neurodiversity impacts the game-theoretic landscape of employee-employer relationships within the macro context of the labor market. This network of concepts has become increasingly defined by a shifting power dynamic whereby employees are finding themselves suddenly with most of the power, and employers are saddled with a series of tough decisions ahead.

No organization is immune to this dynamic. The supply-demand function defining the labor market is a macro effect. It varies somewhat from industry to industry, but the ultimate source of the fundamental pressure is about demographics across the entire economy.

The distribution of stored wealth and passive income in the developed world at present, and the aging of the population in that world overall, have all conspired to neatly set the stage for a structural shortage in the supply of qualified workers relative to the forward path of demand for goods and services.

Centrally, it's an imbalance. And it is structural, not cyclical.

It may be temporarily alleviated to some extent if and when unemployment ticks higher. But it won't go away altogether and will likely roar back to prominence during any putative subsequent recovery. And in some industries, it may not temper at all during a recession.

In other words, the analysis suggests no help is coming, from luck or circumstance, for organizations struggling with the labor shortage. Winning organizations will be those capable of innovating within the domain of human resources.

Like our apple pie entrepreneur, businesses should reexamine their fundamental assumptions about the universe of resources they may tap to do business. The supply of skilled workers can be expanded by embracing universal design principles and the authentic inclusion of people from all points along the spectrum of human neurodiversity.

It's a choice open to all organizations. But it must be handled right. And I will show you how to do it right in Part III of this book and with online resources available to purchasers of this book. When implemented effectively, the reward can extend beyond just a widened pool of talent to include intangible gains in motivation and loyalty, not to mention the potential benefits of expanded creativity, innovation, and fresh ideas, as well as a built-in defense against groupthink.

Key Takeaways

- One of the most powerful arguments for embracing authentic neurodiversity inclusion is rooted in recent developments in the evolution of the supply of labor in developed world economies. The US alone is home to approximately 60 million neurodivergent people, the vast majority of whom are unemployed and many of whom are motivated and skilled job seekers with unique talents and perspectives that carry enormous value potential.

- At the same time, most businesses are struggling to find enough qualified workers. How will this translate to the bottom line? Increased costs, tighter margins, and a generally tougher operating environment.

- Prospective neurodivergent workers seeking gainful employment that provides a level of responsibility and compensation commensurate with their experience and skill level have been chronically excluded from the economy. And yet, in a labor shortage context, they represent an enormous undervalued and untapped resource that

(continued)

The Economics of Neurodiversity Inclusion

(continued)

can be unlocked through the principles of authentic inclusion and universal design.

- According to researchers from the United States Federal Reserve, the labor shortage hinges on a combination of factors including an aging population, a wave of early retirements due to the pandemic, the tragic loss of hundreds of thousands of potential workers due to Covid deaths, and a historic drop in immigration that has been based, in part, on rising nationalism and Trump-era policy changes that have a base of popular support among US voters. But the most important factor is demographic.

- The labor shortage is not likely to be a short-term dynamic. Leaders need a long-term plan to mitigate its impact.

- The labor shortage has consequences that stretch far beyond simply not being able to find enough workers. It creates a game-theoretic landscape that fosters other problems related to motivation and loyalty.

- Offering greater flexibility around working from home for neurodivergent employees can have an enormous payoff in terms of productivity, loyalty, motivation, and innovation.

- The analysis suggests no help is coming, from luck or circumstance, for organizations struggling with the labor shortage. Winning organizations will be those capable of innovating within the domain of human resources.

- The supply of skilled workers can be expanded by embracing universal design principles and the authentic inclusion of people from the rich tapestry of talent found in neurodivergent job seekers.

Chapter 4

The Hitchhiker's Guide to Cognitive Diversity

"Logic will get you from A to B. Imagination will get you everywhere."

—Albert Einstein

Over the past 25 years, I have worked closely with thousands of neurodivergent people spanning a wide spectrum of cognitive diversity. It has been humbling to be exposed to the rich tapestry of so many uniquely talented minds during many years of research, business operations, advocacy, and consulting.

Every step of the way, I have become increasingly convinced that an open mind to new ways of thinking and new ideas is the path that leads out of Flatland. But that journey is best undertaken after taking the time to be armed with at least a rudimentary understanding of the range of different cognitive strategies on display across the human neurodiversity landscape. We live our lives surrounded by them. They define our relationships, our experience of culture on macro and micro scales, our interactions with others, our institutions, and even our own interior lives. And yet, they are typically as invisible to us as water is to fish.

In my experience, the different cognitive techniques, skills, and modes of thought individuals employ to solve problems, make decisions, and understand concepts are rarely appreciated or examined in their full diversity. This is especially true within the strategically managed communities that make up our large corporations and organizations, even though this may be where they can yield the greatest value.

As we have also discussed, accelerating economic and technological change will introduce more urgency into this equation. Cognitive diversity stands to become an increasingly important organizational asset. All employers should be strategizing about how to recruit unique talent, including neurodivergent workers. According to a recent PwC report, it is anticipated that AI will contribute approximately $15 trillion to the global economy by 2030.[1] At the same time, current forecasts estimate that 30% of existing positions across the economy will be automated away while we may see more than 90 million new roles arise by the mid-2030s.

Creativity is a core human asset for organizations navigating the future we can look forward to from here—a point that needs little justification. Unsurprisingly, it is one of the five skills emphasized by the World Economic Forum as crucial for success in the future. Recall in Chapter 2, I suggested that employers should be hiring a cognitively diverse talent pool, where the community-level impact of complementarity is a higher priority than the individual-level absence of divergent traits or tendencies—where some people have stronger strengths, unique talents, and more significant challenges balanced by others with more evenly distributed, less spiky strength-weakness profiles.

Strategically, the goal for the future involves examining cognitive assets at the group, team, or community level within an organization to foster a workforce that possesses enough cognitive diversity to generate strong gains in innovation, imagination, originality of perspective, and unique pathways to optimal productivity.

Perpendicular Thinking in Flatland

This perspective necessitates a rethinking of the entire edifice of human resources on a wide scale. While that is beyond the purview of this book, my team and I have begun to research and employ a process of examination, evaluation, and recommendation derived from cognitive science that can lead to the optimization of what I refer to as an organization's Cognitive Talent Matrix. This involves researching organizational goals and how the inherent complementarity of cognition involved within an organization's most important asset—its people—can better facilitate the achievement of those goals.

Given the rapid advancements being made in AI, we include the assumption that an increasingly important piece of this matrix will be represented by nonhuman cognition as we move toward the future, and how new roles associated with this transition are likely to arise and will come to involve complementarity between human and artificial intelligence assets as well. To put this in perspective, as a cognitive scientist, I was curious how AI-driven art might try to illustrate human cognition. I asked a bot to visualize some aspects of my own cognition, which I would describe, in part, as systems thinking with strong empathy, pattern detection, and hyperfocus. My experience of interior life when problem-solving is almost like being surrounded by invisible whiteboards where I can project, rotate, and combine ideas in conceptual space. I can also see music as colorful moving shapes. While I was reading fluently by age 3, I had tremendous challenges when I was younger. As a teenager, I struggled to fit in socially and also experienced sensory sensitivities that I have since learned to manage. My profile of strengths and challenges has changed somewhat over the years, especially due to forced adaptations after losing both of my parents at a young age. You can see how AI summed this up in the result in Figure 4.1.

Figure 4.1 AI-generated art representing systems thinking.

This AI-generated pictorial representation doesn't sync up very well with the vivid richness of my subjective inner experience, nor does it represent any cognitive or emotional nuance. There is no sense of creative conceptualization; no imaginative leap toward anything narrative or insightful. It's what you might expect to see in a brochure for some kind of tutoring service. At best.

I enlisted colleagues and friends with divergent cognitive traits to try the same exercise, including a friend with sensory processing disorder and language processing difficulties who relies on her memory of tactile features in her environment, such as the wood on a conference table or the feeling of a soft sweater, to reliably remember spoken communication during meetings. An innovator-scientist friend who experiences conceptual synesthesia tends to project visual-spatial imagination to entertain hypotheses in mind and fuel discoveries. Another colleague who is dyslexic worked with the AI through a series of creative prompts to see if he could steer it toward visually representing the concept of a deep instinct for exploratory behavior.

There were others as well, each with a unique perspective and a different approach to prompting. We all repeated it many times over the course of a day, widely varying our strategies. The result? Everyone came away with the sense that this type of process—which boils down to a machine translating the abstractly colorful and richly experienced into a concrete visual representation—showcases what appears to be a fundamental limitation to the current AI paradigm.

Another point all of us agreed upon was that the task offered plenty of opportunity for capturing a sense of the profound. One might argue that this isn't a limitation of the AI model but a point about humans and what we intersubjectively find profound. It's an interesting debate waiting to happen. But, in some sense, it's moot because humans will dominate the end-user role in the marketplace for AI technology for the foreseeable future. In that light, AI art isn't successful unless it results in something that resonates with humans.

These are all different ways of making the point that we appear to be charting a course toward a world powered by a synergy between artificial intelligence and human intelligence, with a premium role to be played by nonlinear human cognitive strategies leveraging the pure speed and processing power of advanced AI to generate peak value.

To the extent that we can prepare for that future, we focused in prior chapters on complimentary cognition, the perils of groupthink, and the economics of authentic neuroinclusion. In this chapter, I focus on walking you through some fascinating examples to showcase the complexity and richness of human neurodiversity drawn from my research, including subjective representations of different kinds of minds.

This is important because, while a values-driven approach is essential to authentic neuroinclusion, getting it right in implementation involves at least some degree of understanding, empathy, and appreciation for the diversity of problem-solving skills and novel approaches that can be brought to the table by the full scope of a human population with a statistically normal distribution of neurotypes.

Human resource tools and checklists focused on neurodiversity are generally lacking in this regard. While they may help you "check the box" of being cosmetically quote-unquote neurodiversity friendly, they won't move the needle at all when it comes to genuinely tapping into unique, and often invisible, talent—the N+1 axis—which requires new methods of understanding, recruitment, and support.

A Guided Tour Through Kinds of Minds

In broad terms, diversity of thought refers to the range of mindsets, thought processes, ideas, concepts, problem solving methodologies, and perspectives that are important in eliminating blind spots and tunnel vision in an organization. While by no means exhaustive, cognitive diversity may include strengths in the following types of problem-solving, perceptual, and analytical tendencies.

Lateral thinking. Traditional linear thinking can be described as a direct path to problem solving—it follows a straightforward, sequential path from premises to conclusion, without loops, jumps, or divergences. By contrast, lateral thinking is the path marked by those loops, jumps, and divergences. It is the way forward when the linear path runs into a wall or a canyon with no bridge.

Lateral thinking may also involve combinatorial thought processes, backward planning, or looking at an old problem from an alternative viewpoint (such as turning a diagram sideways in one's mind and drawing unique conclusions).

A classic example of linear reasoning can be recast as a new example of lateral reasoning: Lewis Carroll's "Two Glasses Problem," which involves the starting condition of one glass of 10 oz of pure water and a second glass of 10 oz of pure milk. In Carroll's puzzle, the question is: if you take a 1-oz spoonful of milk from the milk glass and stir it into the water glass, what do you do next to recreate a situation where the amount of milk in glass two is the same as the amount of water in glass one? The answer, somewhat counterintuitively, is to take a 1-oz spoonful of the water/milk mixture and stir it back into the milk glass. The math works out. Look it up.

However, let's ask a different question: if you go back to the starting condition of one glass of pure water and one glass of pure milk, how do you proceed to get an end result where both glasses have the same amount of both milk and water? The linear approach would be to use finely tuned measuring tools and incorporate the relative physical properties (mass, density, etc.) of milk and water and then engage in a trial-and-error process until the desired end-state is reached.

The lateral thinking solution, by contrast, might be to pour some milk into the water glass and stir thoroughly, then empty the rest of the milk glass onto the ground, and then pour half of the milk/water mixture from what was originally the water glass back into the now-empty milk glass.

Lateral thinking often relies on stepping outside the imagined boundaries of the puzzle or turning some factor upside down or backward to reveal a different perspective.

Another example harkens back to a key point made in the Introduction in this book: find a place on a world map where a major landmass tapers to a triangular point that points straight upward. The only way to solve that question is to turn a world map so that South points upward. The answer is South America.

Associative thinking. Associative thinking and lateral thinking can go together as they both involve nonlinear cognitive processes. Associative thinking is focused purely on connecting the similarities and drawing connections among two or more concepts by combining or associating concepts that don't typically go together (i.e., analogical thinking). In the words of an autistic man diagnosed at the age of four: "Thinking is associative and experienced like the branches of a tree." There is an image below in the section of this chapter on Graphic Depictions of Kinds of Minds that is based on his hand-drawn art of how different ideas combine in his mind.

A very different kind of associative thinking is common with synesthesia where the senses cross different cognitive pathways. These experiences can take a variety of unique forms with over 80 different types of synesthesia documented. Some people taste shapes, others experience letters or numbers as different colors, and still others experience sound as color or taste flavors as sound. Some people, like me, experience ideas as shapes or movement. Tasting shapes or hearing flavors is an example of one of the rarer forms termed lexical-gustatory synesthesia, which occurs in about 0.2% of the population.

Example from interviews: "When I eat, I notice that different flavors, especially strong ones, have their own sound. Spicy foods are experienced as high-pitched musical soundwaves while sweet foods are baritone and fruits sound like white noise." —Male teenager with synesthesia

It is more common than realized for musicians, scientists, and artists to have synesthesia. Tori Amos, who started composing music at 3 years old, has described seeing music as distinct structures of light. Nobel laureate Richard Feynman, a synesthete, perceived mathematical symbols as colors.

Hyperfocus. The ability to intensely focus attention on a task for long stretches of time, especially on tasks and topics of particular interest. Here is the testimony of a young male diagnosed with Tourette's syndrome and strong autistic traits: "At my job, I can concentrate intensely and show a kind of single-mindedness my peers do not. I work in software testing where I find and report bugs. I can do this for many hours straight with only short breaks."

Here is a different testimonial example that more closely exemplifies hyperfixation on a special interest from an Australian woman who was diagnosed with Asperger's syndrome (now part of the autism spectrum) at age 10: "I love gemstones and as a young girl, I collected thousands of stones, learning everything I could about each one, its history, and unique properties. I even won First Place at the state science fair, which made me realize I wanted to be a scientist."

Mental rotation and 3D visualization. Mental rotation (MR) allows for the interior visualization of mental objects in three-dimensional space. It confers a strength in the ability to imagine via mental transportation how an object would appear in space from a particular perspective versus alternative perspectives (such as what that same object looks like when rotated in space at a new orientation or from a new perspective).

An example of mental rotation based on interview material reported in my doctoral thesis at University of Oxford: "If I need to fix something and need the right screwdriver, I would be making and changing pictures of different size screwdrivers and what might fit the screw slot . . . If I am pleased with the choice of screwdriver and want to express it to myself, I might think of a picture of patting myself on the back."[2]

Visual thinking. Visual thinking is exactly what it sounds like—a strength in visualizing information in the mind much in the way that Dr. Temple Grandin, perhaps the most famous living autistic person, describes in her book *Thinking in Pictures*. It can accompany verbal thinking approaches (such as inner speech) but can also be the dominant interior mental life for some neurodivergent people such as Grandin. Superior visual thinking, or "thinking in pictures," allowed Dr. Grandin access to unique insights that she leveraged to transform the US cattle industry.

Visual thinking has been reported as being experienced in the following ways, according to my research interviews with neurodivergent people across the globe:

"I visualize all concepts and ideas in pictures like a library in my head."

"I do think in speech, but my thinking is mostly done with visual images. Sometimes my thinking can be so visual that I might forget what I want to say unless I draw a picture of it in the air."[3]

"I am very easily disoriented. I get lost easily if someone says to get somewhere verbally. If I have to remember words (place names or street names). I can't recall those quantity and detail. I know I'll get lost. My stress shoots up. If I see the map [in mind]. Identify where I am, I try to see in mind and so I cope better."

Dyslexic thinking. Dyslexic thinking encapsulates skills such as creative problem-solving, empathy, synthesizing information, big picture thinking, and leadership. In the EY Value of Dyslexia Report published in 2018, it was suggested that the dyslexic brain was "hard wired" for the skills of the future. Four years later, in 2022, it was announced that dyslexic thinking would officially be recognized as a valuable skill on the platform LinkedIn. Sir Richard Branson has been an early champion for the official recognition of dyslexic thinking as an asset, especially in the context of important future skills as laid out by the World Economic Forum. Richard Branson described his own dyslexia as essential to his success, which "shaped Virgin right from the beginning and imagination has been the key."

During my research and listening tour, I met countless innovators and entrepreneurs, many who struggled with school but found success due to a focus on strengths and the common experience of constant problem solving and "workarounds" when facing challenges. Here is an example.

> We just raised our Series B for our AI-driven data company. I have no doubt that dyslexia and my struggles growing up because of how I learn differently made me more innovative and more persistent—two skills that are important as an entrepreneur. Dyslexic thinking helped me see connections that other people missed, which led to key patents that our proprietary technology is based on. —Dyslexic entrepreneur, male

First-principles approach. First principles thinking, which is sometimes referred to as reasoning from a first-principles methodology or approach, starts with breaking down a problem or issue into its most basic or essential elements. Then assumptions are challenged by asking critical questions with the goal of understanding the most fundamental factual truth. In my experience, this process can be understood as evolving inside a person as a consequence of uneven or insufficient access to top-down conclusions that may be more readily available to neurotypical individuals through social transmission during development.

> I sometimes have an idea that flashes in my mind. If it is interesting enough, I can stick with it and try to understand it based on core properties rather than what I might have read or heard

about how to do something. I might build a model to understand it more deeply. This has really been important to coming up with ways of doing things that other people have not thought about. —Autistic-ADHDer (AuDHD) nonbinary innovator

One way to think about this approach to problem solving is that there may be a gap in knowledge of social rules or instructions that has not been fully processed or appreciated. The information gaps are then compensated for, resulting in the emergence of a habitual process of reasoning from a first-principles perspective to solve the problem. Over time, this method, from my experience and interviews, sometimes develops into a gift that is not as easily accessible to neurotypical peers, who have had an easier time following instructions during their development.

Pattern thinking. Pattern thinking is a cognitive process where observation of hidden patterns becomes clear to the observer and connections between concepts, events, or objects form into a meaningful patterned arrangement in the mind. Pattern thinkers often see connections between disparate things that others don't and can possess powerful insights.

Bottom-up thinking. Bottom-up thinking differs from what we call "top-down" conceptual processing, which is believed to be the norm for many neurotypicals. Example of bottom-up thinking: perceiving (at first glance) all the individual trees and seeing all the unique details, including noticing how each tree is slightly different from each other— rather than first perceiving the more general concept of a forest.

Pattern thinking can sometimes be influenced by bottom-up information processing. For example, the National Geospatial-Intelligence Agency values the unique pattern thinking skills of autistic analysts who have used exceptional pattern finding skills to identify minute details within massive data sets.

Reverse engineering. Reverse engineering often involves starting in the mind with the end result and working backwards to dissemble and grasp all the component parts, which can then be rearranged or reassembled in the mind. Like pattern thinking, this method of problem solving also uncovers hidden structures and reveals important details about how an idea, product, or object was initially designed, as well as how it can be reformed or redesigned in a different way.

Graphic Depictions of Diversity of Minds

Here I include additional fascinating examples of how some neurodivergent people relate to and experience their own mental life. These illustrations and graphic depictions below should enrich your

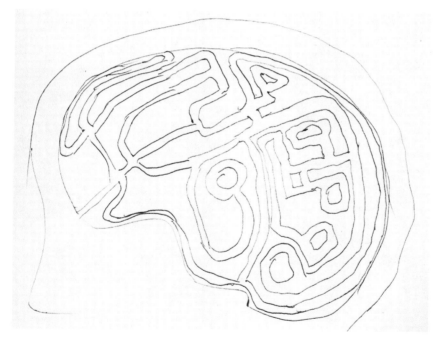

Figure 4.2 Graphic depiction of mind highway system
(*Source:* Maureen Dunne, 2008, raw research material, "Visual and Verbal Thinking," PhD Diss., University of Oxford.)

understanding of the rich diversity of thought and cognitive abilities among neurodivergent people—and how different and unique each individual is.

Figure 4.2 depicts a mind that works like connecting images and words on a highway.

Time-Space Synesthesia is when time is experienced as physical or conceptual space where events, specific times, or calendar months are perceived along visual-spatial dimensions or as existing as points in space. A drawing from an adult depicting her experience with this type of synesthesia is shown in Figure 4.3.

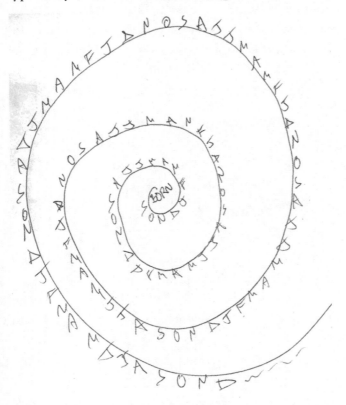

Figure 4.3 Time as points in conceptual space.
(*Source:* Dunne, 2008, raw research material, "Visual and Verbal Thinking," PhD diss., University of Oxford.)

Figure 4.4 depicts an autistic person whose thinking is associative and experienced like the branches of a tree.

Figure 4.4 Thinking is associative and experienced like the branches of a tree.
(*Source:* Dunne, 2008, raw research material, "Visual and Verbal Thinking," PhD diss., University of Oxford.)

Figure 4.5 illustrates the mind of an autistic person experienced as various files with vast information consciously stored and accessed daily. The files would be searched for, and relevant files would be opened in the mind while solving problems at work, socializing with people, and giving lectures.

Or examine Jory Fleming's depiction of his mind and where he feels present at the center (see Figure 4.6), as shared in his book published in 2021, *How to Be Human: An Autistic Man's Guide to Life*. I have been very fortunate to work closely with Jory, an

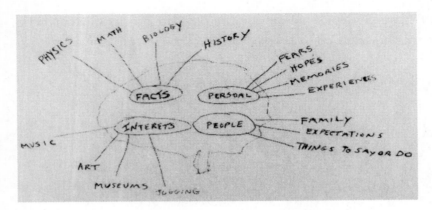

Figure 4.5 Graphic depiction of visual thinking from an autistic adult. (*Source:* Dunne, 2008, raw research material, "Visual and Verbal Thinking," PhD diss., University of Oxford.)

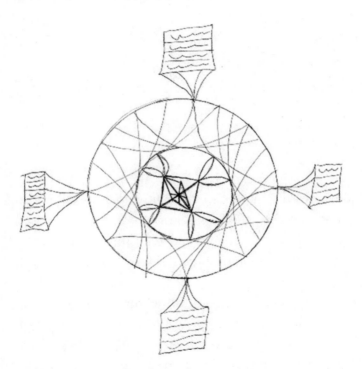

Figure 4.6 Jory Fleming's depiction of his mind. (*Source:* Fleming, 2021, *How to Be Human: An Autistic Man's Guide to Life.*)

The Neurodiversity Edge

extraordinarily gifted autistic Rhodes Scholar; I recruited him to be part of my team for my work helping to launch LEGO Foundation's $20 million Accelerator Fund for Neurodiversity.

Here is how Jory describes his illustration:[4]

> I drew a circle with a lot of lines going everywhere. I didn't draw any of these lines to be straight because I feel like nothing in my brain is especially straight. The larger outer circle is where I envision the conceptual me might rest. The objects on the edges are databases for storing memories or facts or whatever. I am located inside, and I pull them in. The second circle in the middle is like a theater—that's where I look at shards of memories or facts. Whenever I want to do something with my thinking process, I'll push the information I need into the middle space so I can visualize or translate it into other mechanisms, like speech. I imagine these outer databases are probably similar to how other people's brains work, but then inside my mind, it all kind of goes everywhere. The conceptual me is moving really, really fast in a circle around and around, until I get to a point where I pick up what I need and push it into the inner circle.

Jory's perspective, along with the rich interview material and graphic depictions of kinds of minds, informed my business case studies for the content of this book. More generally, the focus is on bringing different perspectives and attributes to the table with a values-based approach to the DEI equation. It often starts with a conscious intention to include cognitive diversity with an acknowledgment that representation is important. But this objective is riddled with risk in the form of what might be called the "check the box" approach to diversity inclusion, as we cover in detail in Chapter 6.

Copernican Moments

Ptolemy was an ancient astronomer who constructed, more than 2,000 years ago, what most historians consider to be the Western world's first fully developed functional model of the solar system.

Back then, he was saddled with the assumption that the Earth was a fixed point at the center of creation—an unassailable cultural axiom. The celestial bodies were all just lights in the sky moving around. But they knew the Earth was at the center of it all.

They also knew the difference between the celestial bodies of the solar system—the planets and the Sun—and other stars much further away because the celestial bodies in our solar system moved around against the backdrop of the rest of the universe in an easily observable sense and could be seen in greater detail even with the naked eye.

Given those initial premises—that the Earth was a fixed point at the center of creation, that there were other celestial bodies nearby that pursued active paths through the sky, and that there were countless other stars much further away that slowly shifted in the sky with the seasons—he constructed his model.[5]

Nowadays, we teach our students that Ptolemy's model (see Figure 4.7) was wrong. However, I would submit that Ptolemy's model wasn't exactly "wrong" per se. It was simply unnecessarily complicated. One might better call it inelegant.

One could make an easy case that Ptolemy's model was a perfectly accurate representation of reality even according to what we now understand because our contemporary understanding includes the notion that everything in the universe is constantly moving relative to everything else. In other words, there are no fixed points in the cosmos. Armed with that notion, you could conceivably take any object as a fixed point, and then assemble a model of movement for

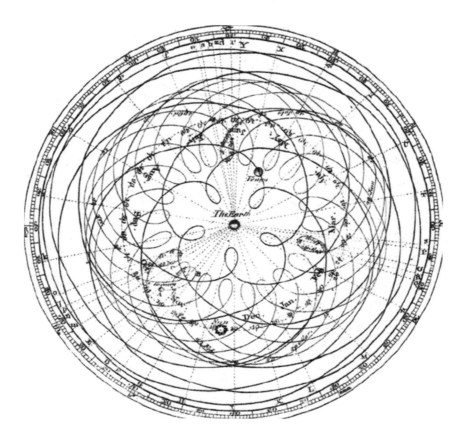

Figure 4.7 The Ptolemaic model of the solar system. (Public domain.)

everything else from that frame of reference and, lo and behold, you would have a basis for perfectly accurate projections once you had enough data in your model.

So, in a sense, the Ptolemaic model was perfectly accurate. But it was absurdly complicated.

To make it work, he had planets moving one direction for a bit and then looping around in circles and moving the other way, zigging and zagging as needed. The sun looped around the Earth and the Moon. The Moon did somersaults. Mars did cartwheels.

However, because his model worked—because it was able to form the basis for accurate predictions—and because no one else had a better model that got the basic job done, no one really questioned it. Planets were simply seen as volatile objects with very strange patterns of movement that couldn't really be explained in a manner that we would now call "algorithmically understandable."

That state of affairs dominated our understanding of the heavens for a long time. In fact, Ptolemy's model stood as the standard-bearer of solar system astronomy for about 1,500 years until a guy named Copernicus came along.

Copernicus rearranged the whole system around a different core assumption: that the Sun was the central fixed point in the solar system. Once that one piece was added to the equation, everything just fell into place. The complexity became unnecessary. Planets moved in big ellipses with no weird deviations. Their movements could now be extrapolated into principles that were universal and algorithmically understandable.

It was a breakthrough in representational parsimony—a more elegant order had been found.

In other words, the data didn't change at all. But seeing that same data through a different lens of interpretation created an epiphany. Sense distilled from nonsense. Intuitive order emerged.

It seems like a long-winded way to begin an explanation of how it feels to realize you are neurodivergent. But this is exactly my own lived experience and the experience of most neurodivergent people.

Your understanding of your whole life and experiences up to that point are seen through one lens analogous to the Ptolemaic model of the solar system. Then suddenly you discover that your sense of self is irrevocably transformed by the epiphany. You find your Copernican moment.

Before that "identity epiphany," life is jumbled into paradoxical theories about yourself, your strengths, gifts, and weaknesses, what constituted realistic expectations about the future, and how other people made sense of you and themselves. Afterward, a new paradigm of the self emerges, and everything simply falls into place.

This is how my husband described his Copernican moment after being diagnosed with ADHD.

> It was like I had been feeling my way around a dark room, wondering whether I was in the attic, or the basement, or the living room, looking for some combination of ideas that made everything fall into place. And then I added this one new piece of information, and it was like turning on the lights. Suddenly, everything made sense.

With cognitive diversity also comes cultural expansion and the rich diversity of unique perspectives that can help teams innovate and solve complex problems. Just as *Flatland*'s main character, A. Square, learned to see a new dimension by being open to taking a journey outside of the confines of his known world, neurotypical people can learn from new ways of thinking and problem solving outside of their direct experience.

Different kinds of minds working together create much stronger teams than cognitively homogenous groups. In this way, both neuro-divergent and neurotypical people alike can share their own kind of Copernican moment. When all kinds of minds are valued and there is a strong foundation of trust and psychological safety, the potential for innovation is ripe.

It is my hope that this book may spark such a paradigm shift, spreading from one organization to another over time.

From Community Level Back to Individual Level

Challenging ourselves to better understand very different perspectives and ways of processing information is helpful not only to developing a powerfully inclusive organizational culture, where neurodivergent people feel valued, but also as a valuable exercise to nudge team members to empathize with a wider range of neurotypes, learning new skills and strategies in the process. It also helps to spur neurotypical and neurodivergent team members to challenge unconscious biases, stereotypes, and presumptions about others.

For example, consider how plotting concepts as visual references in space may be natural to some neurodivergent minds. Exposure to this kind of visual mnemonic cognitive strategy may help to expand the mental resources that neurotypicals can bring to bear on new challenges and opportunities as well as to strengthen working memory.

Both neurodivergent and neurotypical people have much to learn from each other. As we covered in Chapter 1, the theory of complementary cognition suggests that we are stronger at a community level when we have a wider field of cognitive diversity from which to draw collectively. However, my own research and experience working with teams over the years strongly suggests that each member of the community also benefits from exposure to cognitive diversity at an individual level.

Ideas and problem-solving strategies are fluid within communities and can be shared, learned, and adopted simply through sustained exposure, shared experiences, and the cultivation of mutual empathy. We cover this in much greater detail, with case studies and stories from client inclusion training sessions, in Chapter 13.

Parts II and III will also include a focus on strategies to challenge limiting stereotypes to better understand why neuroinclusion, when cultivated on a foundation of psychological safety, trust, and transparent 360-degree communication, holds the potential to drive innovation and team success. In The Neurodiversity Edge online resource library, I also include thought experiments, perspective-taking tools, and templates that can be used during organizational trainings and retreats.

Key Takeaways

- An open mind to new ways of thinking and new ideas is the path that leads out of Flatland. But that journey is best undertaken only once armed with at least a rudimentary understanding of the range of different cognitive strategies on display across the full spectrum of human neurodiversity.

- Accelerating economic and technological change will introduce more urgency into this equation.

- The goal for the future involves examining cognitive assets at the group, team, or community level within an organization to foster a workforce without powerful downside that possesses enough cognitive diversity to generate strong gains in innovation, imagination, originality of perspective, and unique pathways to optimal productivity.

- We appear to be charting a course toward a world powered by a synergy between artificial intelligence and human intelligence, with a premium role to be played by nonlinear human cognitive strategies leveraging the pure speed and processing power of advanced AI to generate peak value.

(continued)

(continued)

- *Lateral thinking* is the path marked by the loops, jumps, and divergences whose absence defines linear thinking. It is the way forward when the linear path runs into a wall or a canyon with no bridge. Lateral thinking often relies on stepping outside the imagined boundaries of the puzzle or turning some factor upside down or backward to reveal a different perspective.

- *Associative thinking* is focused purely on connecting the similarities and drawing connections among two or more concepts by combining or associating concepts that don't typically go together.

- *Hyperfocus* refers to the ability to intensely focus attention on a task for long stretches of time, especially on tasks and topics of particular interest.

- *Mental rotation (and 3D visualization)* allows for the interior visualization of mental objects in three-dimensional space. It confers a strength in the ability to imagine via mental transportation how an object would appear in space from a particular perspective versus alternative perspectives (such as what that same object looks like when rotated in space at a new orientation or from a new perspective).

- *Visual thinking* is exactly what it sounds like—a strength in visualizing information in the mind much in the way that Dr. Temple Grandin, perhaps the most famous living autistic person, describes in her book *Thinking in Pictures*.

- *Dyslexic thinking* encapsulates skills such as creative problem-solving, empathy, synthesizing information, big-picture thinking, and leadership. In the EY Value of

Dyslexia Report published in 2018, it was suggested that the dyslexic brain was hardwired for the skills of the future.

- *First principles thinking*, which is sometimes referred to as reasoning from a first-principles methodology or approach, starts with breaking down a problem or issue into its most basic or essential elements. Then assumptions are challenged by asking critical questions with the goal of understanding the most fundamental factual truth.

- *Pattern thinking* is a cognitive process where observation of hidden patterns becomes clear to the observer and connections between concepts, events, or objects form into a meaningful patterned arrangement in the mind. Pattern thinkers often see connections between disparate things that others don't and can possess powerful insights.

- *Bottom-up thinking* differs from what we call top-down conceptual processing, which is believed to be the norm for many neurotypicals. An example of bottom-up thinking would be perceiving (at first glance) all the individual trees and seeing all the unique details, including noticing how each tree is slightly different from each other—rather than first perceiving the more general concept of a forest.

- *Reverse engineering* often involves starting in the mind with the end results and working backwards to dissemble and grasp all the component parts, which can then be rearranged or reassembled in the mind. Like pattern thinking, this method of problem solving also uncovers hidden structures and reveals important details about how an idea, product, or object was initially designed, as well as how it can be reformed or redesigned in a different way.

(continued)

97

The Hitchhiker's Guide to Cognitive Diversity

(continued)

- The transition from the Ptolemaic to Copernican model was an epiphany because it contained the same data and the same predictive value but accomplished it with just a handful of algorithmic rules. It snapped together and could be understood in terms of principles. It could be represented in full in just a couple sentences. Ptolemy's model would take pages of instructions to describe in sufficient detail to not lose the predictive value.

- This epiphany serves as an uncanny metaphor for the epiphany many neurodivergent people experience when they learn of their neurodivergence and compare their past experiences and feelings with those of others in their tribe—it is often a personal revolution in self-understanding: a new model is discovered that explains everything with a simplicity and elegance previously unimagined by the individual.

- Both neurodivergent and neurotypical people have much to learn from each other. As we covered in Chapter 1, the theory of complementary cognition suggests that we are stronger at a community level when we have a wider field of cognitive diversity from which to draw collectively.

- My own research and experience working with teams over the years strongly suggests that each member of the community also benefits from exposure to cognitive diversity at an individual level.

- Parts II and III will also include a focus on strategies to challenge limiting stereotypes to better understand why neuroinclusion holds the potential to drive innovation and team success.

Chapter 5

From Why to How

"When you've decided you don't have a culture, you've got one...The question is: Do you want to influence it or not?"
—Joel Peterson[1]

U p to here, we have focused on the *Why*—the value proposition of embracing neurodiversity inclusion to drive cognitive diversity, innovation, an expansion in available talent, improved immunity to groupthink risk, and gains in loyalty, motivation, and reputational status. All of these concepts also have further significance in relationship to the context that defines the world now and over coming years—a context defined by a structural labor shortage and revolutionary advances in emerging technologies that promise truly world-changing implications over the next decade separately and, more dramatically, in combination.

It is also a world more divided by cultural and political forces than we have seen in generations, and one where decades of reputational capital can be destroyed in an afternoon. This last factor shouldn't be entirely overlooked. In that vein, neurodiversity inclusion is a universally supported cause celebrated by all cultural tribes because it impacts households regardless of religion, political party, region, socioeconomic status, race, gender, sexuality, or education level. Intersectionality is also incredibly important as many neurodivergent people belong to multiple underrepresented or marginalized groups.

Every community has a stake in this movement. And every organization would benefit from embracing it. I rest my case on the *Why* here. Now, it's time to focus on the *What* and *How*.

For the rest of this book, we will focus on defining an effective set of goals and achieving them through powerful strategies and tactics that incorporate input from neurodivergent voices across the globe. In this chapter, we will focus specifically on defining goals capable of providing a path to manifesting the value of authentic neurodiversity inclusion. As with every other part of the process espoused in this book, the focus must be on changing organizational culture at its deepest level to achieve a sustained transformation.

When an organization commits to becoming more inclusive, the process begins with "The Three C's"—Codification plus Conduct drives Culture (see Figure 5.1). In subsequent chapters, our focus will become more granular as we delve further into the framework of objectives this chapter introduces. We will also explore different strategies and tactics designed to achieve inclusion goals.

Finally, it is impossible to fully understand how to assess and measure progress without utilizing a system of data collection and metrics. This book's related online resources offer customizable templates for strategic planning, assessment, and evaluation as further guidance toward this end.

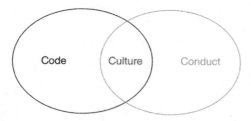

Figure 5.1 The Three C's of Codification, Conduct, and Culture.

Culture Is as Culture Does

Every organization has a culture. That culture may be the result of intentional design, or it may simply be something that grew into the vacuum left by the lack of that intentional design. Either way, there is a culture. An organization that tells itself, "We don't have a particular culture," has a culture defined by (1) the idea that organizational culture is unimportant and (2) the unwillingness to commit to any specific values, which is a statement in itself.

In his lectures at Stanford Business School, Joel Peterson makes the core point that there are good and bad corporate cultures. The essential factor differentiating those designations is ultimately about integrity—do the expressed values of the organization match the actions that define it in day-to-day life?

A company's *expressed* values are important: they either act as a legitimate North Star to navigate by in all other aspects of the organization or they act as a contrast to the demonstrated nature of the organization in its dealings with itself, its customers, and its surrounding community.

In other words, no matter what you say in an email or on a bulletin board or in an interview in the *Wall Street Journal*, your values are reflected by how you actually deal with the world and how you allocate your strategic resources (time, money, and mindshare). If your demonstrated values match your expressed values, then you have an effective culture. If they don't, you don't.

"The Three C's"—Codification plus Conduct drives Culture.

Peterson gives the example of a statement made by Isadore Sharp, founder and CEO of Four Seasons, to capture the secret of Four Seasons' success. Sharp publicly claimed his secret was the Golden Rule—just treat people well, the way you would like to be treated, and they will do the same.

Peterson then brings up the fictional what-if scenario imagining that Sharp made this statement at a keynote speech and then went back to the office and started yelling at his secretary, shoving the cleaning lady out of his way, and chewing out a hotel manager.

The point here is not just that he would be acting rudely, it's that he would be acting that way after making such a statement. If you make a statement like that and then clearly act in a manner that contradicts it, and do so in front of your whole organization, you are planting very deep seeds of cynicism in your organizational culture. It says, we are an organization that says one thing and then does another.

That would be a bad culture.

I bring up this example here because one of the most important elements of a strategic plan to build authentic neuroinclusion into an organizational culture is to enshrine a value statement supporting and committing to that concept. We will cover that step in more detail in a later chapter. But I wanted to bring it up here to "pre-enforce" the sense of the stakes involved. A values statement generally begins with aspirational goals, but organizations will benefit to the extent they hold themselves accountable in terms of exhibiting those values in practice.

Building on what we concluded above, the fictional Sharp would be building a culture, clearly one that espouses the value of duplicity.

Moreover, a viable organizational culture built on integrity is a prerequisite to everything else we will discuss for the rest of this book. It only works if everyone buys in. And that will only happen if everyone is part of a culture built on integrity. That comes ultimately through trust—trust that buying in will be good for each member of the team, trust that leadership will hold itself to the same standards that it demands from everyone else.

These ideas are fundamental, not just to ethical ideals but to performance. Everything follows from trust. This should be accepted as axiomatic.

As Peterson notes, a company's vision is a meta-concept that supersedes all of these layers. The alignment of organizational culture is the process of manifesting that vision. You won't have a truly successful business—you won't be able to achieve your vision—without strong alignment connecting values, goals, strategies, tactics, and measurables.

The vision, then, is the raison d'être of the business—we will serve whom with what and in what unique way. Presumably, every serious business has an answer to that question. Organizations seem to misfire or go off the rails when they have a wrong idea, or no idea, about how to achieve that vision, in principle—about what values should be adopted as North Stars to guide all investments, actions, personnel decisions, and communications; about how to define goals and achieve them through strategies and tactics; about how to build alignment across all of these concepts; and about how to get everyone to fully buy into that program.

Building alignment is about eradicating gaps between each step in the flow that orients and connects values, goals, strategies, tactics, and metrics. If those concepts are all manifestly aligned on a day-to-day basis, you have something that can work over the long term. The word for that state is *integrity*.

Time, money, and mindshare are the soldiers directed by this alignment. They are measured and kept in check by the controls, while being guided by strategic and tactical plans directed toward the achievement of well-conceived goals, which are premised upon the values held as sacrosanct by the organization.

In keeping with this framework, this book is an effort to demonstrate that authentic neuroinclusion is an underrated and powerful value to embrace and one that can be embodied by any organization on a sustained basis provided this process is taken seriously by all levels of the organization.

Scrum Mates

Setting vague goals is a waste of time. They need to be **specific**. Furthermore, if you can't **measure** a goal, you can't define the terms of achieving it. Goals should also be **aligned** with your value system like a ship sailing for the North Star. They should be **realistic** because they have to translate into strategies—targeting a sub-50 round of golf isn't going to yield any strategic options. Finally, goals should be **timebound** to coordinate people, processes, and planning for future goal setting and, perhaps more importantly, to establish a definite criterion for failure for all conceivable goals.

The **SMART** system is fine for personal goals.

But for organization-wide objectives, there are other dimensions that might be included as well, ideally: simple, clear, understandable, easily communicated, and memorable. When you are setting goals for yourself, the goal only has to live in one brain—yours. When you are setting a major objective for an entire organization, it has to live in intersubjective space, within and among the group mind, present in discussions and in quick-access memory in every individual brain involved. That won't be the case if your SMART goal is complicated, difficult to interpret, tough to describe, and hard to remember.

As an example of the ADHD mind at work, my husband looked at this list and almost immediately came up with "SCRUM MATES" as an acronym for all of these criteria together: specific, clear, realistic, understandable, memorable, measurable, aligned, timebound, easily communicated, and simple.

While this is probably overkill, I include it here because, as he pointed out to me a minute after devising it, it works on multiple levels given that SCRUM is a system for project management to help teams structure and manage work, and objectives are certainly MATES of that concept.

More importantly, though, the main takeaway is this: SMART isn't enough for effective organization-wide objectives unless you want them to be known by only about two out of every five members of your organization. In other words, on a meta level, objectives need to be effective in and of themselves as objectives, but they also need to be effective as memes within the culture of your organization so everyone is on the same page.[1]

This is especially true for the types of objectives we will be discussing here.

The Pyramid of Neuroinclusion

Figure 5.2 shows the product of two decades of research, thought, active listening, interviews, and firsthand experience working to help foster a paradigm of organizational management philosophy that better aligns with the reality of human neurodiversity. I first presented a much more basic version of the Pyramid many years ago while at the University of Chicago where I worked with Professor Dan Freedman, who was mentored by anthropologist Gregory Bateson and psychologist Abraham Maslow.

In the Introduction, I noted that access on a sustained basis to the fruits of authentic neurodiversity inclusion—a significantly wider pool of talent, a massive expansion in diversity of thought and lived experience, and groupthink immunity, among other dynamics— could not be attained with merely a practical toolbox and guide for neurodiversity office hacks.

Figure 5.2 shows a layered set of objectives that, in my experience, must all be cemented into place to bring about lasting authentic neuroinclusion and its many benefits. That doesn't necessarily mean they need to be put in place precisely in that order. However, an organization without a firm foundation of psychological safety

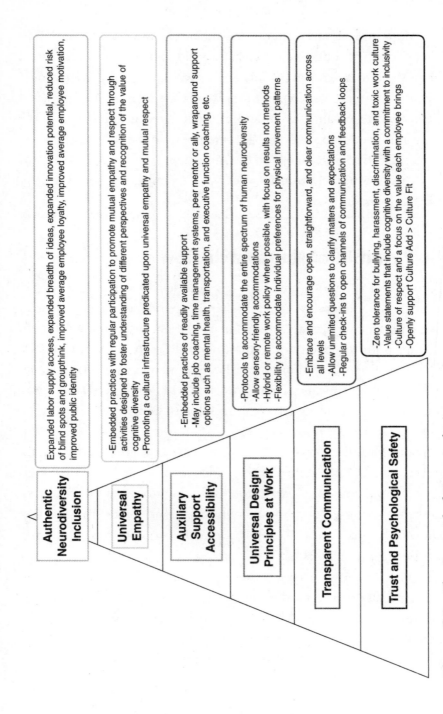

The Pyramid of Neuroinclusion.

Authentic Neurodiversity Inclusion

Expanded labor supply access, expanded breadth of ideas, expanded innovation potential, reduced risk of blind spots and groupthink, improved average employee loyalty, improved average employee motivation, improved public identity

Universal Empathy

-Embedded practices with regular participation to promote mutual empathy and respect through activities designed to foster understanding of different perspectives and recognition of the value of cognitive diversity
-Promoting a cultural infrastructure predicated upon universal empathy and mutual respect

Auxiliary Support Accessibility

-Embedded practices of readily available support
-May include job coaching, time management systems, peer mentor or ally, wraparound support options such as mental health, transportation, and executive function coaching, etc.

Universal Design Principles at Work

-Protocols to accommodate the entire spectrum of human neurodiversity
-Allow sensory-friendly accommodations
-Hybrid or remote work policy where possible, with focus on results not methods
-Flexibility to accommodate individual preferences for physical movement patterns

Transparent Communication

-Embrace and encourage open, straightforward, and clear communication across all levels
-Allow unlimited questions to clarify matters and expectations
-Regular check-ins to open channels of communication and feedback loops

Trust and Psychological Safety

-Zero tolerance for bullying, harassment, discrimination, and toxic work culture
-Value statements that include cognitive diversity with a commitment to inclusivity
-Culture of respect and a focus on the value each employee brings
-Openly support Culture Add > Culture Fit

Figure 5.2 The Pyramid of Neuroinclusion.

and transparent communications protocols won't benefit much in terms of recruiting and retaining neurodivergent talent by simply providing sensory accommodations and auxiliary support resources.

A garden won't grow, no matter how much sunlight and water it gets, if the soil is toxic.

Each of the layers in this pyramid can be construed as an actionable framework for generating specific objectives. For example, an organization might personalize the bottom layer as "Achieve perfect score on anonymous 'Trust and Psychological Safety' survey throughout all departments at all levels, separately and overall, within three months."

That step is up to each organization based on its own appraisal of its idiosyncratic reality. However, I can present a good example. And, importantly, this example demonstrates how multiple layers of the pyramid can be engaged by a single goal.

Case Study: Neuroinclusion from the Ground Up

In 2021, I received a request from the CEO of a technology company. For the purposes of this passage, I will refer to him as Mark.

When we finally got on a call, he told me that his firstborn child had recently been diagnosed as on the autism spectrum, and that diagnosis spurred him to devour every piece of research he could get his hands on. He said the research he did into neurodiversity, in general, was perhaps the biggest eye-opener.

He wasn't aware of the term or the notion that there was this vast community of people all sharing a similar kind of separateness from the rest of the world because of a degree of divergence in cognitive profile, many of them believing they have something special to offer while chronically swimming against wind and tide in terms of participation in the economy.

He was quick to jump on board with the idea of authentic neurodiversity inclusion, probably spurred by his son's diagnosis and a desire to help build a world that would work for him. But I think it also had something to do with Mark's struggle to find enough new talent to take advantage of the demand growth function that defined his current prospects.

In any case, he knew enough to know he needed someone to help him translate that sense of opportunity into an actual business transformation.

By the time he and I first talked, he had already tried to get the ball rolling by bringing on a consultant with a checklist who conducted a few training sessions with managers and the HR team. Basic stuff: What is ADHD? How to accommodate sensory hyperstimulation concerns with autistic employees. Detecting bias in the interview process.

But he didn't feel that the project was progressing well. "What are we missing here?" he asked.

"Education is critical," I replied. "And introducing accommodation is necessary. But these steps are on the surface. I have a friend who owns an estate winery business. He has rapidly expanded over the past five years, buying up new land and scaling up his production. When he starts a new vineyard, he says the bottle he eventually produces from that new plot will only be as good as the land where the grapes are grown. Most of the work from land deal to the corking of the first perfect bottle from that land is spent preparing the site: getting the pH balance right, creating slopes for drainage, adding potassium and lime, growing cover crops for a year ahead of first grape seeding. If you underinvest in that part of the process, nothing you do later will make much of a difference."

He was nodding as I talked. He seemed to get it right away and make the crucial connection with his organization.

I went on to explain that the work he had been doing—introducing basic accommodation measures, handing out educational materials, instituting sensory-friendly environmental options, occasionally holding a mandatory training session or showing a video—was helpful. But it could be a bit like trying to fix cracks in a building's foundation with nothing but landscaping and paint. If there is a gap at a deeper level that needs to be addressed, then that's where the process needs to begin.

In the same way, you won't get traction with neurodiversity inclusion unless practical measures are introduced into a context where they connect with an underlying foundation of psychological safety, genuine acceptance of cognitive diversity, and a culture that celebrates transparent communication. If those dynamics are truly in place, then more practical steps will be able to take root and help the entire team flourish, no matter where any given person fits on the spectrum of human neurodiversity.

Mark was willing to accept this premise wholeheartedly and commit to the entire process. At that point, I knew this was going to be a successful story because it was clear to me that his team trusted him. The rest of the process was just details.

I visited his team next and conducted a neurodiversity inclusion audit to set a baseline for future comparison. He had a diverse team in all respects and a culture built for celebrating new ideas and new perspectives. Challenging the status quo was to be rewarded. That was a great starting point.

His organization also already espoused a culture of wide-open communication. No one would ever be penalized for "asking a stupid question" or voicing concerns of any kind about the company, its culture, and its vision.

One thing we added to this foundation was an official value statement in support of a strength-based perspective on neurodiversity, advertising it widely—a step I will cover in more detail in

Chapter 10. Remember the Three C's? The first C is about codifying values, policies, and protocols. The second is conduct—the everyday habits, choices, and actions taken by all members of an organization as an aggregate. For the most part, an organization's culture can be roughly boiled down to the harmony or dissonance between code and conduct.

I keep harping on this point because if code and conduct aren't aligned, there isn't much that can be done to address challenges, opportunities, or vision. It's a bit like imagining trying to drive somewhere in a vehicle with a steering wheel and pedals that are disconnected from the rest of the car. There isn't much point in concepts such as "navigation" under such conditions.

However, in this case, Mark was a tremendous executive leader. He understood his team, had earned their genuine respect and buy-in, was always fair, and never asked more from his subordinates than he was willing to ask of himself. And it showed. Given all of that, adopting an official value statement in support of a strength-based perspective on neurodiversity was an impactful idea. To extend the analogy, Mark's steering wheel and pedals were soundly connected to the engine, steering column, axles, and wheels. Hence, the value statement was tantamount to handing the driver specific navigational instructions.

Beyond the value statement, my neuroinclusion audit revealed that his organization was already aligned with psychological safety and transparent 360-degree communication and very accepting of inclusion and diversity. But a key piece was missing—a domain-specific appreciation of the strength-based perspective on neurodiversity—which represented a barrier in getting this project off the ground.

After some further discussion, we settled on a strong goal to target this gap:

Within two months, all team members will deeply under-stand and be able to articulate the strength-based framework of neurodiversity and tell a story that highlights the strengths of at least one neurodivergent person they know about.

One important point to make about this goal is that it impacted almost all layers of the Pyramid of Neuroinclusion, cementing the foundational first two layers in a manner that provided rock-solid support for layers three and four, and making strong strides toward establishing the fifth crucial layer of authentic universal empathy throughout the organization regardless of neurotype.

The strategy to attain this goal was simply to tell people they would be regularly asked about this in impromptu one-on-one conversations and would be required to explain it in their own words whenever asked. Tactics included an interactive session for education led by me, distribution of educational materials, and the fact that Mark, himself, would be the one to start these conversations, tell positive stories that defy stereotypes about neurodivergent people, and even informally administer pop quizzes in a one-on-one format randomly and without notice when walking around the office each day just before midday. He showered praise and sometimes even prizes for impactful responses.

Answers to Mark's pop quizzes were graded on a scale of 1 to 5, with 5 being the highest. A "5" would only be scored if the answer showed real passion for the subject and contained nuance, depth, and breadth without repeating anything verbatim from my training session.

Word spread. After six weeks, the organization had achieved its objective. Everyone at Mark's company really understood the strengths-based perspective on neurodiversity, how that reframing opened up worlds of potential, and how embracing that new framework effortlessly translated into feelings of respect and empathy for neurodivergent teammates at the company, which inspired reciprocation and a much more powerful foundation for universal empathy.

The next step was to work with the Human Resources team to revise outdated policies and to further codify new protocols to encourage psychological safety and acceptance for neurodivergent people at all levels of the company. We made sure that neurodiversity was specifically mentioned in policy handbooks. We added in a strong anti-harassment and anti-bullying policy that applied to neurodivergent traits and cognitive diversity. We revised protocols to give managers more authority to allow flexible working conditions whenever possible. The goal was to build a solid foundation so that all employees could be free to be themselves and to work in the way that would allow each to thrive.

In Chapter 9, we delve deeper into evidence showing how this type of foundation directly drives innovation in any organization.

As is so often the case, it further transpired that Mark already had far more neurodivergent employees than he was aware of. Employees that were previously hesitant to reveal their neurodivergence by taking advantage of supportive resources and protocols out of fear of being ostracized began to overcome that concern.

One of his employees privately confided in me that he felt as if a weight had finally been lifted from his shoulders. He had ADHD and now felt, for the first time, that he could talk about it openly without taking a career risk. He felt valued, and that empowered him further. His loyalty and appreciation for the company grew tremendously. Neurodivergent employees began to add to Mark's positive stories, openly communicating about their differences. And, perhaps most important of all, neurotypical employees began to notice and appreciate the upside that their neurodivergent peers were bringing to the table.

Shortly thereafter, a transformation naturally took root in many facets of the company's culture and operations: several neurodivergent hires took place, and a neurodivergent employee was advanced into a management role with significant new responsibilities. This later development further signaled to new neurodivergent hires that they were joining a company that valued them in all aspects, creating a sense of real belonging and inclusion and a willingness to contribute their unique strengths in service of the company's success. In the process, prevailing stereotypes about neurodivergent people were exposed and overshadowed by the bright light of first-hand exposure.

But the breakthrough moment was that first goal and Mark's hands-on approach to achieving it. Since that time, I have made it a central strategic recommendation, wherever possible, to promote the idea that organizational leaders should be visibly all-in on the process of ensuring everyone in an organization embraces authentic neurodiversity inclusion. If your leader is all-in, you take it more seriously.

That's what leadership is all about.

I followed up with Mark several times over the next two years, and I can attest to the fact that the seeds we planted then have sprouted and blossomed. Mark has also suggested to me that the investment of time and energy devoted to that process has had other positive effects beyond neurodiversity inclusion as well.

"There's just a better chemistry overall. It's a happier, more productive, more innovative organization, and people from all sorts of backgrounds have come on board, settled in well, bought into our vision, and show up every day with real passion."

Key Takeaways

- Part I focused on the value proposition of neurodiversity inclusion—cognitive diversity, innovation, an expansion in available talent, improved immunity to groupthink risk, and gains in loyalty, motivation, and reputational status.

- Parts II and III will focus on defining an effective set of goals and achieving them through proven strategies and tactics that incorporate input from neurodivergent voices across the globe.

- When an organization commits to becoming more inclusive, the process begins with "The Three C's"—Codification plus Conduct drives Culture. In subsequent chapters, our focus will become more granular as we delve further into the framework of objectives this chapter introduces. We will also explore different strategies and tactics designed to achieve inclusion goals.

- Every organization has a culture. That culture may be the result of intentional design, or it may simply be something that grew into the vacuum left by the lack of that intentional design. Either way, there is a culture. If your demonstrated values match your expressed values, then you have an effective culture. If they don't, you don't.

- One of the most important elements of a strategic plan to build authentic neuroinclusion into an organizational culture is to enshrine a values statement supporting and committing to that concept. A values statement is something you will be held accountable for, within and outside of your organization.

- The Pyramid of Neuroinclusion is a layered set of objectives that must all be cemented into place to bring about lasting authentic neurodiversity inclusion and its many benefits. An organization without a firm foundation of psychological safety and transparent communications protocols won't benefit much in terms of recruiting and retaining neurodivergent talent by simply providing sensory accommodations and auxiliary support resources. A garden won't grow, no matter how much sunlight and water it gets, if the soil is toxic.

- Each of the layers in this pyramid can be construed as an actionable framework for generating specific objectives. For example, an organization might personalize the bottom layer as "Achieve perfect score on anonymous 'Trust and Psychological Safety' survey throughout all departments at all levels, separately and overall, within three months."

- You won't get traction with neurodiversity inclusion unless practical measures are introduced into a context where they connect with an underlying foundation of psychological safety, genuine acceptance of cognitive diversity, and a culture that celebrates clear transparent communication.

- The breakthrough moment in the chapter's case study was the implementation of the first goal and Mark's hands-on approach to achieving it. Organizational leaders should be visibly all-in on the process of ensuring everyone in an organization embraces authentic neurodiversity inclusion. If your leader is all-in, you take it more seriously.

Chapter 6

Thinking Outside Check-the-Box

"Don't say things. What you are stands over you the while, and thunders so that I cannot hear what you say to the contrary."
—Ralph Waldo Emerson[1]

At 2:15 a.m., I awoke abruptly, my right elbow frozen from the weight of my hip, as my phone moved along the rail of my bunkbed, buzzing.

I picked up the call with a groggy, "Um . . . Hello?"

"I just spent several hours reverse engineering the scoring algorithm. Why were our scoring decisions valued so much lower than other teams?" It was my autistic friend, Dave, a former CTO, and a member of my team of neurodivergent advisors—we were flown to Switzerland to be part of a committee of judges in a pitch review session at the headquarters of a financial firm that was launching a neurodiversity innovation program.

Simultaneously, multiple texts came through from Jim, my other autistic friend and teammate. There were lots of capital letters and exclamation points.

As part of the committee, our job was to evaluate candidates for a large funding award. The committee advertised that selections would be made through a process that included heavily weighted input from neurodivergent people with deep lived experience—that was our job.

Based on how the prior day had played out, Dave and Jim had each smelled something fishy and wanted to figure it out. They had taken different routes of analysis but had both arrived at the same disappointing conclusion at basically the same time.

An accomplished geologist by training, Jim said, "Why didn't they just tell us from the start that they were planning to underweight our opinions and then add weighted factors for geographic considerations! If I knew this was the plan, I would have scored things differently. Or maybe not bothered to come in the first place. I'm not sure why I'm here at this point."

He sounded crushed. I was angry. Why were we even invited to the table if our voices mattered less than the others on the committee?

The next morning, I voiced my concerns. When asked what we had expected, I responded, "Authentic inclusion."

"What does that mean?"

"In this case, one person, one vote. Nothing less."

Our group also discreetly brought up the concern that there was an apparent conflict of interest brewing from the fact that other members of the selection committee had apparently begun negotiating contractual relationships with candidate organizations up for funding even though the selection committee had not yet completed its work.

In short, the situation was rife with corrosive opportunism and perverse incentivization at the individual level and little oversight of the organization's interests at the corporate level, with millions of dollars up for grabs.

After we pushed back openly for all to hear, a committee member who apparently had not known neurodivergent voices had been secretly strategically devalued, blurted out the obvious point.

"We are here to allocate resources to organizations under the banner of making the world more inclusive for neurodiversity, and our first step is to strategically disenfranchise and dismiss the voices in the room of those with lived experience? Really!? Where is this program headed?"

After a lengthy and uncomfortable silence filled with paper shuffling and searching glances, the context and the rules started to change. Mistakes were acknowledged. The process was reformed. And neurodivergent voices were upgraded back to "mattering."

In the process, one candidate organization slated for selection was exposed as a massive brand risk for the project and dropped from the running. Had this not happened, the client company could have suffered enormous brand damage.

Nonetheless, months later, the real verdict hit home: my two brilliant autistic professionals were not invited back to serve on the next selection committee.

We had won the battle but lost the war.

Checking the Box

The mid-level managers in charge of this project wanted to control the outcome while paying lip-service to neurodiversity inclusion along the way. My team had figured this out and effectively shamed them into a performative display of authentic-inclusion-in-practice for about six hours. In effect, we were placated to avoid a backlash. But no genuine commitment to authentic inclusion was ever really under consideration. They had "seen the error of their ways" and thanked us so very much for our keen insights and commitment to their interests. And then they asked us to stay home next time around.

This story is not uncommon and represents a shortsighted approach destined to lose in the long run.

Had the CEO, a Board Director, or other fiduciary been in the room that day, these two talented autistic experts would have been promoted rather than fired from their roles. Their brilliant sleuthing analysis alerted the client corporation to significant and substantial organizational risks. They not only detected those risks but also figured out that the cards were stacked to exclude our opinions while including our team as token features for marketing purposes. We then maneuvered to overcome this, help the client, and present an object lesson in the value of authentic inclusion along the way.

Their reward? Complete exclusion in the next iteration.

I told this story to a neurotypical friend who also happens to be the CEO of a major construction supply company with a tremendous track record of growth and success. I prefaced the story by pointing out that my favorite metaphor for diversity of thought in business is the idea that Steel is stronger than Iron—something I have used in multiple keynotes over the years—and that I thought this point should resonate with him in particular given his line of business.

He responded with an interesting point of view. "My first thought was: that sounds unfair, but I kinda get where they were coming from. A lot of people in the business world have an instinct toward controlling the outcome as the highest priority. It's a stupid instinct and a loser's mentality. But it's hard to get away from. Especially when you're talking about a project being run by mid-level players and they're just told to handle everything and make it work. Control becomes the main objective."

"And your second thought?" I asked, riveted by his perspective.

"My second thought is that, yeah, Steel is stronger than Iron. Alloys are always superior. You can't have a bunch of Iron in there trying to exclude the Carbon or you won't get the benefits of Steel. In other words, that sense of control is an illusion. You need to let new voices into the analysis, especially if they are very different kinds of voices. You want that control to be challenged. That's the winner's mentality in business. Bring it on! You end up with something better 99 times out of a hundred."

Of course, it's true. Steel is superior to iron in just about every measurable dimension that matters for metals engineering. In fact, alloys are almost always superior to pure metals when it comes to strength, fracture resistance, corrosion resistance, and other key properties.[2]

You can think of an alloy as basically a metal that is committed to authentic diversity inclusion: not every atom has to be the same. And the strength comes from different substances with different properties working together. Similarly, as noted previously, I argue that authentic inclusion in neurodiversity is more than just a moral imperative. It's a functional driver of superior performance (see Figure 6.1).

That will be a recurring theme in this book: neurodiversity is an asset, not a trade-off. Organizations are stronger and have access to a competitive advantage when authentic inclusion is encouraged and embraced.

Figure 6.1 Steel is an alloy that derives strength from elemental diversity.
(*Source:* Keynote Presentation, 2022 Stanford Neurodiversity Summit, Maureen Dunne).

Thinking Outside Check-the-Box

Even if it is uncomfortable at times to allow unfamiliar or seemingly risky perspectives into the closely guarded confines of strategic decision making where real value is on the line, businesses that embrace diversity of voices in the room end up winning over those that don't.

The importance of diversity in general as an asset to business performance has been documented and highlighted in many publications. *Harvard Business Review* reported that diverse teams make decisions twice as fast and deliver 60% better results because diversity on a team translates into a stronger focus on facts and incorporates a wider range of experiences and backgrounds.[3]

A McKinsey report also showed that companies ranked in the top 25% for diverse executive teams are 21% more likely to outperform on profitability.[4] As a result, diverse teams are more likely to uncover blind spots, which is something we will talk more about shortly.

So why have businesses and organizations of all sizes been slow to embrace neurodiversity inclusion? I believe that change can only truly get traction once an organization explicitly recognizes diversity of thought as a core value.

Siemens AG: Unlocking the Potential of a Strength-based Approach

Siemens is a good example of an organizational culture making strides to align itself with a strength-based framework for human diversity, including neurodiversity.

Over recent years, this German-based global engineering and technology behemoth has worked with a consultancy firm, Strengthscope, to help align individual recruits with roles and career trajectories where an individual's strengths form the foundation of the relationship.

Employees can opt in or out of the Strengthscope assessment during recruitment. While it isn't a complete solution, it is a clear enhancement to the interview and placement process for neurodivergent candidates because it places strengths front and center in the decision-making process.

Siemens started with a pilot program with Strengthscope and has since expanded the relationship to reach across 27 countries and six languages.

Courting Disaster

Returning to the story, our neurodiversity team was invited to the selection committee to participate for the wrong reasons: while being invited under the pretext of including cognitive diversity in the selection process, it became clear that my team of neurodivergent consultants had actually been invited simply so the organization could "check the box" that people with lived neurodiversity experience were involved.

You can imagine the thought process going on here: The whole project had to do with neurodiversity. So, naturally, it might look bad if they couldn't confidently assert that neurodivergent individuals with lived experience were involved in key stages of the process. After all, the autistic community is well known for its "nothing about us without us" philosophy. And, given the well documented struggles neurotypical people have historically had in intuiting the inner workings of the autistic mind, that philosophy is clearly driven by solid reasoning and important to respect.

So they checked that box. But they still wanted to control the outcome without having the results contaminated by "unpredictable outside ideas." Their solution, as we have seen, was to include neurodivergent people on a superficial level—make us feel like part of the process and perhaps benefit from some social media exposure showing that inclusion—but to then cut us out of having any real impact on the outcome.

In other words, they wanted the cosmetic benefits of inclusion without committing to authentic inclusion. This entirely misses the point and presents a major risk.

Naturally, it then came as a surprise when the organization's hidden structures were unearthed through reverse engineering conceptual techniques to spotlight flaws in the scoring system, serving to both expose the inherent flaws in how they were operating and earn the ire of the very people they were trying to superficially placate.

Neurodivergent people should be included as equal participants because of the value we bring to the table in the form of cognitive diversity, passion, and problem-solving skills, not as token features of a public relations agenda.

Going back to the metaphor of iron versus steel, no one would spend time making an alloy consisting of a pure metal and some other component that was included but had no impact on the behavior or characteristics of the material.

In short, representation without authentic inclusion is a recipe for disaster.

It boils down to the importance of prioritizing a values-based approach to inclusivity rather than a technical box-ticking one. DEI programs are common, but organizations often stop short of investing the effort and creativity necessary to spark and sustain authentic inclusion.[5]

Another report from The Valuable 500 further showed that while organizations and companies pitch themselves as committed to Diversity and Inclusion, there is often little attention paid to surveying customers on issues related to neurodiversity or in making products or platforms more inclusive from an accessibility and disability standpoint.[6]

Setting out targets regarding the proportion of new hires that should be women, ethnic minorities, or other underrepresented groups can be productive and will often serve to maintain momentum. This is made clear by further McKinsey data that indicates that likelihood of outperformance increases proportionally to rates of diversity. Companies with women accounting for more than 30% of executives tended to outperform companies where the percentage ranged from 10% to 30%.[7]

In short, authentic neurodiversity inclusion unlocks value that far exceeds its implied costs. In the chapters that follow, we will distill the various components that should help you and everyone in your circle better understand why diversity of thought should and must be a core value that underpins organizational culture.

That value will be felt in many ways, including avoiding groupthink, driving greater innovation, accessing a wider pool of available workers, and avoiding the brand risk that comes with being on the wrong side of history as 20% or more of the global population increasingly realizes a shared identity and sense of purpose.

In the pages ahead, we will explore in more detail how the adoption of a strength-based perspective, powered by a framework of authentic neurodiversity inclusion, opens the door to competitive advantages in a world increasingly defined by tight labor supply, heightened groupthink risk, a huge and rapidly growing premium on innovation, and an increasingly large, cohesive, powerful, and vocal neurodiversity community.

None of these factors should be underestimated or ignored.

Key Takeaways

- A check-the-box version of inclusivity is as fruitless as it is common. I have seen this most often in situations where control over all internal outcomes is deemed as a higher priority than information or honesty.

- When mid-level managers are given discretionary control and no guidance other than what results to shoot for, diversity of ideas, experiences, and cognition are unlikely to receive authentic consideration. This is when brand damage and legal risk can mount for fiduciaries.

- This can also be viewed as the costs when fear of failure supersedes the drive to achieve great success. This is known as loss aversion and represents a continually present risk. Fear of failure often manifests as excessive concern over controlling the outcome of even those processes that are meant to be about intel or discovery.

- The outcome in the case of the story told in this chapter was the worst of all worlds—the neurodivergent contractors proved to be especially smart and resourceful but the organization excluded them from providing that value. In addition, the contractors were part of the community that the project was meant to please, but the outcome of this instance achieved the opposite.

- Steel is superior to iron in just about every measurable dimension that matters for metals engineering. In fact, alloys are almost always superior to pure metals when it comes to strength, fracture resistance, corrosion resistance, and other key properties.

- You can think of an alloy as basically a metal that is committed to authentic diversity inclusion: not every atom has to be the same. And the strength comes from different substances with different properties working together. Similarly, as noted earlier, I argue that authentic inclusion in neurodiversity is more than just a moral imperative. It's a functional driver of superior performance.

- Even if it is uncomfortable at times to allow unfamiliar or seemingly risky perspectives into the closely guarded confines of strategic decision making where real value is on the line, businesses that embrace diversity of voices in the room end up winning over those that don't.

- Neurodivergent people should be included as equal participants because of the value they bring to the table in the form of cognitive diversity, passion, and problem-solving skills, not as token features of a public relations agenda.

Chapter 7

Neurodiversification Versus Culture Fit

*"For organizations seeking to plant the seeds of a transforma-
tion toward long-term—and sustainable—authentic diversity inclusion, there is no path more powerful than to hire
and advance, and celebrate as an asset, the broadest possible
range of diversity of lived experience. Such a focus needs no
other justification than that of expanding the breadth and
depth of crucial perspectives, ideas, experiences, and cognitive profiles an organization has access to when it comes
face-to-face with new existential challenges or its next defining opportunity, or just another typical day at the office when
some new game-changing idea is dancing just out of view on
the edge of discovery."*
—Dr. Maureen Dunne, unrecorded presentation, 2009

It turns out that one of the most powerful strategies for embracing authentic neurodiversity inclusion, in practice, is to target
"neurodiversification."

In finance, portfolio managers focus on the concept of diversification. The big point of diversification in portfolio management is
to ensure that not all assets are correlated with each other because
correlation leads to the risk of catastrophic losses when market conditions deteriorate.

In other words, if a group of investments are all correlated, there's a huge downside risk. This is because when a portfolio of investment positions is highly correlated, they are likely to all respond to some new change in economic or financial conditions in the same way. For example, high-yield bonds, commodities, and speculative technology stocks have all historically performed poorly when interest rates are rising rapidly. Hence, a portfolio made of only oil producers, gold futures contracts, junk bonds, and early-stage small-cap growth companies could return strong profits over any given period. But it contains the seeds of its own destruction if the wrong market conditions arise.

We can think about neurodiversity in similar terms. As we covered in Chapter 2, groupthink is a serious risk for all organizations. Failing to spot and address the emergence of a groupthink dynamic can be devastating. As we noted in that discussion, an active program of proactively embracing neurodiversity inclusion can act as a tremendous hedge against this risk.

An organization that takes this seriously and implements neurodiversity inclusion as a strategy to protect against homogeneity of perspective can be thought of as "neurodiversifying" its human resources portfolio.

The significant point to make here is that such a strategy, in my experience, will exhibit a positive feedback dynamic: by proactively targeting diversity of thought across an entire organization, authentic neurodiversity inclusion will become second nature. Such an organization will have an easy time attracting and retaining new neurodivergent talent because decision-making teams at all levels will be accustomed to neurodiversity to an extent sufficient to defuse conscious or unconscious unproductive biases that typically act as a barrier to inclusion.

In other words, neurodiversification deployed as a hedge against groupthink is an extremely effective strategy to foster authentic neurodiversity inclusion as a sustainable organizational habit of the heart.

At the outset, I made the case that the effort to embrace neurodiversity inclusion must be approached not as organizational culture cosmetic surgery but as organizational culture gene therapy. Otherwise, nothing stands to be gained. The focus of this chapter provides a good example of the nature of strategic action in that context. But there's a catch.

As much as targeting neurodiversification can be understood as a value-added strategy for embracing authentic neurodiversity inclusion across the board, one key hurdle must be overcome in its successful implementation: bucking the standard of *culture fit* in hiring, firing, and organizational advancement decisions.

Culture Expansion > Culture Fit

One can make a strong argument that the primary obstacle preventing mature organizations from finding new break-out success is the deeply ingrained practice of prioritizing culture fit in hiring and promoting team members.

Companies have traditionally valued cultural compatibility when assessing new hires or advancement potential, often dedicating a portion of the interview process specifically to this aspect. There is often even at least one interview within the interview series dedicated to this goal alone. However, allowing a focus on culture fit to guide recruitment and assessment of new and existing talent may stifle upside potential for the organization as a whole over time. It turns out that the best path may be to simply flip this conventional wisdom and target *culture expansion* instead.

According to research from Stanford University's Baron and Hannan in 2002, culture fit may actually help early-stage start-ups that already have a disruptive idea and just need to scale. But that recipe quickly turns sour. As the company matures past this early stage, the premium shifts from homogeneity to heterogeneity.

In his 2017 Stanford eCorner presentation, "Hire for Culture Fit or ADD?," Wharton management scholar Adam Grant notes that, as companies grow, they start to encounter disruption from the outside and have to adapt to a context defined by constant change driven by external factors. "After they go public, the ones that hire on culture fit grow at the slowest rates. . . . Culture fit is code for hiring a bunch of people who 'think the same way I do.' And it leads to groupthink and weeds out diversity of thought."[1]

The solution? Hiring for culture add instead of culture fit. This implies a proactive search for team members who bring new ideas, backgrounds, and cognitive tendencies.

But it isn't easy to kick the culture fit habit. It's slippery and has many faces. In Chapter 8, we will cover a range of prevalent cognitive biases that obstruct attempts to embrace diversity of all kinds, and culture fit wears most of them in one form or another among its disguises.

Note: I am not suggesting an organization should actively recruit a new addition with a history of dishonesty and flawed character artifacts to challenge a culture of honesty and integrity. Another caveat is that culture fit is an important factor to the extent it is limited to sharing an appreciation for the organization's fundamental values. In other words, if you are an organization built on the value of caring for the natural environment, I am not suggesting you go out and hire someone who actively disdains nature and environmental care. Or, if you are a venture capital firm, I am not suggesting you go out and hire an ardent socialist who disdains private enterprise.

However, within those boundaries and within reason and common sense, bringing on new talent with very different backgrounds, assumptions, and cognitive tendencies is quite possibly the only way an established company can break through to a new level of success.

Stop and read that last sentence again. Give it some thought.

In many cases, the same kinds of inputs are going to lead to the same output. You have been driving through the same neighborhood for many years. The only way out may be to take a left turn where you have been taking right turns for all that time. People like to find common ground with other people. People also dislike tension and conflict, even if it's productive. This is especially true in the workplace. The people in charge of hiring new team members are just people, too. If they tend to gravitate toward what they know—toward the familiar, the homogenous, the comfortable—then they are holding you back.

To approach this same point from a different angle, consider what drives Darwinian evolution. Evolution works by variation and selection. Often, a major evolutionary change that provides enormous survival or selective advantages comes from variations that wouldn't have made immediate intuitive sense at that stage when analyzed in retrospect.

For example, there are frogs in Alaska that evolved the ability to produce and store lots of extra glucose. While this makes sense from an energy standpoint, it turned out to lay a foundation for intracellular cryoprotection of cell volume. The upshot is that these same frogs can now freeze during the winter. Their hearts stop. They turn to ice. And then they thaw out in the spring and go on living.

That's a breakthrough adaptation that opens powerful new optionality and potential success. And that power is derived from the variation—from exploring the matrix of all possible designs. The "selection" part of the process is just the weed-out. The value enters the equation in the "variation" part of the process. The more variation, the more potential for breakthrough value. I firmly believe the same logic applies to diversity of thought and lived experience. The main customary force preventing this is the traditional habit of prioritizing culture fit when making key human resources decisions.

Ditching culture fit for culture expansion is an active choice to embrace enough added variation to drive the next evolutionary leap of progress in an organization that may otherwise be at risk of stagnating. Naturally, this discussion is ultimately aligned with authentic neuroinclusion, which is the epitome of embracing culture expansion in team building.

In my experience, which includes working with many different companies in an advisory capacity—including Fortune 500 powerhouses, colleges, start-ups, and small businesses—companies and organizations that have strategically prioritized culture expansion over culture fit demonstrate a clear edge over time, both in terms of innovation potential and immunity to common pitfalls.

It's team-level hybrid vigor.

Neurodiversification Is Culture Expansion

One of the most important mechanisms in translating the objective of culture expansion in the hiring process into more effective inclusion is the impact it has on unconscious bias and how much leverage biases have over an organizational culture.

Hiring for culture fit encourages and nurtures unconscious bias because biases that are already established within a culture are less likely to be challenged. Culture fit, as a concept, is a carapace protecting whatever is under the surface of an organizational culture—both bad and good.

Unconscious biases are mental shortcuts. We will discuss strategies and tactics to uncover such biases in subsequent chapters, which in my experience often starts with a neurodiversity organizational audit. Unconscious biases are harmful to productivity and organizational culture because they allow us to make value judgments without having to think things through. It saves time and mental energy to just outsource a judgment to a preexisting mental shortcut built to produce sweeping conclusions on nothing more than superficial impressions plugged into preinstalled Pleistocene-based "HumanOS" decision-making brain-ware.

You can see how unproductive this dynamic may be for a business with stretch goals and active competition, especially when it's protected, and effectively endorsed, by the insidious "culture fit" brain-app.

In other words, pursuing culture fit as a priority in the team-building process not only tilts organizations toward limitations in diversity of thought but protects and nurtures unconscious biases that reinforce themselves by stripping the organizational culture of necessary checks and balances that might otherwise emerge via rational examination of the results of prior decisions. A slippery slope.

But there's another very important derivative disadvantage of an organizational culture with culture fit acting as a core guideline for hiring, firing, and advancement decisions: it will almost certainly actively repel neurodivergent talent. Those that manage to get hired will actively feel they don't fit in, which will, in turn, force them into a masking position, all but extinguishing any hope of cultivating authentic neurodiversity inclusion.

In other words, an organization built through strong reliance on a conscious or unconscious bias toward culture fit will be destined for high groupthink risk, homogeneity of perspective, and very little access to the ocean of undervalued and motivated neurodivergent talent looking for an organizational home.

As we discussed earlier, targeting neurodiversification can spark a self-reinforcing feedback dynamic that gives rise to robust authentic neurodiversity inclusion. However, by the same token, failure to root out culture fit as a core factor in personnel decisions can spark just the opposite.

In my experience, the most effective way to cut off this downward spiral toward homogeneity, stagnation, and lack of access to the expanded talent pool offered by embracing the whole spectrum of human neurodiversity is to proactively prioritize neurodiversity in leadership. If neurodiversity is represented at the leadership level—especially if it is openly disclosed and visible—it sends a powerful message throughout an organization that cognitive and experiential diversity is valued, and quirky team members have no reason to waste valuable time and energy with masking behaviors.

We will discuss this point in further detail in a later chapter, but it is worth emphasizing here. To drive organizational health, stability, and performance, diversity in all its forms is inherently valuable while conscious or unconscious biases that foster cultural homogeneity are obstacles. Both of these points can be mobilized by hiring and promoting practices that prioritize culture expansion over culture fit.

Implementation

A core thesis of this book is that one of the most powerful ways neurodiversity can add value to organizations is by adding different cognitive, perceptual, and analytical abilities to the equation.

But the most important point is the diversity itself.

In other words, neurodivergent minds are often uncorrelated with the group, more likely to bring unconventional ideas or perspectives into the equation, and less likely to be influenced by potential loss of social status.

A group of people who all have similar backgrounds, educational achievements, and cognitive tendencies may perform very well on any given task. But that arrangement contains the seeds of destruction under the wrong conditions, as highlighted in Chapter 2. When all minds in a group are highly correlated in terms of experiences and cognitive tendencies, the potential for overlapping conceptual blind spots becomes a primary risk.

Neurodiversification is the hedge against that risk.

It is crucial to include people at all staff levels who are best equipped to uncover such blind spots by bringing in fresh perspectives, including a trusted senior advisor, board member, or senior member of management.

In this book, I make the case that authentic neurodiversity inclusion is not only the most effective hedge against those risks but also an essential strategy to stay competitive. As a simplistic thought experiment, consider a group trying to solve a problem or question that centers on a circle. But they only think in different types of rectangles. And on the outside, excluded from the conversation, is someone who has different-shaped thoughts (see Figures 7.1 and 7.2).

In other words, this team was built for an operating context that presented a lot of rectangle-shaped problems and opportunities. They were unaware of the possibility that non-rectangular problems and solutions even existed at all—this was an unknown but significant risk as a blind spot.

Naturally, eventually they run into a circle-shaped problem, and they're stuck.

Including different-shaped thoughts in the conversation spurs new avenues of conceptual exploration among the group, leading to a solution that would have been less accessible in the absence of cognitive diversity.

However, it's important to understand that you can't derive that value without authentic inclusion—it's not enough to shoehorn a neurodivergent person into an otherwise homogenously neurotypical cultural context and force them to spend all their energy just trying to fit in.

When this happens, as we discussed in Chapter 1, so much mental effort is expended on masking that the productive value that

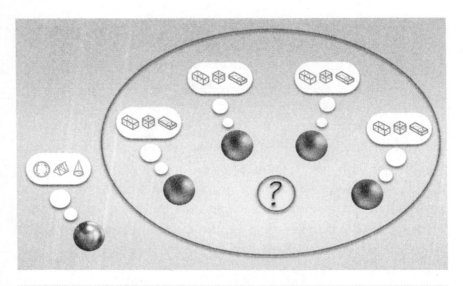

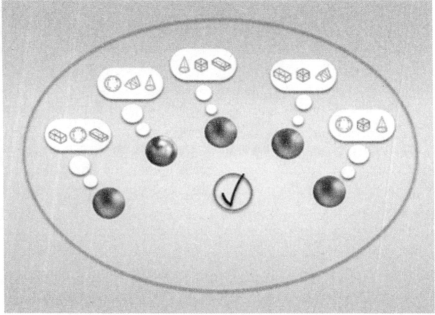

Figures 7.1 and 7.2: Breaking free from groupthink.

individual may otherwise have been able to contribute never surfaces, and you are left, instead, with an unhappy, stressed out, anxious, depressed team member confronting a gauntlet of unhealthy obstacles, including the daily experience of a lack of belonging.

In other words, the damage wrought by the tyranny of culture fit doesn't stop at the door, it also stifles the potential value of any cognitive diversity that manages to slip through the filter of the interview process. It should also be noted here that research has shown that the experience of not belonging is a top reason talented employees quit (whether neurodivergent or neurotypical).

The upside here is only available when neurodiversity is allowed to thrive under conditions of authentic inclusion, where people are embraced for who they are, where cognitive diversity is valued, and where different cognitive strengths and unique skill sets are allowed to shine through.

However, there is a critical point to note as you are implementing your organizational strategy: *neurodiversity is NOT monolithic.*

There is a richness and diversity *both between* different cognitive typologies (such as ADHD, autism, dyslexia, hyperlexia, synesthesia, and dyspraxia) and *within* any specific typology. No two autistic people, for instance, are the same, and it is important to remain receptive to learning from every neurodivergent person you meet. There is also more documented overlap between different neurodivergent traits than is generally assumed. And, of course, intellectual giftedness may also accompany all or some of these traits. When that is the case, it is often referred to as "twice exceptional" or "2e."

Let's go back to the paradox outlined in the initial chapters—how it is that the neurodivergent have been perhaps overrepresented among many of our historical innovators but, simultaneously, underappreciated as participants in our economy? This is a question we will continue to explore throughout the book. What does emerge is that our future economy—and organizations everywhere—will come to depend more and more on these unique skills, including lateral thinking and creativity. We are headed for a world where a higher premium will be placed on including cognitive diversity for an innovative edge.

It is important to note that the paradox has existed for centuries with many examples of trailblazers throughout history displaying strong neurodivergent cognition. Take, for example, the unique cognitive profile of Leonardo da Vinci as illustrated by author Thomas West in his 1997/2020 book *In the Mind's Eye: Visual Thinkers, Gifted People with Dyslexia and Other Learning Difficulties, Computer Images and the Ironies of Creativity*.[2] On page 181, West asserts:

> To gain a sense of how he worked, it is useful to look at just one of his many inventions. One of his lesser-known innovations provides an excellent example of the power of simple mental rotation and the application of similar structures to similar forces in a very different context. Leonardo used a concept that he took from the architecture of buildings—the simple, triangular arch. He rotated it in his mind and found that it was ideally suited to providing a self-sealing gate for a canal lock. In a building, the arch supports the weight of the roof and its own structure. The weight of the arch pushes the two parts of the central joint tightly together. Similar principles apply in a canal. In the lock gate, the water pressure comes from upstream rather than from above and keeps the gate tightly shut, in a perfectly analogous fashion.

In subsequent chapters, we will revisit the importance of neurodiversification in the context of strategies and tools you can utilize to effectively implement authentic neurodiversity inclusion. We will also cover how standardized verbal interview processes often miss the hidden talents that are needed for a neurodiverse workforce. I will offer some alternative suggestions and strategies you can employ and more effective ways to tap into unique talent that ultimately will be a value-add and competitive advantage.

In other words, the topic of this chapter is that neurodiversification is a strategy for achieving immediate and tangible organizational performance objectives. And deploying this strategy is, itself, a tremendous strategy for laying a foundation with long-term viability in the pursuit of authentic neurodiversity inclusion, and in fact, authentic inclusion of diversity in all its forms.

As a final point, even if you don't lead a business or manage a staff or organization, you can still play a significant role strengthening neurodiversification. Leadership does not come from a title, role, or position. It comes from action and the ability to influence. This book is aimed to arm you with the knowledge and tools, whatever your official title, to become a proactive strategist and influencer in creating a more inclusive world.

The Neurodivergent Leader Paradox

In the process of engaging neurodiversification as an engine of cognitive diversity and authentic neurodiversity inclusion, organizations will eventually confront the question of neurodiversity leadership as an openly disclosed and visible dimension.

Paradoxically, for many organizations, this aspect of the process may be experienced the other way around. To explain what I mean, we must set off on a minor tangent.

Why do we see so few examples of neurodivergent people in top organizational leadership roles? Surely, if all we have discussed in this book thus far holds water, there should be many examples that fit this description—even in your own organization. What gives?

In physics, there's something called "the Fermi paradox" that should be appreciated here:

- There are billions of stars like the Sun in the Milky Way galaxy.
- With high probability, some of these stars have Earth-like planets in a circumstellar habitable zone.
- Many of these stars, and hence their planets, are much older than the Sun.
- If Earth-like planets are typical, some may have developed intelligent life long ago.
- Some of these civilizations may have developed interstellar travel, a step that humans are investigating even now.
- Even at the slow pace of currently envisioned interstellar travel, the Milky Way galaxy could be completely traversed in a few million years.
- Since many of the Sun-like stars are billions of years older than the Sun, the Earth should have already been visited by extraterrestrial civilizations, or at least their probes.
- However, there is no convincing evidence that this has happened.

In other words, any logical extrapolation of these facts points to a thriving galaxy full of alien civilizations with the ability to reach out and say, "Hi!" Yet, no one has. What explains this seemingly illogical outcome?

There are basically three common ways to resolve this paradox: inherent rareness, developmental filtration, and incentive to remain hidden.

In other words, intelligent extraterrestrial life is extremely rare *or* all intelligent civilizations eventually reach some point in development where most destroy themselves making the average intelligent extraterrestrial civilization extremely short-lived *or* they are out there but have some incentive to remain hidden from each other and us.[3]

We can look at neurodivergent talent in a similar way: if there are all these advantages to neurodivergent talent and all these ways that neurodivergent people can help to drive organizational success, then why don't we see lots of neurodivergent executives on display in the corporate world?

We can even postulate the same three resolutions: neurodivergent talent at the executive level is extremely rare *or* neurodivergent executives eventually end up being ousted from their roles due to some critical mistake or failure *or* they are out there but have some incentive to remain hidden from view.

We may never know how to resolve the Fermi paradox, but the neurodivergent leader paradox is an easy one: they are out there but have some incentive to remain hidden from view.

During my listening tour, I met countless examples that fit this description: senior executives and leaders who were neurodivergent but reluctant to disclose.

Recently, it has been revealed that there are senior intelligence officers and leaders in the military that are neurodivergent but are unable to live as an openly neurodivergent leader due to exclusionary policies. Neurodivergent leaders are indeed everywhere. They are hiding in plain sight.[4]

I was recently asked about this topic in a *Forbes* interview and here was my response:

> Unfortunately, there is a chicken-and-egg problem. The high neurodivergent unemployment rate is on people's minds, and we still live in a world where it doesn't always feel psychologically safe to disclose due to lack of understanding and potential for negative bias, especially among younger neurodivergent adults who may be less established in their careers.

Neurodiversification Versus Culture Fit

The problem, of course, is that, without broad representation included in key leadership positions, inaccurate biases and stereotypes are more likely to get reinforced.

Let's cook that chicken and boil the egg.

This amounts to a situation where people will feel much more comfortable disclosing their neurodivergent status once others do the same and that experience is normalized. While that can be seen as a Catch-22 situation preventing movement from some sort of game-theoretic equilibrium, it also contains the embryo of a self-reinforcing feedback loop. It's almost a network effect phenomenon: the more people that do it, the more that will.

In practical terms, we will be living in a more functional world once that feedback loop has fully run its course and everyone out there in high-level positions who wants to disclose their neurodivergent status feels completely comfortable doing so. This will inspire a Copernican moment on a social scale. It will become more widely known how skilled this population really is and empower neurodivergent youth to feel more comfortable from the start while nudging employers toward a greater appreciation of neurodiversity. In other words, once that feedback loop is triggered, everyone wins.

This is one of the primary motivating factors for me in writing this book. Openly acknowledged neurodivergent leadership is one of the surest paths to attracting and retaining neurodivergent talent and tapping into all the associated benefits that can follow.

Nature survivalists know that healthy freshwater shrimp are a strong indicator that water in a running natural stream is potable, because they generally can't survive otherwise. By the same token, neurodivergent talent will gravitate toward organizations with visible neurodiversity among the executive ranks—if a company has an openly neurodivergent C-suite leader, you can bet it's a friendly place to work if you're a neurodivergent person looking for a new organization to call home.

It's a beacon of light shining out at the neurodivergent community.

Key Takeaways

- It turns out that one of the most powerful strategies for embracing authentic neurodiversity inclusion, in practice, is to target "neurodiversification"—an active program of proactively embracing neurodiversity inclusion as a hedge against the risk of groupthink.

- "Neurodiversification" as a strategy can spark a positive feedback dynamic: by proactively targeting diversity of thought across an entire organization, authentic neurodiversity inclusion will become second nature as new neurodivergent hires enter an organization where neurodiversity is represented widely.

- The source of this dynamic is acclimation. Neurodiversification deployed as a hedge against groupthink drives authentic neurodiversity inclusion as a sustainable organizational habit through exposure, which destroys negative stereotypes and drives a wider range of empathy.

- But there's a catch: As much as targeting neurodiversification can be understood as a value-add strategy for embracing authentic neuroinclusion, one key hurdle must be overcome in its successful implementation: bucking the standard of culture fit in hiring, firing, and organizational advancement decisions.

(continued)

(continued)

- One can make a strong argument that the primary obstacle preventing mature organizations from finding new break-out success is the deeply ingrained practice of prioritizing culture fit in hiring and promoting team members.

- Allowing a focus on culture fit to guide recruitment and assessment of new and existing talent may stifle upside potential for organizations over time. The best path to eradicate this risk is to simply flip this conventional wisdom on its head by targeting culture expansion instead.

- According to research from Stanford University's Baron and Hannan in 2002, culture fit may actually help early-stage start-ups that already have a disruptive idea and just need to scale. But that recipe quickly turns sour. As the company matures past this early stage, the premium shifts from homogeneity to heterogeneity.

- This step isn't as easy as it sounds: we all come with pre-installed social software that includes unconscious biases that work against kicking the culture fit habit. It turns out we are deeply programmed by nature to bias toward in-group biases. We cover this dynamic in detail in Chapter 8.

- Bringing on new talent with very different backgrounds, assumptions, and cognitive tendencies is quite possibly the only way an established company can break through to a new level of success.

- Ditching culture fit for culture expansion in recruiting and advancement decisions expands an organization's access to a variety of personalities, ideas, experiences, and cognitive strengths, which expands the matrix of diversity that fuels evolutionary leaps of progress in an organization that may otherwise be at risk of stagnating.

- Hiring for culture fit encourages and nurtures unconscious bias because biases that are already established within a culture are less likely to be challenged. Culture fit, as a concept, is a carapace protecting whatever is under the surface of an organizational culture—both bad and good.

- When all minds in a group are highly correlated in terms of experiences and cognitive tendencies, the potential for overlapping conceptual blind spots becomes a primary risk. Neurodiversification is the hedge against that risk.

- It's important to understand that you can't derive the value of cognitive diversity without authentic inclusion—it's not enough to shoehorn a neurodivergent person into an otherwise homogenously neurotypical cultural context and expect that situation to bear fruit. As we covered in Chapter 1, inauthentic inclusion isn't productive as so much energy must be invested in simply fitting in.

- The damage wrought by the tyranny of culture fit doesn't stop at the door, it also stifles the potential value of any cognitive diversity that manages to slip through the filter of the interview process.

(continued)

(continued)

- People feel much more comfortable disclosing their neurodivergent status once others do the same and that experience is normalized. While that can be seen as a Catch-22 situation preventing movement from some sort of game-theoretic equilibrium, it also contains the embryo of a self-reinforcing feedback loop.

- This is one of the primary motivating factors for me in writing this book. Openly acknowledged neurodivergent leadership is one of the surest paths to attracting and retaining neurodivergent talent and tapping into all the associated benefits that can follow.

Chapter 8

Tricks Minds Play

"Protect me from knowing what I don't need to know. Protect me from even knowing that there are things to know that I don't know. Protect me from knowing that I decided not to know about the things that I decided not to know about. Amen.

Lord, lord, lord. Protect me from the consequences of the above prayer."

—Douglas Adams, *Mostly Harmless*, 1992[1]

"We take great care to assess each new candidate according to a truly objective set of standards, and we have worked hard to ensure we are not allowing *any* built-in biases to interfere with that process."

It's hard to argue with that kind of blanket statement. But, in my experience, being told something like that, in language that even roughly approximates that kind of rhetoric, is a sure sign that there may be a problem.

Unconscious cognitive biases are extremely tricky enemies to battle. Imagine a species of invisible cockroach: very hard to detect or be aware of, and very hard to eliminate.

One interesting dynamic here is that human resources professionals appear to know they have an invisible cockroach infestation, but they aren't sure what to do about it. In my research reinforced by a listening tour, I found that an overwhelming percentage of human resources professionals truly believed that unconscious biases represented a major barrier to diversity and inclusion in the workplace. And more to the point, they also believed their organizations had no effective strategies in place to address this problem.

This is an interesting conundrum because they understand there's a battle to be fought. But they also know that their own organizations aren't engaging in that battle.

In my experience, the first step to engaging in that battle is simply about cultivating a strong understanding of the enemy—knowing it well enough to spot it in action and counter it by making different cognitive choices.

The idea of "the invisible cockroach" is a good jumping-off point because it harkens back to evolutionary design. And that's likely the source of all the unconscious cognitive biases we discuss below. They are, effectively, shortcuts—time- and labor-saving cognitive devices that have become installed functions of our evolved cognition over hundreds of millennia.[2]

One of the most important points to make here is that those hundreds of millennia were mostly spent in small kinship tribes of diffusely genetically related populations in sub-Saharan African grassland environments.

In other words, in most cases, these unconscious cognitive biases were useful tools that promoted an individual's Darwinian fitness by reducing the time and energy needed to make snap judgments about situations and other people when tribal membership meant everything, and genetic similarity was the defining factor for knowing who to trust in a game-theoretic landscape defined almost exclusively by competition for scarce resources.

Now, by contrast, they are simply analogs for appendicitis risk—legacy functions that only serve to limit our ability to function in a very different world: a complex, multifaceted, and multilayered social environment where tribalism and superficial judgment almost always lead to costly errors.

In short, unconscious cognitive biases are there to produce conclusions without tying up much mental energy or time—they offer a lazy path to something that purports to be, but no longer reliably approximates, knowledge.

From biology right down to underlying physics, nature favors whatever will accomplish a given need or task in a minimally sufficient sense with the least investment of time and energy.

If you study evolution enough, you will find that "laziness" is often a good approximator for the logic that powers change. If a system can accomplish TASK-X with CONFIGURATION-1 using less energy than with CONFIGURATION-2, then it's a safe bet that CONFIGURATION-1 is going to win the Darwinian duel over sufficient iterations in generational population genetics.

To the extent we have built-in instinctive biases, they are probably just *shortcuts that approximate logical thought,* rather than *actual instances of sound logical thinking,* for reaching conclusions that worked well enough most of the time across any given sample of instances in our environment of evolutionary adaptation.

However, once you change the context, it takes a long, long time for evolution to catch up. And the world we are dealing with now in no important way resembles the world that formed the context for the evolution of instinctive programming in the minds of *Homo sapiens* for hundreds of thousands of years before civilization got its roots dug in.

In other words, if you travel back in time 50,000 years, your instinctively preinstalled unconscious cognitive biases will probably be right on the money in terms of steering you toward productive assumptions and actions with a minimum of effort or time spent in deliberation.

But in today's world, the only function they serve is to trick you into forming conclusions that will work against you most of the time.

With that said, it's time to set out on our quest to identify the primary species of unconscious cognitive biases that limit our ability to effectively assess others and destroy our chances at realizing genuine inclusivity in our organizations.

A Safari through the Jungle of Cognitive Bias

As noted, unconscious cognitive biases are common patterns of thinking that can lead to errors or distortions in judgment and decision-making. In the context of authentic inclusion, certain unconscious cognitive biases can get in the way of progress even when an organization has committed itself to achieving authentic inclusion across all departments and functions.

Unconscious attitudes or associations that influence our perception and decision-making can perpetuate stereotypes and contribute to discrimination or exclusion. Recognizing and addressing these biases forms the backbone of any attempt to foster inclusivity in any environment where people are being evaluated so that those evaluations end up reflecting individual merits rather than predetermined stereotypes.

On our safari trip, we will be looking out for several different species of unconscious cognitive biases known to stymie progress toward inclusivity.

Following is a brief overview of the main species on our list. We will look at each in greater detail as we go, focusing specifically on how each tends to prohibit authentic inclusion, briefly touching on some of the more interesting ways researchers have found to identify and better understand these invisible cockroaches of the mind.

Confirmation bias: This term refers to our instinctive predilection to seek out, interpret, and/or recall data about the world in a way that confirms our existing beliefs.

Availability bias: This is one we covered in our overview of the factors that lead to groupthink disasters. It has applications here as well. It refers to the tendency to rely on readily available information or examples that come to mind easily when making judgments or decisions.

Attribution bias: This is the tendency to attribute our own successes to our own abilities and our failures to external factors. But it applies to our appraisal of others just as absurdly—we tend, unsurprisingly but clearly problematically, to attribute the successes of others to external factors while seeing their failures as a function of their own flawed abilities.

Halo effect: Here we are dealing with the tendency to let our overall impression of someone influence our assessment of their individual qualities.

In-group bias: We all seem to have a built-in tendency to bias toward others who seem to belong to our own social tribe. It has obvious benefits in a sub-Saharan savannah grassland context 30,000 years ago. But the opposite is now true as we seek to build inclusive organizations.

Anchoring bias: Another preinstalled bias that can be hard to delete or reprogram is the tendency to over-rely on the first piece of information we encounter when assessing something in the world around us—even if that first piece of data is entirely arbitrary or totally unrelated to the situation at hand.

If organizations are going to win this game of implementing authentic inclusion—whether related to neurodiversity or to race, gender, sexuality, or any other social dynamic—one of the most important steps will be to identify and deeply understand this list of different species of unconscious bias. Only then will we be able to immunize our organizational structures and systems against the powerful deforming impact they bring to bear as we work to cultivate authentically inclusive environments that value and promote diversity in all its aspects.

This is a worthwhile project not only for our collective well-being as a society but also for the cultivation of competitive edge among those best able to rapidly achieve such a peak feature of organizational culture.

Confirmation Bias

Confirmation bias refers to our tendency to seek out, interpret, and remember information in a way that confirms our preexisting beliefs or assumptions about people and the world around us.

In the context of authentic inclusion, confirmation bias can lead to selective perception and a reluctance to consider diverse perspectives or to challenge our existing beliefs and biases. To foster authentic inclusion, it is important to be aware of confirmation bias and actively seek out diverse viewpoints and experiences.

People tend to seek out information that confirms their existing views, while ignoring or downplaying information that contradicts those views. This bias can lead to a narrow and limited understanding of complex issues and can perpetuate exclusionary behaviors.

One widely cited example is shown in an experiment conducted in 1979 on the topic of capital punishment. It included participants who were in support of and others who were against capital punishment.[3]

All subjects were provided with the same two studies. After reading the detailed descriptions of the studies, participants ended up all still holding their initial beliefs and were quick to argue in support of those beliefs by citing the provided research—both those in support of and those against capital punishment recited confirming evidence from the studies as robust and rejected contradictory evidence as in some way flawed.

In many cases, we will fight like hell to preserve our existing beliefs, even if it means accepting a certain degree of irrationality into the equation. That's obviously not healthy. And anyone with any real stake in the prospects of an organization should be very interested in rooting out confirmation bias as quickly as possible.

We noted earlier that there's some overlap with the biases we covered earlier when discussing groupthink. While confirmation bias wasn't specifically discussed in that section, it certainly resonates with that medium of self-destructive organizational behavior.

Why it has relevance for neurodiversity inclusion efforts should be obvious at this point: we all tend to prefer interpreting new information in a way that helps us avoid the work of reconfiguring our foundational assumptions and beliefs. But the instinctive inclination to avoid that work can play havoc with our attempts to become more inclusive.

In other words, this book wouldn't need to exist if authentic neuroinclusion was the path of least resistance.

But it's not, so it does. In fact, authentic neurodiversity inclusion is accessible only by confronting and challenging our shared assumptions to find a better way of understanding the relationship between neurodivergent cognition and the social fabric we inhabit and enlist in our endeavors.

In my own experience working with organizations, I have noted many instances where hiring managers tended to exhibit confirmation bias by focusing more on information that confirmed their initial impression of an applicant and less on information that challenged that impression. Clearly, this pattern of behavior has the potential to drive unfair hiring practices and limit inclusivity by favoring individuals who fit preconceived notions of what a successful candidate should be. Research has also been conducted on how confirmation bias drives stereotyping—how individuals justifiably feel concerned that social interactions may serve to unfairly bias others by confirming negative stereotypes associated with social group identity.[4]

This research highlights how confirmation bias can lead to exclusion by perpetuating stereotypes and creating self-fulfilling prophecies.

Since then, we have seen these conclusions replicated, confirmed, and further developed. At this point, you will be hard-pressed to find anyone in the cognitive sciences that dismisses confirmation bias as a critical force in driving irrational decision-making behavior within and among groups.

It isn't difficult to imagine how this bias might play havoc with attempts to adopt an inclusive hiring process. Simply put, people are more likely to remember information that confirms their existing beliefs and forget information that contradicts them. This can lead to people making decisions that are biased in favor of their existing beliefs, even if they have been exposed to plenty of information and evidence to the contrary.

By the same token, we also tend to trust information from sources that we agree with and distrust information from sources we don't often agree with. We see this playing out dramatically in the formation of echo chambers in the relationship between media outlets and political news. The upshot is the tendency to seek out information from sources we know and like because they are sure to confirm our existing beliefs.

Recognizing the presence of confirmation bias and actively seeking diverse perspectives and information can help overcome this bias and promote a more inclusive organizational culture.

One particularly interesting implication of this bias is that you will be more likely to remember and trust *what you just read about* if you came into this chapter already a believer in the power of unconscious biases and how they interfere with our ability to gauge the world around us objectively and rationally.

In other words, if you already accepted the idea that unconscious biases are real, impactful, and potentially dangerous forces within our minds, then this chapter is likely to stick with you much more forcefully than if the reverse were true.

Availability Bias

Availability bias can limit inclusivity by favoring familiar or dominant narratives and overlooking less visible or underrepresented perspectives. The term was first coined in 1973 by Nobel Prize–winning psychologist Daniel Kahneman and his colleague Amos Tversky.[5]

Overcoming availability bias requires actively seeking out diverse sources of information and deliberately considering a broad range of experiences. Simply put, availability bias can lead to the exclusion of diverse perspectives and the reinforcement of existing narratives or dominant ideas through mere familiarity or emotive power—which are powerful forces when making unconscious snap judgments.

Probably the most common way the availability heuristic infringes on efforts at diversity and inclusion in the workplace is simply due to the fact that most people are primarily exposed to diverse social groups through news and media consumption, rather than personal or professional interactions. And, quite simply put, what you pick up through news and media consumption is likely to be skewed toward whatever equivalent to clickbait is most applicable, depending on specific medium of transmission.

In other words, media of all kinds tends to be geared toward delivering a high-value audience to advertisers rather than high-value content to an audience. To be maximally effective at its job, narratives, imagery, and characterizations in any form of media tend to skew toward sensationalism or exaggeration to ensure the cultivation of an audience of sufficient size.

Given that most of us are primarily exposed to members of truly different social groups through such media experiences, the availability bias/heuristic wreaks havoc on our ability to pass sound judgment in real-life situations on individuals representing very different social groups to our own because those judgments are, in part, infected by our media-based and sensationalized preconceptions.[6]

It turns out that individuals with limited exposure to diverse perspectives or experiences tend to over-rely on easily accessible information or examples that come to mind readily. It isn't hard to imagine how this tendency can work against efforts at authentic inclusion. The main enemy such efforts must battle is favoritism of the familiar leading to the exclusion of the less visible or underrepresented in past experiences.

I have witnessed or personally experienced countless occurrences of the availability bias at work in daily life. In many instances, neurodivergent people I know, or even myself, have been conveniently typecasted based on some preconceived ideas due to unrepresentative examples of what neurodivergent people look like. It is one of the reasons I have always aimed to be very visible in leadership positions. It is critical that the broad masses have experiences that shatter stereotypical categorizations based on a hyperactive neighbor, their clumsy nephew, or Sheldon from the tv show "The Big Bang Theory."

Attribution Bias

First introduced by Lee Ross in 1977, this is the tendency to attribute our successes to our own abilities and our failures to external factors. But it applies to our appraisal of others just as absurdly: we tend to attribute the successes of others to external factors while seeing their failures as a function of their own flawed abilities.[7]

This can lead to our underestimating the abilities of autistic job candidates. For example, in an interview, when autistic job candidates do not perform well, we may assume they are not capable of doing the job, when the real problem could be that the interview questions were not remotely related to the skills required for the role.

In essence, it is a flaw in our extrapolation process.

Attribution bias can limit inclusivity by influencing the way individuals perceive and attribute the causes of others' behavior. This bias can lead to unfair judgments, stereotypes, and discriminatory attitudes based on inaccurate or biased attributions.

This has enormous implications for neurodivergent job seekers. After all, if an achievement that comes as an exhibition of unique talent is chalked up to luck or special accommodations, some employers may never learn to appreciate the special gifts of their neurodivergent workers. Allowing this bias to go unnoticed and unchallenged stands to directly limit inclusivity by perpetuating stereotypes, reinforcing discriminatory practices, and hindering equal opportunities.

In short, attribution bias can work to limit inclusivity by influencing judgments, stereotypes, and discriminatory attitudes. Recognizing and challenging attribution biases, promoting empathy, and fostering a deeper understanding of the complexities behind individuals' behavior can help overcome these biases and create more inclusive environments.

Halo Effect

Here, we are dealing with the tendency to let our overall impression of someone influence our assessment of their individual qualities.

First coined in 1920 by a behaviorist, the halo effect can lead to us overlooking the strengths of neurodivergent job candidates because

161

we are overly focused on their perceived or assumed weaknesses.[8] For example, if an interviewer just so happens to have a generally negative impression of autism, that person may be less likely to hire an autistic job candidate once certain markers are identified, even if the specific individual being appraised is clearly qualified for the job.

The problem isn't anything to do with the actual person being interviewed. Instead, the problem is simply that the candidate has been sized up in a general sense, and from that general sense, the interviewer has unconsciously made a lot of assumptions about specifics without any evidence.

The halo effect can limit inclusivity by influencing perceptions and evaluations based on a single trait or characteristic of an individual or group. This bias can lead to the oversimplification of complex individuals or groups, overlooking their full range of abilities or qualities.

The classic study demonstrating the impact of the halo effect is Nisbett and Wilson's 1977 research on subjective judgments. The study asked participants to rate a college instructor based on a brief video interview. The instructor was played by the same actor, but he was given different personality traits in each interview. For example, in one interview he was portrayed as warm and friendly, while in the other he was portrayed as cold and distant.

Nisbett and Wilson found that participants who saw the warm instructor rated him more favorably on all dimensions, including his competence, intelligence, and trustworthiness. In contrast, participants who saw the cold instructor rated him more poorly on all dimensions.[9]

This suggests that people tend to make global judgments about others based on their initial impressions, even when there is no evidence to support those impressions.

Now, extrapolate that to the job interview process where two candidates—one neurotypical and extroverted and one autistic and introverted—are both under consideration for the same job as a financial market analyst. You can probably see where I'm going here and intuit a reasonably well-founded outcome distribution centered around the question: Just how much more qualified would the autistic person in this example need to be to get that job?

The answer probably isn't "none."

In my experience, the halo effect bias is one of the most damaging and difficult to overcome for organizations committed to achieving authentic neurodiversity inclusion. It carries the potential to completely wrong-foot us in some of our most important decisions, both personal and professional, leading to bad investments, poorly conceived alliances, and hiring errors.

The halo effect can work to limit inclusivity by influencing perceptions, evaluations, and decision-making based on a single positive trait or characteristic. Recognizing and challenging the halo effect, promoting a comprehensive understanding of individuals and groups, and considering a broader range of qualities and contributions can help foster inclusivity and reduce the impact of this bias.

But, once again, the key idea here is to take a proactive approach.

In-Group Bias

If you want to go straight to the heart of evolved unconscious bias that comes preinstalled in "*Homo sapiens* OS" when your brain switches on for the first time, you don't need to look much further than in-group bias.

In-group bias is the tendency to favor individuals who belong to one's own social group. It had obvious advantages 35,000 years ago on the plains of equatorial sub-Saharan Africa. You trust your kinship group—which basically represents your extended family—and you don't trust anyone else. The risk/reward ratio on violating this heuristic just doesn't pay off over the large sample.[10]

However, that same instinctive bias is now a major hurdle to successfully navigating the world. The upshot is the creation of divisions and barriers to the formation of inclusive relationships. To promote authentic inclusion, it is important to recognize and challenge in-group bias, actively seek out diverse perspectives, and foster connections with individuals from different backgrounds.

It can be countered proactively. But if left unchecked, the research suggests we are driven toward intergroup conflicts and the perpetuation of exclusionary behaviors, with obvious implications for neurodiversity inclusion at the organizational level.

If you pair this dynamic with the double-empathy problem covered in Chapter 13, you have a relatively clear path to understanding why in-group bias is another major hurdle to confront for organizations striving to achieve authentic neurodiversity inclusion.

However, one should also note that these studies show us a path forward every bit as much as they show us the obstacles in our way: the key is in working to promote a sense of the whole range of cognitive diversity as the many facets of a single in-group tribe.

Anchoring Bias

Anchoring bias is one of the most robust effects in psychology. It occurs when individuals rely heavily on the first piece of information they encounter when making judgments or decisions, even if that information is arbitrary or unrelated to the situation at hand. This bias can influence perceptions and lead to unfair treatment or exclusion based on initial impressions. Overcoming anchoring bias requires consciously considering a variety of information sources and avoiding snap judgments.[11]

A common example is the $1,200 T-shirt. If that's the first T-shirt you ever see for sale, you're going to think $100 T-shirts are cheap.

But, by the same token, if the first ADHDer you ever met turned out to be very unreliable, and you are interviewing someone for a position at your firm, and that person is up-front about an ADHD diagnosis, there's an awfully good chance you aren't going to be fair in how you evaluate that person's fitness for the role.

In the context of hiring, anchoring bias can lead to hiring managers making decisions based on their initial impressions of candidates, rather than on the candidates' qualifications and experience. For example, if a hiring manager has a negative impression of a candidate based on their name or appearance, they may be less likely to give the candidate a fair chance.

Anchoring bias can also lead to hiring managers overlooking qualified candidates from underrepresented groups. For example, if a hiring manager has a preconceived notion that women are not as qualified for technical roles as men, they may be less likely to interview qualified female candidates.

Summary

As we have covered in this chapter, there are many different species of unconscious cognitive biases that undermine our capacity to be inclusive, objective, and rational in our evaluations of others. But there are some commonalities that should be highlighted.

The foremost unifying theme is that our brains run on an instinct operating system designed by evolution predominantly in the Pleistocene epoch. Much of our social instinctive preinstalled software was designed to give us an edge when navigating the challenges faced by early hominids living in small kinship-based tribal communities in a savannah grassland environment over many hundreds of millennia. In that context, anything approximating what we consider to be "civilization" is very recent—not nearly enough time for genotypic change driven by Darwinian selective pressure. In other words, we are still running a preinstalled Pleistocene Human OS version 1.0 despite living in Civilized World 10.0. We update that software through cultural downloads throughout our lives. But the instinct layer is hard if not impossible to entirely delete and replace with updated protocols.

There's a basic functional mismatch problem between a fundamental design feature we all share and the new context in which that feature is being engaged in our daily experiences. Those deeply embedded cognitive shortcut "apps" were designed as time- and labor-saving algorithms to help us make snap judgments that were mostly accurate in the context of our world as it was thousands of years ago. But most of them are now out of date and counterproductive.

Another commonality among many of these biases is the fact that we live in a world completely dominated by media and social media. Much of our perceptual anchoring for diverse groups stem from some instance of media or social media consumption, where reality has been actively distorted and sensationalized to cultivate a wider audience.

In short, not only are we equipped with woefully out-of-date and counterproductive cognitive shortcut apps in our social experiences, but we are also subject to massive sampling bias risk as we attempt to make sense of the world we live in today.

Unfortunately, those deficiencies carry over into our professional experiences, and authentic inclusion efforts suffer as a result.

Understanding this and taking proactive measures to counter these biases is a key step in building a truly inclusive culture where neurodivergent people are valued and inaccurate assumptions are regularly challenged and overwritten by more effective strategies.

Unconscious biases sneak into our thought processes and contribute to the construction and maintenance of deeply rooted barriers preventing authentic inclusion of the neurodivergent in our organizations. Part III will offer strategies to combat the risks they pose while encouraging perspective-taking, positive stories that focus on strengths, and increased opportunities for shared experiences across any organization so that everyone, regardless of neurotype, will be empowered to succeed.

Key Takeaways

- Unconscious cognitive biases are mental shortcuts—time- and labor-saving cognitive devices that have become installed functions of our evolved cognition over hundreds of millennia.

- Now, however, they are legacy functions that only serve to limit our ability to function in a very different world from the context that guided their design. Today, they dependably guide us astray in our present complex, multifaceted, and multilayered social environment, where tribalism and superficial snap judgments consistently lead to costly errors.

- To the extent we have built-in instinctive biases, they are probably just shortcuts that approximate logical thought, rather than actual instances of sound logical thinking, for reaching conclusions that worked well enough most of the time across any given sample of instances in our environment of evolutionary adaptation.

- Confirmation bias refers to our instinctive predilection to seek out, interpret, and/or recall data about the world in a way that confirms our existing beliefs.

(continued)

(continued)

- Availability bias refers to the tendency to rely on readily available information or examples that come to mind easily when making judgments or decisions.

- Attribution bias is the tendency to attribute our own successes to our own abilities and our failures to external factors. But it applies to our appraisal of others just as absurdly—we tend, unsurprisingly but clearly problematically, to attribute the successes of others to external factors while seeing their failures as a function of their own flawed abilities.

- Halo effect refers to our tendency to let our overall impression of someone influence our assessment of that person's individual qualities.

- In-group bias is our tendency to bias toward others who seem to belong to our own social tribe.

- Anchoring bias is the tendency to over-rely upon the first piece of information we encounter when assessing something in the world around us—even if that first piece of data is entirely arbitrary or totally unrelated to the situation at hand.

- There are many different species of unconscious cognitive biases that undermine our capacity to be inclusive, objective, and rational in our evaluations of others. But there are some commonalities that should be highlighted.

- First, the counterproductive skew that characterizes their impact is likely, in each case, an artifact of the mismatch between the social demands of the world of our evolutionary adaptation tens of thousands of years ago and the very different sociocultural context we live our lives in today.

- Second, we live in a world completely dominated by media and social media. Accordingly, many of our anchoring or most available references for diverse groups stem from some instance of media or social media consumption, where reality has been actively distorted and sensationalized to cultivate a wider audience. Hence, our instincts guide us to make referential shortcuts to data points that do not accurately represent anything close to median reality.

- In short, not only are we equipped with woefully out-of-date and counterproductive cognitive shortcut apps in our social experiences, but we are also subject to massive sampling bias risk as we attempt to make sense of the world we live in today.

- These unifying flaws and the biases that manifest them represent enormous barriers to neuroinclusion and unfair obstacles for the neurodivergent. Overcoming them is a persistent objective for all successful, inclusive organizations.

- Part III will offer strategies to combat the risks posed by unconscious biases while encouraging perspective-taking, positive stories that focus on strengths, and increased opportunities for shared experiences across any organization so that everyone, regardless of neurotype, will be empowered to succeed.

Tricks Minds Play

Chapter 9

Building a Sturdy Foundation

*"Kindness is more than deeds. It is an attitude, an expression,
a look, a touch. It is anything that lifts another person."*

—Plato

One day, out of the blue, I received a private communication over social media from an online acquaintance of mine named Anna, a bright, late-diagnosed autistic individual and an accomplished professional with over 15 years in senior leadership positions. She said she was desperately searching for her tribe and wondered if I could help her put together a support group of neurodivergent women.

"They say it's lonely at the top," she said. "But few will ever understand the isolation of being an openly neurodivergent person in leadership."

It turned out that she had recently mustered the courage to disclose her autism diagnosis at work and was devastated by what followed, especially since she expected her colleagues and managers to rally behind her. After all, she had helped spearhead an internal "Neurodiversity at Work" program about a year ago and with great success. Sensory-friendly policy: check. Hybrid work policy: check. A process to implement nontraditional interviews to include neurodiverse talent: check.

On the surface, the company appeared to be doing some amazing work and made several changes that should have facilitated a solid path toward authentic neuroinclusion and belonging. The company had updated several policies and procedures that were neurodiversity-friendly. All employees had access to noise-canceling headphones, could select their desk location in the office, and were welcomed to request light and temperature adjustments. This was a huge step in the right direction and led to the successful recruitment of new neurodivergent staff. Some employees, depending on their role, were also given flexible work options, both remote and hybrid. This same company was previously very much against any remote or hybrid work arrangements as soon as the pandemic subsided, so this last step was a clear signal that neurodiversity inclusion was a genuine priority.

So what was the problem?

When I met with Anna over Zoom later that same day, her face looked pale and tired, as if she hadn't slept in days. I had always considered her a calm person, a bold thinker, and a straight shooter. But the person on my screen that day was a mess—nearly too distraught and anxious to speak.

Apparently, once she disclosed her diagnosis, everything changed in her professional life. She was bullied and gaslighted on a daily basis. Peers mocked her behind her back. And she was quickly being strategically marginalized in terms of her status and responsibilities at her organization. She had also become the default scapegoat for anything that went wrong with the team. Every hiccup became cast as her failure to properly understand something crucial. Her boss started to belittle her ideas to her face and then incorporate them into his own presentations.

The problem was rooted in deep organizational culture challenges that had not been apparent to her before her disclosure. While the company on the surface seemed committed to valuing neurodivergent people, the habits and actions of bad-faith players suggested otherwise. Like all employees, Anna just wanted to feel accepted and valued for who she is and for her contributions.

Having worked as a marketing executive for many years, she had excellent organizational and communication skills and her quirkiness was previously perceived as "delightfully refreshing." She is one of the clearest communicators I have ever met. Her staff always appreciated her communication style and the fact that they never had to guess what her expectations really were. She always said what she meant.

Now, people began to doubt her managerial and client-relationship skills. Whereas she used to be asked to weigh in on a range of corporate decisions regularly, she was now only rarely invited by the CEO and Senior Vice President to provide her strategic input.

As she later confessed, the last straw occurred the day before she contacted me. Apparently, she was exiting the elevator midday on her way to grab a cup of soup for lunch when she overheard a burst of laughter coming from the cafeteria. She looked in the direction of the laughter just in time to see someone she thought of as a loyal colleague rolling her eyes and clearly saying, "Yeah, but now we know Anna is a retard!" This was followed by more laughter.

She was heartbroken. She loved her job. Work was so much of her identity. But she felt demoralized and wanted to quit to salvage what was left of her mental health.

As we later learned, Anna was but one example of this kind of treatment at the company. Management had become complacent—content to pat themselves on the back for checking the inclusivity box while turning a blind eye to the toxic nature of the organization's culture under the surface.

We now know that Anna's mistreatment turned out to be the beginning of the end for the company.

Psychological Safety Is Paramount

After working in this space for over two decades and having lived experience as well, one of the most important principles I have learned along the way is this: while there are many elements to crafting an organizational culture in which all can thrive, there are some basic foundational parameters that must be in place for any of the other elements to matter. This is why I put *trust and psychological safety* as the foundational layer in the Pyramid of Neuroinclusion, which we covered in Chapter 5.

Harvard Business School Professor Amy C. Edmondson, a leading researcher in this niche for several decades, defines psychological safety as "a belief that one will not be punished or humiliated for speaking up with ideas, questions, concerns, or mistakes."[1]

As I define the concept in the neurodiversity context, psychological safety is the belief, evidenced in daily experience, that one will not be devalued, humiliated, gossiped about, subjected to gaslighting, or strategically disenfranchised by others in the group for displaying neurodivergent traits or behaviors or disclosing neurodivergent status.

All aspects of the Pyramid of Neuroinclusion are vital to a thriving neuroinclusive culture. But psychological safety is the foundation. In its absence, the workplace can quickly become a toxic environment for everyone. No amount of practical neurodiversity-friendly policies can cancel out the trauma of not being able to authentically reveal one's identity without fear of repercussions or prejudice.

Imagine trying to build a house without a foundation. It won't hold up even if you have the best windows, doors, bricks, and quality flooring. The same holds true for building an organizational culture that espouses a commitment to neurodiversity inclusion.

Throughout this book, I argue that authentic neurodiversity inclusion checklists, in and of themselves, are ineffective. So why did I include a "Neurodiversity-Friendly Organizational Culture Checklist" among the tools on offer in the Appendix section and the online resource associated with this book?

I did so because I believe checklists can be utilized productively but in a very different way than they have generally been used in the past. They should be used as one tool within a vast toolbox and with their purpose being to force us to ask ourselves difficult questions. In other words, they should be used as devices that guide us to question where we stand in process-based ongoing deliberations somewhere on a path toward authentic neuroinclusion and belonging.

The checklist I provide, for example, should also be used as a starting point rather than an end result, and the questions that appear there will be expanded and updated online as new research and data become available over time.

Here is a sample of the kind of process-based questions that appear on the Neurodiversity-Friendly Organizational Culture Checklist:

- Have you adopted a Neurodiversity Inclusion Value Statement?
- Does your organization have anti-bullying and anti-harassment policies that explicitly cover neurodivergent people?
- Is transparent communication encouraged, valued, and rewarded?
- Do you offer flexible work arrangements, such as remote only, remote first, or hybrid?
- Does your organization offer alternative interview processes that are not biased toward traditional communication and social skills?
- Do you conduct trainings for staff at all levels to promote a neurodiversity-friendly organizational culture?

Two points are important to keep in mind. First, a perfect score on a neurodiversity inclusion checklist is meaningless in practice in the absence of a culture of psychological safety if the goal is to foster authentic neurodiversity inclusion and belonging—just ask Anna. Second, psychological safety is the bedrock of growth and innovation, as we shall see in the next section.

Permission to Think Freely?

In reviewing the Pyramid of Neuroinclusion, psychological safety is the most foundational layer because, without it, all other levels become meaningless. It's a bit like Maslow's Hierarchy of Needs in that respect. What good is "friendship" if you don't have access to oxygen or water?

When the foundational layer of psychological safety is shaky, communication can't be transparent because it will be taking place in a context of fear and insecurity. And without transparent communication, the feedback mechanisms necessary to establishing supportive needs will be disrupted and accessing accommodations or auxiliary supports will invite discrimination and social exclusion, destroying any semblance of empathy among and between all members of the organization. The result: tribal divisions, alienation, and a culture completely incapable of producing innovative solutions due to the widespread sense that being different, challenging existing assumptions or the group hierarchy, or expressing an original idea isn't worth the risk.

In short, without a sturdy foundation of psychological safety, an organization is living on borrowed time.

When I was advising an investment fund several years ago, the CEO of one of the fund's more mature portfolio companies set an internal goal to hire a minimum of 10 new autistic employees over a two-year period as a strategy to spark new ideas by broadening

Ble ~~#~~ 4

rlllb   4

Z   43r

Tutoring Log - _____

Email: _____

First and last name:

How many hours di

the company's pool of cognitive diversity. He hired a general HR consultancy firm and assembled a plan that looked feasible. Senior leadership at the executive and board levels appeared unanimously committed to the idea. There was even an "Introduction to Neurodiversity" training workshop for his current staff.

With the company suffering from a lack of innovation, Steve, the company's first new hire as part of this program, seemed like a perfect fit. An autistic software engineer and product designer known for implementing very original ideas and getting winning products to market, Steve was well-known in venture capital circles. As such, he thought he had earned the respect of his peers by his accomplishments and that the days of being bullied were long gone.

Yet, when he came on board and got settled into his new role, there came a day when he challenged the team to consider taking a different approach to a new product concept. In response, the manager made an exaggerated show of rolling his eyes before moving on with the discussion as if Steve had never said a word. Instead of rewarding this talented new employee for having the courage to express an alternative perspective that challenged the view favored by everyone else in the room—by being willing to contribute his vast experience and deep conviction despite it being a professional risk—the group's leader made an effort to signal to the entire team that Steve wasn't worth listening to.

Later, another employee recorded a video of Steve "stimming"—something many autistic people do that should be accepted; examples include rocking back and forth, hand-flapping, or repetitive hand or finger movements, to name a few—and shared it with other employees over a group Skype chat to make fun of him.

From that point on, Steve went into a shell. He decided he could not do the work he was hired to do in an environment where he did not feel welcomed and appreciated for who he was, quirks and all. He left the company a short time later. As I recall, the CEO's goal of expanding the company's pool of cognitive diversity ended with Steve's departure.

Bullying Continues in Adulthood

Bullying of the neurodivergent is unfortunately very common. Autistic people are far more likely to be bullied than their neurotypical peers, with some research suggesting bullying rates may be as high as 94%.[2]

During my listening tour and throughout the interviews I conducted for this book, stories about bullying and harassment of the neurodivergent both at school and in the workplace were all too common. Sometimes it happens covertly in all the subtle ways people signal to each other that someone's credibility should be undermined. Sometimes it is far less subtle. The unfortunate result is much higher suicide rates among the neurodivergent than among neurotypical people.

When someone is bullied because of a disability or perceived disability, it counts as a form of harassment. Harassment in the workplace should never be tolerated, not only because it creates a toxic workplace, but also because it is illegal.

It is crucial that neurodivergent people have access to opportunities to be productive at work in environments where they are valued and where they can trust that their behavioral idiosyncrasies or diagnoses will never be used against them. Over the years, I have met many hundreds of neurodivergent senior leaders who were afraid not only to explicitly disclose their neurodivergence but even to simply relax and be themselves, quirks and all, around their coworkers because they believed they would suffer social and professional discrimination as a direct result.

Recall all the different ways unconscious cognitive biases can sneak in through the basement window and distort judgment in our experiences, as we surveyed in Chapter 8. No one is perfect, and we all fall victim to unconscious biases in the course of our daily lives. It's impossible to entirely avoid. That's why it's so important to know thine enemy—to know what bias at work looks like in action and to assiduously avoid making unfounded presumptions about the capabilities or limitations of neurodivergent employees and coworkers based solely on awareness of their neurodivergent cognitive profile.

It is not only neurodivergent people who benefit from an organizational culture that prioritizes psychological safety. Everyone throughout the organization stands to gain. A 2022 study by Bain & Company found that today's young professionals are feeling more stress with greater mental health vulnerabilities than prior generations. In the same year, Gallup reported that 54% of Gen Z workers feel disengaged or ambivalent at work.[3]

A healthy culture built on a solid foundation of psychological safety and transparent communication standards may mitigate some of the challenges and anxieties that the working generation currently faces with accelerating social, economic, and technological change. Organizations that reinforce this core value with daily action will inspire everyone to feel comfortable in showing authenticity, sharing new ideas, taking risks, making mistakes, and genuinely embracing differences.

Given the premium on innovation we are likely to see over coming years, I would also argue that all organizations and boards should prioritize the conditions that will create the most fertile cultural soil for attracting, retaining, and authentically including all kinds of minds. Prior research has shown that the most innovative companies, teams, and boards all celebrate a culture that embraces new ideas and challenges to the status quo—where courage to explore new directions is rewarded, rather than chastised and marginalized.

Google Project Aristotle, for example, studied 180 of their own teams up close and found that "psychological safety" was more closely correlated with high performance and innovation than either "intelligence" or "resources."[4]

Risk Requires Trust in Safety

Psychological safety occurs when someone feels included, accepted, valued, and safe to contribute to and even challenge the status quo without risking abuse when in a group setting. In the context of neurodiversity, it also means that all kinds of minds are valued, and that neurodivergent people feel empowered to contribute without being ridiculed.

In his book, *The Four Stages of Psychological Safety*, Timothy R. Clark proposed a framework where high-performing teams progress through four stages to ultimately arrive at a state capable of spurring innovation while also valuing challenges to the status quo. Clark sums up psychological safety as something that arises in an organizational culture "of rewarded vulnerability."[5]

The four stages are depicted in Figure 9.1. I will briefly summarize each of the four stages of psychological safety and then discuss its applications to neurodiversity and the central themes of this book.

1. *Inclusion safety:* Inclusion safety is the first stage and refers to respect for all human beings as well as open acknowledgment that everyone deserves to be included. The only criterion for inclusion is as a fellow human being at the start.

2. *Learner safety:* The second stage allows for an environment where questions can be asked and where failure is not only tolerated but rewarded. The expectation is that an organization will grow to become more collaborative and innovative when employees feel comfortable asking for help or clarification without fearing negative consequences.

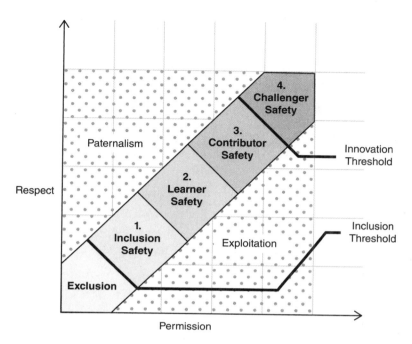

Figure 9.1 The four stages of psychological safety.
(*Source:* Clark, 2020. Berrett-Koehler Publishers.)

   3. *Contributor safety:* The third stage is earned by demonstrated
   performance. It's basically an exchange of risk: if you consistently deliver results, you'll be trusted to do your thing. This
   can become a chicken-and-egg problem.

   4. *Challenger safety:* The final stage is challenger safety, which is
   generally an organizational prerequisite for achieving the capacity to innovate on a serial basis. If someone on the team challenges a viewpoint or offers a new idea and is penalized as a
   result, then the culture will be one of fear, and no one will want
   to do anything to rock the boat. However, if dissent is appreciated and the engagement in alternative ideas is rewarded, then
   a culture of innovation can take root and blossom.

Building a Sturdy Foundation

How do we apply psychological safety frameworks to neurodivergent people at work? Anna's story at the beginning of this chapter presents an important case study because she experienced psychological safety even at the level of the fourth stage, where she could innovate and challenge assumptions, until she openly disclosed that she was a late-diagnosed autistic.

Her impeccable work ethic, vast experience, exceptional track record, and extraordinary skills—qualities she was openly recognized for before her disclosure—didn't suddenly stop being true facts about her when she opened up about her neurodivergence. Yet, after her disclosure, she was suddenly ostracized and excluded from the opportunity to contribute at anywhere near the same substantive level as before. At that point, she was relegated back to square one on the psychological safety ladder, fighting for basic inclusion safety—to simply be treated with the respect due to any fellow human being.

I wish I could write here that this was a turning point for Anna's company and that everything turned out for the best. Unfortunately, things only progressed in the wrong direction. A few key people in her organization had a very narrow understanding about autism and attributed characteristics to her based on the two or three people they had previously met personally or had been exposed to in movies.

The more she voiced her concerns, the more she was excluded. Even though she was "out" as an autistic, she felt more pressure than ever to hide her neurodivergent traits and thought she just needed to work harder. She tried to advocate for herself but to no avail. Eventually, the stress of masking, disproportionate performance standards, and her constant sense of social trauma at work left her burnt out and she succumbed to pressure to quietly resign.

She did have allies and friends at the company, but only one publicly spoke up to defend her. This ally remarked that the company had no idea what they were doing and that without Anna the company would suffer. This is exactly what happened, but the company's senior leadership decided the best path was to pretend none of it was real—that the autistic woman "just couldn't hack it after all."

A year later, Anna contacted me to tell me she had heard from some of her former colleagues that the company experienced an exodus of talent in the aftermath of her resignation. Whether they spoke out about it or not, clearly many of her coworkers were acutely aware of her story and the lesson it contained: namely, that the organization that employed them embraced a culture of bigotry, discrimination, bullying, and senseless animosity toward people who are different or atypical in how they think and act; a culture that has no qualms about treating its hardest working, most dedicated, and most talented employees with truly striking injustice.

Not a good look.

Fortunately, Anna's story has a happy ending. After a challenging but short-lived search for a new role similar to her prior one, she started her own consultancy firm as a very in-demand expert in her field doing plenty of business with her prior company's largest competitor.

This is another important point drawn from her story: although there is strong evidence that some neurotypes—particularly ADHDers and dyslexics—appear to be naturally attracted to entrepreneurship, I have met countless neurodivergent founders like Anna that were effectively railroaded into entrepreneurial success by necessity and prejudice rather than choice.

Anna's story lies at the extreme negative end of the spectrum, but it is invaluable as a case study because it provides an unambiguous example of an organizational culture that appears healthy at a glance but turns out to be rotten to the core under the surface.

Neurodiversity and Entrepreneurship

Several years ago, I cofounded the Neurodiverse Entrepreneur Program, an equity free grant and support program for neurodivergent founders or start-up companies with an inclusive culture and at least one neurodivergent leader in a C-suite position.

According to my data spanning the past three years, roughly 65% of surveyed applicants to the program to date have stated that they are pursuing entrepreneurship as their first career choice, while 35% would prefer to utilize their unique talents and innovative mindset at an established company if given the chance but had no luck in finding or maintaining a role commensurate with their qualifications.

To balance her story, I have also worked with many organizations over the years that represent the opposite end of the spectrum, like Mark's company, which we covered in Chapter 5. These organizations recognize the importance of doing the deep work to become psychologically safe and neurodivergent-friendly right down to their DNA. And those efforts have generally translated into a competitive advantage expressed through increased productivity, new innovative products, lower turnover, and a culture of respect, tolerance, and employee satisfaction.

How to Get There

At the absolute minimum, make sure there is a clear anti-bullying and anti-harassment policy that explicitly covers neurodiversity or perceived neurodivergent characteristics. As discussed earlier, the best windows, doors, walls, and roofing tiles can't compensate for a faulty foundation. When mutual respect and trust are in place, there is room to correct misunderstandings, express innovative ideas, ask for help, and advocate for oneself.

Dos and Don'ts to Promote Psychological Safety

Dos:

- Codify clear anti-bullying and anti-harassment policies that cover neurodiversity;
- Adopt a neurodiversity inclusion value statement;
- Reward people who take intellectual risks;
- Encourage creativity and innovation;
- Make neurodiversity training available throughout the organization;
- Tell positive stories about neurodivergent people, focusing on strengths;
- Reward and encourage transparent communication;
- Show leadership in celebrating differences;
- Encourage respectful, dissenting opinions;
- Facilitate team-building exercises that help value difference and bridge understanding;
- Employ neurodivergent people at all levels of the organization;
- Combat limiting stereotypes about neurodivergent people;
- Promote a culture that rewards honesty and transparency;
- Demonstrate that honest mistakes and misunderstandings are okay;
- Reframe shortcomings and mistakes as opportunities to learn;
- When things go wrong, facilitate honest discussion in the form of postmortems;

(continued)

(continued)

- Have a no-interruption rule to allow all voices to be heard;
- Consider training peer navigators, mentors, and allies to welcome divergent views and perspectives;
- Actively model empathy and respect at the leadership level;
- Always include neurodivergent people as co-participants.

Don'ts:

- Don't turn a blind eye to bullying, gossip, or harassing behaviors;
- Don't exclude neurodiversity protocols from HR employee handbooks, anti-bullying or anti-harassment policies;
- Don't reward people who demand compliance through fear and intimidation;
- Don't allow people to be stereotyped or reduced to categorical characteristics;
- Don't make it emotionally, psychologically, or financially risky for people to speak up;
- Don't use ambiguous language;
- Don't reward criticism of neurodivergent traits;
- Don't give presentations without encouraging questions or different perspectives;
- Don't demonstrate behavior that you don't want to see on the team;
- Don't make demeaning comments to "motivate" the team or reward others who do;
- Don't exclude neurodivergent people from conversations affecting the team, their role, or neurodiversity more generally;

- Don't force neurodivergent people to disclose to ask for simple adjustments;
- Don't treat neurodivergent people differently if they do disclose, and don't reward anyone who does.

In my experience, one of the hurdles organizations will face in making this type of transformation is simply about inertia. As a general rule, people are resistant to change. So it's critical to get the authentic buy-in of existing employees, advisors, and board members as early as possible in the process.

Veteran employees in the organization are accustomed to a certain way of doing things. And they may become anxious about how transformative changes might influence their professional status and prospects, the products they have helped to build, or their value to the organization. It may be necessary to target this issue—it's different for different organizations—to help everyone understand what the goal is and why psychological safety and honest, transparent communication are important and can provide a foundation for neuroinclusion, which benefits everyone.

Clark's model implies that the kind of psychological safety needed for anyone in a group to comfortably express a dissenting opinion is developed over time, progressing through more rudimentary stages first. Companies don't benefit from what Clark refers to as the "innovation threshold" until organizational cultures reach this final stage.

Neurodivergent people are generally less correlated to the group in terms of analytical, perceptual, and cognitive skills, and many have spiky profiles, meaning that they have heightened abilities and strengths in some areas and greater challenges in others. This doesn't mean they make poor teammates. However, it does imply that there must be at least some level of psychological safety in place before neurodivergent people will be able to manifest their true value.

Key Takeaways

- While there are many elements to crafting an organizational culture in which all can thrive, there are some basic foundational parameters that must be in place for any of the other elements to matter. This is why I put trust and psychological safety as the foundational layer in the Pyramid of Neuroinclusion, which we covered in Chapter 5.

- In the neurodiversity context, psychological safety is the belief, evidenced in daily experience, that one will not be devalued, humiliated, gossiped about, subjected to gaslighting, or strategically disenfranchised by others in the group for displaying neurodivergent traits or behaviors or disclosing neurodivergent status.

- No amount of practical neurodiversity-friendly policies can cancel out the trauma of not being able to authentically reveal one's identity without fear of repercussions or prejudice.

- Neuroinclusion checklists should be used as one tool within a vast toolbox and with their purpose being to force us to ask ourselves difficult questions—as devices that guide us to question where we stand in process-based ongoing deliberations somewhere on a path toward authentic neurodiversity inclusion & belonging.

- Two points are important to keep in mind. First, a perfect score on a neurodiversity inclusion checklist is meaningless in practice in the absence of a culture of psychological safety if the goal is to foster authentic neurodiversity inclusion and belonging—just ask Anna. Second, psychological safety is the bedrock of growth and innovation.

- Absent a sturdy foundation of psychological safety, trust, and transparent 360-degree communication, the pyramid crumbles into tribal divisions, alienation, and a culture completely incapable of producing innovative solutions due to the widespread sense that being different, challenging existing assumptions or the group hierarchy, or expressing an original idea isn't worth the risk.

- Bullying of the neurodivergent is unfortunately very common. And the unfortunate result is much higher suicide rates among the neurodivergent than among neurotypical people.

- It is not only neurodivergent people who benefit from an organizational culture that prioritizes psychological safety. Everyone throughout the organization stands to gain.

- Prior research has shown that the most innovative companies, teams, and boards all celebrate a culture that embraces new ideas and challenges to the status quo— where courage to explore new directions is rewarded, rather than chastised and marginalized.

- Google Project Aristotle studied 180 of their own teams up close and found that "psychological safety" was more closely correlated with high performance and innovation than either "intelligence" or "resources."

- Psychological safety occurs when someone feels included, accepted, valued, and safe to contribute to and even challenge the status quo without risking abuse when in a group setting.

(continued)

(continued)

- In his book, *The Four Stages of Psychological Safety*, Timothy R. Clark proposed a framework where high-performing teams progress through four stages to ultimately arrive at a state capable of spurring innovation while also valuing challenges to the status quo.

- Clark's model implies that the kind of psychological safety needed for anyone in a group to comfortably express a dissenting opinion is developed over time, progressing through more rudimentary stages first. Companies don't benefit from what Clark refers to as the "innovation threshold" until organizational cultures reach this final stage. This is especially true for neurodivergent employees.

Chapter 10

Recruiting for Cognitive Diversity

"If knowledge is power, knowing what we don't know is wisdom."

—Adam Grant[1]

In prior chapters, we discussed The Three C's and how codification and conduct can align to foster a culture that authentically supports neurodiversity inclusion, which in turn supports improved cognitive diversity, innovation, and groupthink immunity, a wider pool of new talent to draw from and gains in employee loyalty and motivation.

Last chapter, we discussed in detail the pivotal idea that a sturdy foundation of psychological safety, trust, and transparent risk-free 360-degree communication is a crucial prerequisite to all of these dynamics. Finally, in Chapter 6, we painted a picture of what I call a check-the-box approach to this process, and how such an approach is ultimately a disaster in the making.

In other words, we have focused a lot on creating a state of affairs defined by a culture tied to formal neurodiversity-friendly codification that is expressed faithfully in day-to-day conduct and rests on a foundation of widely established and perceived psychological safety, where employees never fear negative career repercussions for being honest about their problems, needs, or interpretive confusion and have access to meaningful feedback and clarification about expectations at any time.

We have also discussed the powerful legitimating implications of advancement—showcasing neurodivergent leadership sends a meaningful signal to current and prospective employees, members of the neurodiversity community, and the general public.

In summary, authentic neuroinclusion is derived from a values-driven approach to inclusivity. The Pyramid of Neuroinclusion introduced in Chapter 5, with its hierarchical approach to an actionable framework for inclusivity, should be front and center as you work on implementing key strategies. When values are codified in both behavior and policies, current employees will feel valued and supported and the organization will be attractive to prospective candidates as a good place to invest significant time and mindshare.

With that foundation in mind, we drill down further in this chapter to cover concepts and practical strategies designed to help any organization successfully attract and recruit neurodivergent talent.

Strategy #1: Demonstrate Commitment with a Values Statement

The neurodiversity community is tight-knit, and many potential employees will likely do their own research on the organization, which will include investigating how current and former neurodivergent employees have been treated. If your track record in the past in this regard is not commendable, it is time to right the ship.

Rather than focus on a bag of tricks to create an outward-facing PR focus as being "neurodiversity friendly," the deeper work must be done to set the stage for a thriving organizational culture able to inevitably attract committed neurodivergent workers. This means working on genuinely getting buy-in across all levels of the organization. An explicit values statement adopted as an aspirational goal by an organization—one that commits to including neurodiversity in all its unique and rich forms of expression—may be a good place to start.

When I served as president of the Illinois Community College Trustees Association (ICCTA), I made it a priority as a statewide leader to make higher education more accessible to as many students as possible. The Illinois Community College System is the third largest in the United States, and the ICCTA represents 48 member colleges in legislative advocacy and trustee education, serving over 700,000 students. I led, with the support of the entire organization and representatives across the state, the adoption of the first ever Neurodiversity Inclusion statement in the world by a statewide education association to influence policy. After lobbying the Illinois state government, our values statement inspired new legislation, HR 219 "Neurodiversity in Higher Ed" in May 2023. The legislation encourages all institutions of higher education across the state to adopt a similar statement in committing to valuing, supporting, and empowering all students, neurodivergent and neurotypical alike, to achieve their full potential.

The values statement that inspired the legislative step purposely included the importance of welcoming and empowering neurodivergent faculty, staff, administrators, and trustees in addition to students (see Figure 10.1). A thriving and diverse organizational culture will allow for the necessary conditions so that people from all levels of the organization can feel welcomed for who they are and comfortable with disclosure should they wish to be open about their neurodivergent status.

With an established foundation of mutual respect, trust, and transparent communication—the foundational levels outlined in the Pyramid of Neuroinclusion framework—your organization will make it on the short list as an especially desirable place to work.

Neurodiversity Inclusion

The Board of Representatives, administration, and staff of the Illinois Community College Trustees Association recognize that neurodiversity * among the students, faculty, staff, trustees, and administrative teams of our member colleges is critical to enhancing the educational experience for our students and providing for a more inclusive learning and operating environment, providing public benefits for our communities.

We believe that, when neurodivergent people are understood, valued, and empowered, we all stand to benefit from their important and unique contributions. This resolution represents our commitment to promoting an authentically inclusive learning environment in alignment with this ideal.

** Neurodiversity is defined as a strength-based paradigm to viewing conditions such as autism, ADD/ADHD, Dyslexia and Dyspraxia as differences in individual brain function and behavioral traits and as part of normal variation in the human population.*

Figure 10.1 Neurodiversity inclusion values statement.

Strategy #2: Don't Let Fear Get in the Way of Hiring Unique Talent

Over the years, I have heard from many managers who were enthusiastic about hiring people with physical disabilities, but when we started to talk about neurodivergent talent, we hit a "discomfort" wall. In short, they feared doing something wrong—of being out of their depth or lacking in-house expertise to deal with so-called invisible disabilities.

They did not even know where to start and felt that their team lacked the expertise and know-how to successfully recruit and support neurodivergent talent.

Emerging themes at the nexus of work, culture, technology, and economics are set to accelerate the impact of dynamics already in play forcing employers to either invest in cognitive diversity or get left behind. Managing that process with superficial checklists, a check-the-box mentality, and cosmetic inclusion won't cut it. This book is a resource to help organizational leaders better understand how and why they are missing out on what amounts to a human resources revolution. There are many inexpensive strategies highlighted here to accommodate neurodivergent employees.

But the process must begin with a full commitment to authentic neuroinclusion.

Faced with high stakes, fear of the unknown has never been a winning strategy.

Strategy #3: Understand Barriers to Recruitment

It starts by gaining an in-depth understanding of the challenges to employment for this group, particularly as they may be manifested within the context of your own organization's recruitment, evaluative, and onboarding protocols in action.

One path to gaining that understanding is through a neurodiversity-friendly organizational audit. You can access a sample organizational audit report as part of the package of online tools that go along with this book. The sample summary report included is based on an organizational audit I completed with a company that had a long way to go to building an inclusive culture.

I have heard countless stories from job seekers, many of whom told me they had interviewed for hundreds of jobs and never heard back at all. The credentials of many of these candidates were competitive, including several with PhDs and MBAs from Ivy League Schools. Nonetheless, unemployment or chronic underemployment despite valuable skills was the most common refrain.

One bright autistic man I met at a summit had a master's degree from a respected university. Where had that gotten him? Working at a company sorting mail for the past 10 years. So, what is going on? For one, many neurodivergent people have a built-in disadvantage when it comes to the recruitment process because many of the outdated processes prioritize social skills and having an instinct for appearing confident and selling themselves in the course of a conversation, being persuasive in a cover letter, and "acting the part" rather than showcasing potential productivity and problem-solving abilities.

Neurodivergent candidates can easily be overlooked in such a process, which leads to exclusion or the acceptance of roles that vastly underrepresent their true capacity to contribute. This state is the very definition of an untapped resource. Employing a more innovative recruitment and evaluation process is the path to harvesting that opportunity.

In other words, the process used to evaluate new prospective candidates may contain biases that filter out people who otherwise may have gone on to become some of your most productive, motivated, creative, and loyal team members. However, there may be other barriers as well. The first step is to understand this and invest in the process of evaluating your own protocols to better understand the extent to which you may be unwittingly filtering out cognitive diversity.

Strategy #4: Offer a Nontraditional Interview Process

As suggested, the standard interview process includes many steps that have nothing to do with the job itself or even the duties of the job. This process puts neurodivergent candidates at a disadvantage, and the lack of flexibility in assessing candidates disadvantages employers looking to tap unique talent. When you are in need of an AI rockstar, a data analyst, or cybersecurity expert, does it really make sense to assess candidates on their interest in making small talk? Of course not. Similarly, if exceptional public speaking skills are most central to a role, does it make sense to deploy a recruitment and talent assessment process that makes sure that candidates are equally as good at other skills that may not be part of the job duties, such as technology skills? Yet, this level of nuance is non-existent from most recruitment efforts—and to the detriment of all stakeholders.

In offering nontraditional interview options, you won't miss out on great talent because your interview processes screened them out based on superfluous and superficial considerations. Even a few simple modifications to how candidates are interviewed and assessed can go a long way. Over the years, I have helped countless organizations, including large multinational corporations, colleges and universities, startups and scaleups, and nonprofits successfully architect and implement new frameworks and processes in a structured and fair manner that give all job seekers the opportunity to shine. Clear communication throughout the process is essential.

Some examples of nontraditional interview processes include providing the questions to candidates ahead of time to reduce anxiety, administering task-based interviews to assess for skills and expertise rather than social skills, game-based assessments, and the option for candidates to talk about and showcase their talents, passions, and interests.

In one 2021 study, the 263 autistic job seekers and 323 job seekers recruited from the general population both took one of two randomly assigned game-based assessments. It was hypothesized that game-based assessment may be one effective recruitment strategy due to the focus on capturing abilities and skills without social communication requirements that disadvantage autistic people. Performance on the game-based assessments was similar across the populations with only small differences detected. The results imply that when the focus is on abilities and the social communication aspects of interviews are reduced or eliminated, the biases that often impede autistic talent from being hired may go away.[2] By offering nontraditional interview processes that focus on the skills required for the role and by allowing candidates to submit evidence of skills, such as a portfolio of prior work results, you are far more likely to end up hiring the best candidate for the job.

Strategy #5: Develop Strategic Partnerships to Grow Your Talent Pipeline

As all industries brace for increasingly transformative change at the hands of emerging technologies, flexibility in core skills will become more important than ever, and so will establishing strategic relationships with institutions of higher education, nonprofits, and other platforms that focus on certification for in-demand skills, upskilling, and reskilling.

After we successfully adopted the Neurodiversity Inclusion statement in Illinois, community colleges across the country are in the process of adopting it to guide more practical steps. Industry partnering with community colleges can be game changers in growing a solid pipeline of available talent given the large percentage of neurodivergent students who begin their higher education journey at community and technical colleges.

Higher education itself is also at an inflection point and many institutions now offer short-term certificates that are eligible for Pell grant funding in areas as broad as cybersecurity, data analytics, machine learning, creative writing, and Python—all areas in demand for the foreseeable future.

Strategy #6: Hire Neurodivergent Talent at All Levels of the Organization—Including Leadership

The importance of leadership and representation at all levels in thought and practice is highlighted throughout this book. As we covered throughout Chapter 7, seeding an organization with cognitive diversity catalyzes a self-reinforcing feedback loop toward more cognitive diversity, especially when this strategy includes representation of neurodiversity at leadership levels.

Strategy #7: Establish Neurodiversity-Friendly Policies, Including Neurodiversity Within DEI

In prior chapters, we discussed the three C's and how codification of policies reinforced by behavioral conduct ultimately determines your organizational culture. The presence of neurodiversity-friendly policies embedded within broader inclusivity strategies, organizational values statements, and Human Resources will translate into a competitive edge in attracting neurodivergent job seekers. It is important for all job seekers, including neurodivergent people, to feel they will be treated with dignity and respect and will be supported by their employer. When a value statement and neurodiversity-friendly policies are in place, neurodivergent people will feel welcomed at your company and, in my experience, be far more likely to recommend your organization to others.

I have helped companies, nonprofits, and colleges craft a neurodiversity value statement often at the beginning of a serious commitment to embracing neurodiversity. A value statement is generally a public facing ideal to which the company, organization, or college aims to aspire and is generally the first step in revising or codifying neurodivergent-friendly human resource procedures. Since code plus conduct ultimately determines your culture, I have also written extensive internal Values training documents to be dispersed throughout the organization to make sure everyone—from the mail room to the board room—is on the same page where neuroinclusion is concerned.

For LEGO Foundation and the LEGO ecosystem, for instance, I wrote the values and mission statements that focused on the importance of valuing, accepting, and empowering neurodivergent people. As part of my process, I included dozens of neurodivergent leaders around the globe to provide their insights and feedback. This is a very effective strategy, especially for multinational corporations, as the final statements benefited from a wide diversity of experiences, with important intersectional insights. These resources and reference guides helped to reinforce healthy conduct and promoted empathy across all levels of the organization.

Adopting a values statements and revising HR policies, when implemented correctly, can be one of the most powerful indicators of an authentic mindset toward neurodiversity inclusion. The other powerful indicator, as described in Strategy #6, is hiring and promoting qualified neurodivergent people to leadership positions. This combination will land you on the short list as a highly desirable place for workers of all neurotypes.

Strategy #8: Offer Sensory-Friendly Policies

It is essential to be sensitive to potential sensory overload issues and to have policies to address this. In the online resources, there are recommended sensory tool kit strategies that every organization should have. While many autistic and other neurodivergent people experience sensitivity to noise, bright lights, colors, and/or smells, everyone is unique.

Using the principles of universal design that we have explored in prior chapters and further explore in the next chapter is critical. For example, evidence suggests that a designated quiet room at the office benefits everyone, not just those vulnerable to sensory overload. In addition, a policy where anyone can use headphones or other strategies to mitigate sensory overload, such as a room with dim lights or the use of fragrance sprays to neutralize strong smells, can be pivotal.

Strategy #9: Offer Educational Opportunities on Neurodiversity for Everyone

If it is only the neurodivergent employee who is expected to participate in training and coaching, then the universal empathy bridges we explore in Chapter 13 will never be built and can never blossom into a thriving and inclusive organizational culture. Educational opportunities and resources about neurodiversity with a non-monolithic approach to understanding spiky profiles should be available across all levels of the organization. As things currently stand, very few organizations offer training and resources throughout the organization (see Figure 10.2).

This is important to create the kind of trust and clear transparent communication that helps everyone thrive, including traditionally marginalized groups. It further goes a long way in helping to recruit neurodivergent people—allowing them to imagine they could belong at your organization by seeing evidence of buy-in by everyone in terms of efforts to understand and value neurodiversity.

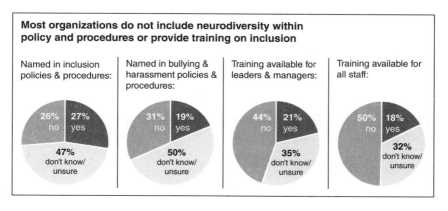

Figure 10.2 Very few organizations offer training and resources throughout the organization.

(Source: The Institute of Leadership and Management.)

Strategy #10: Job Postings and Application Process Should Be Simple, Flexible, and Inclusive

Job postings should be clearly worded and lead to a streamlined application process stripped of unnecessary and superfluous steps.

Be very specific about the job description. For instance, if the job is for a data analyst or a visual designer, do you really get relevant information from an extensive cover letter? Such a device is destined to be evaluated with a bias toward culture fit, which can be an engine for organizational stagnation over time.

Allowing for some flexibility for the job seeker to showcase strengths, skills, and personality, and to demonstrate the capacity to be successful in the role advertised will provide more relevant information in deciding on a hire. This is particularly important in recruiting neurodivergent applicants, who can be an enormous source of imagination, creativity, and original ideas.

Being upfront in the posting that the job seeker is invited to send a link to showcase what they can do, and to submit examples from prior work that back this up, would be a signal that you are neurodiversity friendly. Tagging employment opportunities as Remote or Hybrid eligibility will also send the message that you are a company or organization that is welcoming to neurodivergent employees.

Strategy #11: Ask Job Seekers about their Strengths and Passions

Involving job seekers in the process to better understand what motivates them will go a long way in creating the best win-win situation with a person-centered approach to hiring and matching tasks to strengths. Being flexible will allow an employer to attract and retain the best talent.

Strategy #12: Value Individuals within a Complimentary Skills Matrix Organizational Framework

The prior point makes the case for the power of neurodiversification. That's the point of teams: each person doesn't need to be good at everything, and hiring with that implicit premise under the surface is bound to lead to teams where the potential for greatness is sacrificed for the protection of universal mediocrity. There may be no surer way to lose in the long run in the Transformation Age.

Allowing for the redistribution of tasks and evolving job descriptions to get the most out of all employees and appreciating the fact that the strengths of one employee may complement those of another allows for an increased overall upside at the group level, as well as a competitive edge and a happier, more motivated workforce.

Strategy #13: Provide Managers with Training and Give Them More Authority Over Day-to-Day Processes

A focus on outcomes rather than methods—on what gets done more than on how it gets done—will allow an organization to support all workers to thrive. If a manager can approve minor adjustments—such as headphone use or working from another area of the office or other changes to roles as needed—important dimensions of flexibility will be unearthed that can translate into gains in productivity, loyalty, and reputational status within the neurodiversity community.

Strategy #14: Demonstrate How You Already Include Neurodivergent Voices

Learn the importance of "nothing about us without us" in co-creating products, services, and policies that affect neurodivergent people. Symbology is also important. If you utilize the puzzle piece symbol in connection with neurodiversity efforts, for example, many autistic people will feel you are suggesting they are broken and will assume you don't listen to or care about autistic voices.

Strategy #15: Become Known as a Neurodiversity-Friendly Brand

The advent of real-time digital networks and the thriving communities that inhabit them has allowed the neurodiversity movement to flourish into a powerful global force. Self-advocates regularly connect online through Facebook forums, LinkedIn, and other online groups, as well as conferences. If your organization is consistent in following the strategies in this book and putting into practice the values-based actionable framework advocated here, very happy neurodivergent employees will enthusiastically champion your brand to the world.

Keep in mind that being known as the kind of brand that hires and supports disabled or neurodivergent workers translates into benefits far behind the opportunity to hire amazing talent. This includes a greater degree of brand loyalty, positive brand association, and a higher performing organizational culture. In a *Harvard Business Review* article, researchers Alemany and Vermeulen reported results of studies that showed that customers thought more positively or became more psychologically bonded to a brand when the company employed disabled or neurodivergent people.[3] One example is the popular Dutch coffee chain, Brownies&downies or B&D. In nearly all respects, the brand is very similar in offerings and pricing to other chains, including Starbucks. The primary differentiator that has been central to the popularity and likability of B&D is its commitment to hiring employees with Down syndrome.

These same researchers collaborated with the Association of Supported Employment in Spain and found that at least 88% of HR professionals reported that their organizational culture improved significantly after hiring disabled workers with 70% in strong overall agreement and 65% reporting that psychological safety improved for everyone.

Follow-up research further showed that such inclusive teams were working more collaboratively than before, which enhanced the overall work environment. There was even evidence that new customers were drawn to the brand. Recent surveys by Gallup, Deloitte, and Tallo also strongly suggest that inclusivity and support for neurodivergent people are crucial considerations in the labor market for all neurotypes, especially among Millennials and members of Generation Z.

That will lay a foundation for a self-reinforcing feedback loop as other talented neurodivergent candidates seek you out for new opportunities.

Key Takeaways

- In Chapters 5–10, we have focused on creating a state of affairs defined by a culture tied to formal neurodiversity-friendly codification embraced and expressed faithfully in day-to-day conduct to build a sturdy foundation of psychological safety, where employees never fear negative career repercussions for being honest about their problems, needs, or interpretive confusion and have access to unbiased meaningful feedback and clarification about expectations at any time.

- In this and subsequent chapters, we focus on attracting, retaining, and supporting neurodivergent talent.

- That starts with the following 15 concepts and practical strategies designed to help any organization successfully attract and recruit neurodivergent talent:

  - Strategy #1: Demonstrate commitment with a values statement;

(continued)

(continued)

- Strategy #2: Don't let fear get in the way of hiring unique talent;

- Strategy #3: Understand barriers to recruitment;

- Strategy #4: Offer a nontraditional interview process;

- Strategy #5: Develop strategic partnerships to grow your talent pipeline;

- Strategy #6: Hire neurodivergent talent at all levels of the organization—including leadership;

- Strategy #7: Establish neurodiversity-friendly policies, including neurodiversity within DEI;

- Strategy #8: Offer sensory-friendly policies;

- Strategy #9: Offer educational opportunities on neurodiversity for everyone;

- Strategy #10: Job postings and application processes should be simple, flexible, and inclusive;

- Strategy #11: Ask job seekers about their strengths and passions;

- Strategy #12: Value individuals within a Complementary Skills Matrix Organizational Framework;

- Strategy #13: Provide managers with training and give them more authority over day-to-day processes;

- Strategy #14: Demonstrate how you already include neurodivergent voices;

- Strategy #15: Become known as a neurodiversity-friendly brand.

Chapter 11

Accommodating Humans

"Fitting in is about assessing a situation and becoming who you need to be to be accepted. Belonging, on the other hand, doesn't require us to change who we are; it requires us to be who we are."

——Brené Brown, *The Gifts of Imperfection*[1]

Clouds parted and we were all momentarily blinded by the blast of mid-morning sunlight that pierced through the high-set clear windows of the conference room. At almost the same moment, a thunderous clatter erupted in the room as the tower of large wooden puzzle blocks smashed back down to the hard oak surface of the conference table. Crash. Thud. Boom.

It would be a bit jarring to the senses for anyone. But I suddenly felt a pang of concern for Jim. Out of the corner of my left eye, I saw him rocking with his hands over his ears and his eyes pinched shut in a rictus of suffering. I seemed to be the only person in the room who noticed his anguish.

How did this happen?

A well-intentioned group leader decided we would begin with "a fun exercise to get us all energized" for the many hours of work we had ahead of us that day helping the firm make capital allocation decisions, which mostly boiled down to listening to pitches from around 30 project leaders focused on programs broadly related to neurodiversity. It was myself and my team of neurodivergent consultants with lived experience, about 10 other advisors with ties to the firm, the project leader at the firm, and the group facilitator who had devised the activity.

We were each given a bag of irregularly shaped wooden blocks. The goal was to stack them as high and as fast as we could. *If*—and more likely *when*—your blocks fall, you're out of the running. The person left with the tallest mountain of blocks when the timer went off would be the winner.

At the start of the exercise, I pointed to Jim and registered my concerns with the group facilitator. But she shook her head and said everything would be fine. "You'll see. This is a great way to loosen up and get our minds into the right gear!"

Sounds like an interesting and innocuous team-building exercise, right? For someone like Jim, with his notable hypersensitivity to sensory stimuli overload, it was torture.

The irony was that we were there to help guide decisions about investments in neurodiversity, but apparently no consideration was given to making our own process inclusive. As we discovered much later, it also turned out that there was an amazing Quiet Zone Garden on the corporate campus. But no one thought to bring it up. It would have been a lifesaver for Jim.

As leaders and allies, it is important to familiarize yourself with the concept of sensory overload to build into any blueprint for an inclusive organizational culture strategy. Many of these strategies often either cost nothing or are very cheap to accommodate. Yet, these simple strategies can make a significant impact on the quality of life of neurodivergent teammates, which, in turn, will translate into increased loyalty and engagement within the organization.

Being an inclusive leader is not about "check the box" solutions where neurodivergent people are merely hired or present at a team meeting. It means learning to become sensitive to the range of environmental stimuli that may be making a work environment intolerable as well as embracing the flexibility to develop policies that allow for the kind of communication feedback mechanisms that employees and employers alike can appreciate and augment continuously over time so everyone can thrive.

I am often asked where a leader, manager, or ally should begin in designing and encouraging more welcoming and neurodiversity-friendly environments.

A good place to start is with this question: Under what conditions will people with diverse backgrounds, strengths, challenges, and sensory experiences be able to express the greatest possible value in this organization? Then apply that process universally with the assumption of an employee base that includes the full spectrum of human cognitive variation.

In other words, it's not about autism or ADHD or dyslexia. It's about universal design, which is a valuable concept that holds that systems can be built from the ground up to accommodate nearly everyone.

This is a profound change from the standard one-size-fits-all model and its many assumptions about which cognitive profiles fit best into the linear world we have constructed in our current post-industrial framework. It is also a necessary shift. As with every approach to improving inclusivity, universal design requires a fundamental resetting of perceptions about value, choice, and context when it comes to building great organizations.

While it may end up being the case that only a small percentage of employees require access to extra supports or different working conditions, if you start out with the premise that those options are necessary to accommodate all possible employees, you will end up with a system that gives you the widest possible access to available human performance and contribution.

211

Accommodating Humans

One candidate for the most basic distillation of the thesis of this book might be: there's a vast gulf between "being willing to hire neuro-divergent people" and "embracing authentic neurodiversity inclusion." However, an even better one might be this: the paragraph directly above this one represents a value-added transaction—organizations that embrace this philosophy proactively will enjoy a competitive advantage, and as more and more organizations come to the same conclusion, the world becomes a better and more functional place.

Remember the world before wheelchair ramps existed? Think about how many people who are not in wheelchairs that also benefit from ramps: elderly people, moms with babies in strollers, pregnant women, young kids, people with visual impairments, people using crutches, those recovering from a stroke or anyone else who would prefer to avoid stairs. Now consider the total value all those people have to offer.

This is universal design at work—everyone wins when everyone can fully participate.

Seven Principles Guide Universal Design[2]

Intuitive use: Anyone can understand without a lot of training.

Flexibility in use: Accommodates the needs and preferences for as many as possible.

Equitable use: The design is easily accessible by people with a wide range of abilities and challenges.

Perceptible information: The design easily communicates important information for effective use for people with different sensory inclinations.

Tolerance for error: Minimal risk of hazards or unintended consequences.

Low physical effort: The design should be accessible and comfortably utilized with minimum physical effort.

How does universal design relate to the world of work and improvement of organizational culture?

A one-size-fits-all approach where everyone sits in a cubicle is *not* how we get there. This design is not centered on the learner's or worker's experience or accessibility given different learning and information processing styles. This is an environment with built-in biases against multisensory or experiential elements that may be critical to all employees performing at their full potential. While standard neurodiversity-at-work programs were an excellent start, many of them still belong to Neurodiversity World 1.0 as they offer a special, separate pathway to employment. Neurodiversity World 2.0 necessities that it is not only the neurodivergent people who receive training and mentorship, but the entire organization that learns to value diversity in all forms, including neurodiversity, from the ground up.

Ernst & Young is an example of a company that has expressed a clear desire to go this route. I informally consulted with them briefly several years ago and suggested this deeper approach. From what I can tell, it would appear the company is actively pursuing this path with positive results.

In workplace environments that emphasize universal design principles, sensory stimulation is varied across space, interactivity is maximized, and there's space for movement. This is an environment that supports both linear and nonlinear ways of thinking and learning. There are earplugs and sunglasses available, as well as light dimmers to accommodate sensory overstimulation.

There are several ways that universal design can be applied to the authentic inclusion of neurodivergent people. For example, workplaces can be made more accessible to neurodivergent employees by providing flexible work arrangements, such as telecommuting or flextime, which will be discussed in detail next chapter. Universal design also means providing accommodations, such as quiet workspaces or access to assistive technology that will benefit everyone.

Accommodating Humans

It is not just neurodivergent people that thrive with access to quiet spaces, but it can be critical for neurodivergent people to be included.

Universal design is a powerful tool that can be used to create more inclusive environments for neurodiverse groups. This also has application in dynamic cultural contexts. For example, events can be made more accessible to neurodivergent people by providing clear and concise information about the event, by providing opportunities for breaks and quiet time, and by making it easy for people to communicate their needs.

Here are some additional examples of how universal design can be applied to the authentic inclusion of neurodivergent people with varied strengths, challenges, and intersectional backgrounds.

- *Using plain language:* When writing or speaking, use clear and concise language that is easy for everyone to understand. Avoid using jargon or acronyms that people may not be familiar with.

- *Providing multiple ways to communicate:* People with different learning styles may prefer to communicate in different ways. Provide multiple ways for people to communicate, such as in person, over the phone, or in writing.

- *Being patient and understanding:* Neurodivergent people may need more time to process information or complete tasks. Be patient and understanding and avoid getting frustrated if someone needs more time.

- *Being open to feedback:* Ask Neurodivergent people for feedback on how you can make your environment more inclusive. This feedback will help you to create a more welcoming and supportive environment for everyone.

Universal design also means providing a variety of options and controls so that one can better customize their environment to be more productive. For technology platforms as well as office environments, this could mean being able to change visual and auditory components or environmental settings such as lighting tone, sound levels, or brightness.

This may mean allowing all employees—regardless of disclosure—to use headphones or natural lighting in the office if that makes them more productive. Optionality is key.

Case Study: Confusion Is a Failure to Communicate

One company I worked with in the past as a consultant presented an interesting case study because they had successfully embedded supportive accommodations using universal design principles into some aspects of everyday work life but were struggling with other important layers, which created an environment where employees felt frustrated. There was a lot of sensitivity, for instance, in encouraging different methods of communication depending on employee preferences (text, phone, virtual, in person). All employees were allowed to wear earbuds, headphones, or even sunglasses while working if it made them more productive. Managers also received neurodiversity training and generally made good faith attempts to be understanding.

However, communicating expectations in a simple, clear manner without the need for the employee to constantly interpret what the boss wanted via vague hints was a major hurdle. The executive leadership was disorganized and seemed to change the goalposts regularly. At the same time, there was also a lot of unnecessary rigidity where all employees were expected to take turns interrupting their workflow throughout the day to greet customers.

On at least one occasion, meetings were canceled less than five minutes before they were scheduled to occur. An external autistic consultant was specifically asked to do some research and write a report only to be told two weeks later that the report was no longer needed and that she would not get paid for the time she had already spent working on it. As I was working on a neurodiversity-friendly corporate audit, I spoke to one of the Vice Presidents and expressed my concerns. They desired an inclusive and productive corporate culture but had practices and habits that were creating a lot of stress on all their employees and consultants, neurotypical and neurodivergent alike. The lack of concrete and clearly communicated expectations made at least one neurodivergent employee quit.

We came up with a plan to reinforce what was going well and to codify new policies and practices to improve those aspects of the organizational culture that were presenting hurdles as a starting point, starting with how expectations were communicated. One critical step was to create a more formal documentation vehicle for logging expectations that executives, employees, and contractors all committed to honoring.

This turned out to be a breakthrough measure that drove clear gains in employee satisfaction, and its biggest payoff was among neurodivergent employees where imprecise or vague messaging about expectations tends to have the most deleterious impact.

Supporting Humans to Their Full Potential

A supportive organizational culture is important for neurodivergent people to feel safe in asking questions, requesting clarification, communicating the need for accommodations, and contributing ideas.

In a recent study conducted in 2023 by INvolve UK, over two-thirds of employees with invisible disabilities reported that they create their own reasonable adjustments and accommodations and tend to source extra support all alone. This finding is remarkable as it suggests that most neurodivergent people feel alone in creating the conditions that allow them to thrive at work. Fifty percent of respondents also reported that the process required to even aim to get support from their employers was not worth it. Thirty-two percent of participants who had not disclosed their diagnosis or needs to their employer claimed that they were concerned that they would be perceived as less capable if they did disclose. In addition, 25% felt that disclosure wouldn't result in any meaningful improvements in their work conditions.[3]

In other words, half thought the process of accessing supports at work was too complicated or burdensome, a third thought the act of accessing supports would negatively stigmatize them on a professional level, and a quarter thought any available supportive resources weren't of value in the first place so why bother.

While not exhaustive, wrap-around support programs, such as the one I implemented over a decade ago called The Transition 2 Success Project, have been very effective. That specific program has since evolved into the Gap2Gain program with evidenced-based supports for postsecondary students transitioning to college, apprenticeship, entrepreneurship, and/or employment. There are several other support programs and platforms as well.

Wrap-around supports in my model have a wide menu of options, including:

- Peer mentors, allies, and navigators;
- Executive functioning coaching;
- Time management and organizational tools;
- Regular check-ins by managers and navigators;
- Mental health support;
- Assistive technology;
- Self-advocacy mentorship;
- Support in self-discovery of cognitive strengths;
- Neurodiversity training at colleges, work, and community organizations;

Accommodating Humans

- Inclusive skill-building and job-shadowing opportunities;
- Sensory-friendly toolkits and strategies for all employees/students to adjust to their needs;
- Templates for everyone to better understand strengths and challenges.

Allies, mentors, and coaches can make a huge difference in supporting neurodivergent students and employees for sustained success and career growth. These are crucial supports that help neurodivergent people feel welcomed and thrive. There is also evidence that employers benefit significantly in terms of productivity and profitability when employees have access to mentors. For instance, a 2022 Deloitte Insights report showed that employers who offered mentoring support to employees with disabilities demonstrated a 16% increase in profitability, an 18% increase in productivity, and a 12% increase in customer loyalty.[4]

Online resources accessible with the purchase of this book include a downloadable and customizable template to help you plan out a broad organizational strategy and better work with individual employees to understand and adjust to their strengths and needs.

Depending on where you reside, there may be tax and other incentives, grants, and programs to help defray the costs of this support. In any case, the support is a small price to pay to retain qualified, loyal, motivated, and uniquely talented workers.

Strategies to Better Accommodate Humans

Strategy #1: Promote a culture of acceptance and belonging.
It starts with effective and inclusive leadership. Everyone at all levels throughout the organization should not only learn about neurodiversity but should be encouraged to celebrate differences more generally.

This includes acceptance of stimming and special interests. This means going beyond neurodiversity training and checklists. Remember that you want to cultivate a thriving organization at the DNA level. This is gene therapy not cosmetic surgery.

Strategy #2: Proactively include employees in creating optimal working conditions. Working environment matters. The best environments will inspire and energize. Ineffective environments will distract and be unproductive. Giving neurodivergent people agency in creating and shaping their work environment to maximize their strengths and productivity will go a long way.

Strategy #3: Be an ally. Anyone can choose to be an ally. This means not only showing your support and acceptance but also refusing to participate in any toxic behaviors by others. To be a true ally that promotes psychologically safe work environments for neurodivergent people, stay clear of participating in any side conversations, gossip, jokes, or dismissive behavior targeting neurodivergent co-workers, managers, or staff.

Strategy #4: Nothing about us without us. Always include your neurodivergent co-workers and staff in decisions affecting neurodivergent people.

Strategy #5: Upward mobility potential. Opportunities for advancement are critical for everyone but many neurodivergent workers struggle to find advancement opportunities commensurate with their skill level. Make sure to never overlook neurodivergent employees for a promotion or a leadership position. Neurodivergent people of all stripes can make good leaders and managers but are sometimes unfairly sidelined due to management's social familiarity with other members of the team or external candidates.

Key Takeaways

- Leaders should familiarize themselves with factors such as sensory overload and others that disproportionately affect neurodivergent employees to build an inclusive organizational strategy.

- Inclusivity requires understanding diverse needs and developing policies that allow everyone to thrive.

- Universal design, which caters to as many people as possible, can be implemented to provide value to everyone.

- Adjusting for sensory hypersensitivities, flexible work arrangements, and access to assistive technology can support an inclusive environment.

- Applying universal design principles such as intuitive use, flexibility, and equitable use can create more inclusive environments for neurodivergent people.

- Universal design benefits all individuals by improving accessibility and helping them participate fully in society.

- The chapter also covers five strategies to help implement accommodations that support neurodivergent team members:

  - Strategy #1: Promote a culture of acceptance and belonging.

  - Strategy #2: Proactively include employees in creating optimal working conditions.

  - Strategy #3: Be an ally.

  - Strategy #4: Nothing about us without us.

  - Strategy #5: Upward mobility potential.

Chapter 12

Workplace Flexibility

"Politics is the art of the possible, the attainable—the art of the next best."

—Otto von Bismarck, *St. Petersburgische Zeitung* interview, 1867

It is more important than ever for organizations to think hard about the true costs and benefits of the workplace protocols they have in place. Leaders may have strong preferences. But consequentialism is an important consideration: if rigid attempts to implement ideal policies lead to eventual self-destruction, then the clear course of action is to reexamine those preferences.

This line of analysis is particularly relevant when it comes to navigating the future where policies around remote, hybrid, or in-office work are concerned. This topic is of special relevance to neurodiversity inclusion.

It's easy to market yourself as a champion of inclusivity. But a failure to put in place substantive measures to support a truly diverse team will resonate as insincerity—a very difficult judgment to overcome.

But it's more than a branding mistake: Organizations that tout inclusivity but fail to implement meaningful measures overlook a significant portion of skilled individuals. As previously discussed, around 15–20% of people are considered neurodivergent, and each person's experience with neurodivergence is unique, making a one-size-fits-all strategy ineffective. For instance, while some neurodivergent employees might find the structure of an office environment calming, others could be disturbed by factors like bright lighting or office noise.

The goal here is to remain flexible and accommodating to the needs of neurodivergent team members to benefit from this untapped and underappreciated talent pool. The pandemic, for all its tragedy, actually provided an interesting laboratory for understanding what has been going wrong in neurodivergent employment and what could pave a better path forward.

The pandemic period was a devastating time for all of us. But it was also undeniably a major event in the evolution of culture, permanently altering how we learn, work, and socialize. In fact, for some—including those who identify as neurodivergent—it also brought about a change in professional working conditions that led to an improvement in flexible employment options.

Neurodivergent employees and job seekers have been pursuing geographic flexibility ever since the advent of the internet. But most organizations stuck firmly to policies steering clear of that kind of flexibility until COVID-19 broke out around the world and social distancing became a primary daily concern.

At that point, work from home (WFH) suddenly suited the needs of neurotypical employees, and everything changed. The result has been a period of increased employment and job satisfaction for many neurodivergent employees, though that state of affairs is up for grabs at present.

The broader disability community saw the highest ever employment figures as remote work opened opportunities that were not previously available. Though this was not the case for all neurodivergent people, many students, and colleagues of mine in the community seemed to thrive when, suddenly, they could control many elements of the "presentation" side of group teamwork. ADHDers I know who run companies felt more productive when they could comfortably turn off their video camera and still participate while pacing around the room. I know one founder/CEO who started to consider cultivating a company culture where this kind of thing was socially acceptable for all his employees when people started to come back to the office. I encouraged him to create flexible policies and demonstrate leadership by creating a model that other companies might follow.

This isn't to say that working from home will ease all the difficulties that arise from being neurodivergent in the corporate world. However, it has introduced greater flexibility and optionality, which has been shown to alleviate some of the struggles faced by neurodivergent workers while, at the same time, helping to highlight unique strengths.

An authentic and meaningful commitment to diversity and inclusion necessitates the cultivation of workplace environments and policies that enable all employees to excel. That's one of the tenets of universal design principles so central to this book: what is necessary for some should be available to all.

Remote, In-Person, or Hybrid?

To work from home or not to work from home: that is the question.

We can attack that question from multiple angles, one of which is simply a consequentialist appraisal of realistic options in the world ahead of us.

Feedback I came across when researching this topic reflects a wide range of views, but it also carries a clear message about the value of optionality for employers concerned about retaining talent and finding new skilled workers. The following comments are all responses to a question posted on Reddit: "Recently, a lot of companies have gone back to in office work as well as some choosing to stay hybrid. If you've experienced this how has the change [affected] your work flow?"[1]

"My previous employer insisted I come back 5 days a week. I quit and now have a new WFH job with a huge raise."

—Ok_Opportunity2693

"Working from home is not for me. Not good for my mental health or productivity. I live single in a one-bedroom apartment and am within a 20 min. walk from my office. Forcing myself to get out of the home and go to the office helps with separating work and personal life. Also I have much better relationships with people I work with in person than those who remote. I've been in the office full time since getting fully COVID-19 [vaccinated]."

—[Name deleted]

"I now get less work done multiple days per week. Between packing all of my stuff to take to the office and the drive to work, I'd say that my 2 days per week in the office mean at least 3 hours less work being done. Also, our conference rooms are still closed so in office we're still meeting over Teams."

—Mustang46L

"I have been hybrid for the last 6 years. When we went fully remote during COVID, I did miss going into the office 1–2 days a week like I was. Last year, we went back to hybrid and I do

enjoy my 1–2 office days per week, but I like the 3–4 remote days as well. It's a great balance for me."

—*cbdudek*

"I've been back in the office since May 2021 after being full remote from March 2020–May 2021. I absolutely hate it. There are so many distractions. I have to commute 35–40 minutes for a job in which I stay on a computer all day anyway (cyber security) and most weeks I don't even talk to my supervisor at all even though she's literally in the same room. We even take meetings on Teams, so why are we here?"

—*The McThief*

As previously observed, recent research analysis from Global Workplace Analytics suggests that 56% of the US workforce is employed in a job that has some component of remote work, while only 3.6% of the employee workforce was working remotely at least half-time prior to the pandemic. That number is projected to rise seven to nine times over, which would result in 25%–30% of the entire workforce working remotely over the long term, notwithstanding any new technological developments that drive an expansion in the percentage of current jobs accessible to remote-work strategies.[2]

Essentially, there's a debate underway in the business world about whether more flexibility in employee work environments pays off. But I will argue here that it's not really an important debate because your organization doesn't exist in a vacuum. You have a competitor right across the street and another just up the road. And how you choose to address this question—let's be honest—is hardly independent of how your competitors choose to address it.

This is acutely true in the context of the labor shortage we covered in Chapter 3.

In other words, if you would ideally prefer to mandate that all employees work full-time on-site in your office because you believe that policy is in alignment with maximizing productivity, information security, and strategic control, then that philosophy is important to articulate if only to yourself. But it still may be disadvantageous to implement because there's an awfully good chance your employees have different ideas about what would be best, and your top competitor is more than willing to cater to their preferences to secure an advantage in accessing talent.

To reiterate, this is "the art of the possible," not "the art of the ideal." You may have strong preferences, but an organization is a voluntary association among different agents, each equipped with personal preferences, each weighing the costs and benefits of some level of proactive compromise for the achievement of goals.

It pays to keep this in mind. This is especially true when it comes to attracting and retaining neurodivergent talent.

This debate has been simmering for more than a decade but has caught fire since the onset of the pandemic as most businesses moved to some form of work-from-home arrangement to accommodate a period when social distancing became essential and Zoom meetings became the norm.

During the pandemic, flexible work arrangements became unavoidable for all businesses capable of operating under those conditions. That circumstantial pressure drove further technology innovations geared toward optimizing remote work productivity.

Now, in the aftermath, we live in a world saddled with both that cultural normalization process and the technology it spawned. There's no going back: both your current employees and your new prospective hires are acclimated to a world where working from outside the office is normal and expected and new technological solutions arise seemingly every day to make that state of affairs increasingly accessible and productive.[3]

When you pair those factors with the labor shortage, and its implications for the balance of power between employees and employers, nursing any delusions about your ideal preferences in this debate as an employer could be disastrous.

Based on my own extensive discussions with a wide range of employers across a broad spectrum of industries in preparation for this volume, I have arrived at the inescapable conclusion that winning companies in the decade ahead will be those who have made peace with the idea that there's no escaping at least some degree of acceptance of flexibility in the geographic definition of "the workplace."

Once you accept that reality, you might as well go all in and apply yourself to the task of maximizing the benefits of being an employer that offers a hybrid or distributed model of workplace protocols. After all, what's the point of being a reluctant late mover when it comes to doing the inevitable?

Getting out in front where this dynamic is concerned offers the opportunity to establish an employer reputation capable of attracting and retaining neurodivergent workers because the neurodivergent community has unambiguously expressed a clear preference for increased flexibility in "how" work is done to best suit individual strengths and challenges. Some people work best in a structured office environment but many employees feel they are most productive with a remote or hybrid option. And, as a major incentive bonus, having remote employees means that you get to spend lease money on something else.[4]

Workplace Flexibility Is Key to Establishing Neurodiversification

If you scan through books focused on neurodiversity in the workplace, you might get the impression that there's also a debate underway among HR professionals about work-from-home and neurodiversity. Specifically, do neurodivergent employees drive more value when given the option of working at least some of the time from home (or some other location of their choosing outside the office)?

Other authors addressing this topic tend to weigh many factors and then inevitably conclude by saying something like this:

"Neurodivergent people benefit from working at home for reasons X, Y, and Z. But many neurodivergent people also suffer from such arrangements for reasons A, B, and C. In the end, our recommendation is that employers offer hybrid optionality and take a person-centered approach."

This is too simplistic of an approach.

Of course optionality, whenever possible, is the right answer. But it is doubly true for neurodivergent workers:

Flexibility: Optionality with regard to remote, in office, and hybrid working conditions allow neurodivergent workers to work from a location that is comfortable and conducive to their productivity. This can be especially helpful for neurodivergent workers who have sensory sensitivities or who find it difficult to concentrate in noisy or crowded environments.

Accommodations: Remote and hybrid working conditions allow neurodivergent workers to make accommodations for their specific needs. For example, neurodivergent workers may need to take breaks more frequently, work in a quiet environment, or have access to fidget toys or other tools that help them focus.

Reduced social interaction: Remote and hybrid working conditions can reduce the amount of social interaction that neurodivergent workers need to engage in. This can be helpful for neurodivergent workers who find social interaction to be draining or overwhelming.

Increased productivity: Remote and hybrid working conditions can lead to increased productivity for neurodivergent workers who have difficulty working in traditional office environments. The flexibility and accommodations that remote and hybrid working conditions provide can help neurodivergent workers to focus and be more productive.

All else equal, for businesses that can manage to function with a hybrid working environment plan, offering that flexibility to employees will certainly help to attract and retain unique talent, including neurodivergent talent. It will also most likely create a context conducive to increased motivation and productivity from neurodivergent employees.

Naturally, as noted earlier, the pandemic was a major factor in casting a spotlight on these dynamics.

In conducting research for this book, I found through many discussions with a variety of different employers across diverse industries that, rather than lose difficult to find talent to competitors, the best case strategy for the time being often is to either extend remote working policies or to introduce some permanent policy involving more flexible hybrid arrangements.

To be fair, as we saw during the pandemic, not every industry has the luxury of offering remote or hybrid work options. I enjoyed a deep discussion on this topic last year led by Charles Evans, then the Head of the Federal Reserve Bank of Chicago at Innovation DuPage with community business leaders and elected officials.

Still, my sense from many of these conversations is that organizational leaders can simply see which way the wind is blowing. The art of the possible.

That said, a not insignificant minority of companies had decided—come hell or high water—to reenforce more traditional protocols, demanding, globally, that employees basically return to the pre-pandemic way of office life.

Apple, Inc. is a great learning example. In early June 2021, Tim Cook, CEO at Apple, announced to his 137,000 employees that they would have to return to the office less than three months later. To be fair, it wasn't a return to full-time in-office-only work. It was a hybrid plan requiring employees to work three set days a week from the office—Monday, Tuesday, and Thursday.

There was a backlash in the form of a now infamous letter to Cook from "the employees of Apple."[5] And it's awfully instructive because the argument the letter makes will resonate powerfully with neurodivergent workers and job seekers.

Dear Tim and Executive Leadership,

Thank you for your thoughtful considerations on a hybrid approach to returning to office work, and for sharing it with all of us early this week. We appreciate your efforts in navigating what has been undeniably an incredibly difficult time for everyone around the world, and doing so for over one hundred thousand people. We are certain you have more plans than were shared on Wednesday, but are following Apple's time-honored tradition of only announcing things when they are ready. However, we feel like the current policy is not sufficient in addressing many of our needs, so we want to take some time to explain ourselves.

This past year has been an unprecedented challenge for our company; we had to learn how to deliver the same quality of products and services that Apple is known for, all while working almost completely remotely. We did so, achieving another record-setting year. We found a way for everyone to support each other and succeed in a completely new way of working together—from locations we were able to choose at our own discretion (often at home).

However, we would like to take the opportunity to communicate a growing concern among our colleagues. That Apple's remote/location-flexible work policy, and the communication around it, have already forced some of our colleagues to quit. Without the inclusivity that flexibility brings, many of us feel we have to choose between either a combination of our families, our well-being, and being empowered to do our best work, or being a part of Apple. This is a decision none of us take lightly, and a decision many would prefer not to have to make. These concerns are largely what prompted us to advocate for changes to these policies, and data collected will reflect those concerns.

Over the last year we often felt not just unheard, but at times actively ignored. Messages like, 'we know many of you are eager to reconnect in person with your colleagues back in the office,' with no messaging acknowledging that there are directly contradictory feelings amongst us feels dismissive and invalidating. Not only do many of us already feel well-connected with our colleagues worldwide, but better-connected now than ever. We've come to look forward to working as we are now, without the daily need to return to the office. It feels like there is a disconnect between how the executive team thinks about remote / location-flexible work and the lived experiences of many of Apple's employees.

For many of us at Apple, we have succeeded not despite working from home, but in large part because of being able to work outside the office. The last year has felt like we have truly been able to do the best work of our lives for the first time, unconstrained by the challenges that daily commutes to offices and in-person co-located offices themselves inevitably impose; all while still being able to take better care of ourselves and the people around us.

Looking around the corner, we believe the future of work will be significantly more location and timezone flexible. In fact, we are already a distributed company with offices all over the world and across many different timezones. Apple's organizational hierarchy lends itself towards offices that often follow the same structure, wherein people in the same organization are more likely to be co-located in an office. At the same time, we strongly encourage cross-functional, cross-organization collaboration, and our organization's many horizontal teams reflect this. Such collaboration is widely celebrated across our organization, and arguably leads us to our best results—it's one of the things that makes Apple, Apple. However, orgs are rarely co-located within walking distance, let alone in the same building, meaning our best collaboration has always required remote communication with teams in other offices and across timezones, since long before the pandemic. We encourage distributed work from our business partners, and we've been a remote-communication necessary company for some time, a vision of the future that Steve Jobs himself predicated in an interview from 1990. This may explain how mandatory out-of-office work enabled tearing down cross-functional communication barriers to deliver even better results.

Did it work?

At first, no. But some months later, one of the top talents at the firm, Ian Goodfellow, director of machine learning—and one of the biggest advocates of remote work protocols—left Apple to join Alphabet (Google), citing the back-to-the-office policy as a key factor in his decision. "I believe strongly that more flexibility would have been the best policy for my team," Goodfellow reportedly wrote, as reported by *The Verge*. One assumes Goodfellow is now heading up a team that enjoys working from home as part of Google's DeepMind subsidiary. Consequentialism, indeed.

Apple management caved soon afterward and delayed the addition of another mandatory day in the office. But that was just a delay. At present, Apple management has doubled down on "return to the office." Where this battle ends up is anybody's guess. But reporting on the issue suggests a war is underway.

Amazon is now locked in a similar battle.

One should note, however, that a job at Apple or Amazon is a prestigious status symbol in today's world. Most businesses don't have that extra ace up their sleeve. If even organizations such as Apple and Amazon are now entrenched in multiyear wars just for trying to get employees to agree to a hybrid setup stipulating a mandated three days a week in the office, the balance of power should be clear around this issue.[6]

To pile on a bit, according to a recent ADP report, nearly two-thirds (64%) of US workers surveyed said they would consider looking for a new job if they were forced to return to an office full time.[7] In other words, workers are now more than ever willing to wave goodbye to their current employers and join a competitor over workplace flexibility.

Remote Control

But just how relevant is this topic in the first place given that much of the economy is still dominated by jobs that cannot be accomplished remotely?

I will let Mr. Gretsky field that question: "Skate to where the puck is going, not where it has been."

Any business deciding now how to align itself where remote or hybrid work environments and corporate policies are concerned should take this advice to heart. Plan for the long term.

Automation, technological intermediation, robotics, connected environments, and real-time AI augmentation are combinatorial forces: they all reinforce and enhance the impact of each other, and they are all very much now active developing themes across every industry. But it's still very early innings. Over the next five years, their impact will grow exponentially. Five more years down the road and you are likely dealing with the exponential enhancement of that already-exponential curve.

It's impossible to know precisely what that world will look like. But the general principle that "what *can* be done probably *will* be done" is the best guide we have. And the upshot is the inescapable conclusion that nearly all jobs will become accessible to remote work arrangements over time.

A good friend of mine from my Silicon Valley days helped me understand this through his "Diner of the Future" thought experiment. He is a partner at a prominent venture capital firm and the founder of three technology companies that were all acquired for eight figures or more, so I tend to take him seriously when he daydreams out loud about the future.

We were at a Starbucks in Menlo Park. I had flown out to meet with a client. He is one of those people I usually catch up with when out there. In the first few minutes, we talked in general terms about how Silicon Valley is changing, and he made it a priority to tell me about an amazing new Turkish restaurant in Palo Alto with live jazz music. He told me to check it out. But when I brought up the topic of remote work, his voice and posture changed. His grey-blue eyes went from "warm grandpa" to "piercing intellectual." We had an enlightening but serious discussion about what the future of work might look like at restaurants:

So, AI, no matter how good it gets, won't be able to fully take over until we transition generationally to a culture dominated by consumers who are more acclimated to dealing with AI for everything. It's a bit like the transition from a pidgin language to a creole language. Your kids are going to get it because they grew up with it. But most of us are set in our ways. So, you're going to see a long transition period where the dominant style is real humans remotely available through some kind of technological intermediation.

A futuristic restaurant is a good device for clarifying. You walk in with your family and are greeted by the face of a host floating on a tablet over a readout screen with a map of the table layout and a waiting list of names.

The host adds your name to the list—you see it pop up on the screen at the bottom—and instructs you to take a pager. When the pager buzzes, you return to the host stand. The readout screen shows a line-drawing map of the tables in the restaurant with one of the table outlines flashing. It looks to be the corner booth. The host instructs you to please be seated and enjoy your meal. You look up and notice that the booth in the corner has a light-strip tracing the outer edge of the seat that is flashing in the same color as the corner booth icon on the readout screen.

Once you're seated, your server's face appears on the tablet in the middle of the table. The server can remotely control the swivel to face in any direction. Your server takes your order—you don't need to type it in or anything. You can ask questions and share what you're in the mood for and ask her advice because she's a real person, like the host. She can tell you about the specials. She sees your kids and flashes up games that appear on the table-top screens like coloring and puzzles, and she tells you that the chicken fingers are "really good" here and you can't miss with those for the kids.

You notice that her face appears on the tablet in the middle of the next table over as soon as it disappears from yours, and you hear, "How is everything? Would you like a refill on that soda?"

The point is everyone is remote except for maybe one busboy and one line cook. You could conceivably get away with two people on site and still provide that comfortable American Diner experience without the coldness of an automated vending restaurant.

Workplace Flexibility

The interesting part of this imagined future, to me, is that none of it depends on technology beyond what we already have. Tablets. Connected devices. Some kind of "diner platform." The limitations are merely cultural. As noted earlier, what *can* be done *will* be done, especially if it helps the bottom line. That is inevitable.

The same vision applies to most of the service sector, especially if we assume minor further advances in robotics. And even in that case, the technology necessary to render a hairdresser, cleaning specialist, line cook, or physical therapist role accessible to remote work strategies is already in place, with an applied strategy only limited by the lack of economies of scale at the cutting edge of the robotics field.

Someday, many aspects of these roles will likely be automated. But in the meantime, we are staring at a transition period where the trend is toward human-mediated technology augmentation. The thing that drops out of the equation is geography. Your waiter or waitress might live on the other side of the country or even the world. But the person attending to your needs where you are eating will still be a human you can relate to, and provided the right technology is in place, that person can fulfill the fundamental value proposition just as well as an in-person waiter or waitress in the legacy model.

This isn't science fiction. As noted above, all the technology necessary to manifesting "the diner of the future" experience is already available, with future innovations likely even allowing the remote work model to spread further to the line cook and the busboy. All it would take, in theory, according to my friend, is a clever kitchen design and some relatively minor advances in robotics—perhaps a track-mounted chassis with VR-controlled arms and hands able to roam around a cooking space on-site all operating under the control of a qualified chef cooking from a computer interface somewhere else in the world. Another friend of mine not that long ago invested in a startup working on a similar robotics platform for cleaning kitchens and bathrooms.

Fully autonomous vehicle functionality is probably 10–20 years away according to analysts at GlobalData in a 2022 report—we still have quite a leap to go before people are comfortable with the idea of a driverless car speeding through their neighborhood while their kids play in the front yard.[8]

But, in the meantime, the natural intermediate step is human moderated remote-controlled semiautonomous vehicles. The term du jour is "teleoperated vehicles." It amounts to remote drivers with multiscreen setups including side, front, and rear camera footage and access to a very responsive ultra-low-latency wheel and pedal input system. The car can mostly drive itself. But professional remote overseers are actively following every step of the way from a remote location with the ability to take full control of the vehicle at any time.

In other words, even the job title "Uber driver" is likely to become accessible to remote-work models.

We can play this game all day long. But the point is: the notion that there is only a limited and static universe of jobs accessible to remote work strategies is rapidly becoming a fallacy. The implications are revolutionary and suggest that we aren't far from a world where the number of jobs that remain entirely immune to remote work models will quickly approach zero, even if asymptotically in the final picture.

Another key point to reiterate here is that the economics of a labor shortage context previously discussed will certainly contribute more pressure toward realizing this vision: geography is a primary limiting factor for service sector labor supply. Businesses able to remove geography as a constraint in the equation will have a clear edge. Remote work is, by definition, geography-agnostic. In a capitalist economy, strategies that are plausible and provide a clear edge over competitors have an awfully hard time remaining unexploited.

There is, admittedly, some degree of speculation in the above section. But hopefully you will agree that the questionable part is the details. The basic trends are already clear. And the logic they rest upon applies to nearly every conceivable vocation.

But don't just take my word for it—ask an AI chatbot. Here's what happened when I posed questions to ChatGPT:

Me: *Given your current capabilities and given the progress curve you estimate for future augmentation of those capabilities over the next 10 years, paint me a narrative speculative picture of how human work may change over the coming decade as progress in sophisticated AI intertwines with progress in networks, robotics, edge computing, and other ascending revolutionary technologies. Please comment specifically on how currently in-person service sector human jobs (i.e., waiting tables, cooking, hairdressing, etc.) may become increasingly accessible to remote work strategies.*

ChatGPT: *As an AI language model, I can speculate on how human work may change over the next decade as AI and other revolutionary technologies continue to advance. It is likely that many currently in-person service sector jobs, such as waiting tables, cooking, and hairdressing, will become increasingly accessible to remote work strategies.*

The integration of AI, networks, robotics, edge computing, and other technologies will enable a greater level of automation and remote access to service sector jobs. For example, we may see the development of advanced telepresence technologies that allow workers to remotely perform tasks such as cooking, serving, or cutting hair. This could be facilitated by the use of advanced robotics and sensors that provide a high level of precision and control, even at a distance.

In addition to remote work, we may also see the development of hybrid work models that combine both in-person and remote work. This could enable workers to perform some tasks remotely while still maintaining a physical presence in the workplace. For example, a hairdresser could use telepresence technology to remotely consult with clients and provide guidance on styling, while still having a physical presence in the salon for hands-on work.

The integration of AI and other technologies could also lead to the creation of new types of jobs that are more focused on the management and maintenance of these systems. For example, we may see the development of AI trainers and data analysts who are responsible for optimizing and improving AI systems, or network architects who design and implement advanced network systems to support remote work.

Overall, the integration of AI and other advanced technologies is likely to transform the nature of work, particularly in the service sector. While some jobs may become automated or shift to remote work, there will still be a need for human workers who possess the skills and expertise needed to manage and maintain these systems. The challenge for businesses and workers will be to adapt to these changes and develop new skills that will enable them to thrive in this new work environment.

There have been several studies and reports that have addressed the potential impact of AI and other advanced technologies on the workforce and employment trends.

According to a report by the McKinsey Global Institute, up to 375 million workers globally could be displaced by automation by 2030. This report also suggests that there will be a shift towards the creation of jobs that require human skills and expertise, such as management, creativity, and social and emotional intelligence.

A study by the World Economic Forum (WEF) has identified the growing importance of "digital skills" and "social skills" in the future job market. This study suggests that workers will need to develop a range of new skills, including digital literacy, critical thinking, and problem-solving, in order to adapt to the changing job market.

There have also been several studies that have addressed the potential impact of remote work on employment trends. A study by Global Workplace Analytics suggests that remote work has the potential to save employers significant amounts of money in office expenses and increase employee productivity. This study also suggests that remote work may become more common in the future due to advancements in technology and changes in workplace culture.

Overall, while there is still much uncertainty about the specific impact of AI and other advanced technologies on the workforce, it is clear that there will be significant changes in the nature of work and employment trends in the coming years.

Again, my point here isn't to play "crystal ball futurist." I'm simply making the case that our current assumptions about the percentage of jobs accessible to remote work strategies are probably poised for a radical rethinking in the years ahead. And organizations contemplating how to address this topic should do so with an open mind and a long-term strategy. The future is nearer than you may think.

The question of remote work environments is defined now by a limited universe of job descriptions. But that universe is expanding rapidly in a trend that would appear to suffer from very few natural barriers given the confluence of technology revolutions well under way right now.

Universal Optionality

From the standpoint of any given employee—neurotypical or neurodivergent—optionality is superior to a lack of optionality. But that much is trivially true. And every business needs to weigh factors and take a business-centered approach.

One caveat: the universal design framework is critical to the implementation of any neurodiversity inclusion transition process that involves extra support or accommodation measures. In other words, don't set up an "extra benefits" vending machine that only takes currency not available to everyone.

To summarize: this book recommends a flexible model and a person-centered approach anchored by the principles of universal design—flexible to work and results-oriented, with access to wraparound supports as necessary.

In other words, arm your team with everything they need to be successful, even up to and including executive functioning and coaching support. In my experience, the organizations that I helped in terms of implementation of such support, when piggybacked by other neurodiversity-friendly practices, were particularly ripe for continued innovation. Arm them also with extremely clear goals and milestones. And then let them figure out the geography side of the equation that will best enable them to deliver the goods.

From the standpoint of your employees—neurotypical and neurodivergent, alike—flexibility, respect, supportive atmosphere, and autonomy will be highly valued. From the standpoint of the organization, results, retention, motivation, and the ability to attract new and unique talent above your competitors are key.

What choices an organization makes to reconcile those values with policy is probably less important than how well the resulting policies are implemented. That said, hybrid, flexible, and results-oriented is a good place to start.

Given the macro trends in place, it will become increasingly clear that the fiduciary responsibility of top decision makers within an organization will boil down to respecting their team members enough to trust their judgment about how they will be most productive and effective over the long term.

In other words, you don't need to conduct therapy sessions with them. You don't need to build a complex psychological profile for each employee and then dictate to them what you believe will be in their best interest. And you certainly don't need to violate their privacy and badger them about an official diagnosis from a brain-care specialist.

Just provide them with clarity in terms of their responsibilities, and then extend to them optionality, respect, dignity, and discreet access to supportive resources as needed. In my experience, you will find that value returned tenfold.

In short, if you want to reduce turnover risk while accommodating a larger pool of potential talent—two major objectives during a labor shortage—then you could do a lot worse than to signal to your entire team a relatively laissez-faire approach to hybrid flexible working arrangements, very well-defined expectations for production, and a willingness, whenever possible to provide additional support as needed.

Key Takeaways

- Weighing the costs and benefits of inclusive workplace protocols for neurodivergent individuals in different work settings (remote, hybrid, or in-office) is crucial for organizations.

- Empty pledges of inclusivity can lead to reputational damage and talent loss, considering a significant portion of the population is neurodivergent.

- The pandemic highlighted remote work's benefits for neurodivergent individuals, underlining the need for diverse and inclusive workplaces.

- Workplace flexibility driven by the pandemic is crucial in today's competitive job market, with winning organizations leveraging this trend to attract and retain diverse talent.

- Despite some companies, such as Apple and Amazon, advocating for a return to traditional work protocols, there has been significant employee resistance. A top talent departure due to lack of flexibility illustrates this challenge.

- According to a 2022 report, a majority of US workers would consider changing jobs if forced to return to the office full-time, highlighting the strong preference for flexible work arrangements.

- The exponential growth of automation, robotics, and AI suggests that most jobs will be accessible for remote work in the future.

(continued)

(continued)

- Although this transition to remote work culture may not be immediate, it is inevitable with younger generations more accustomed to AI and remote services.

- The integration of AI, networks, and robotics can enable remote access even to traditionally location-specific service sector jobs. Moreover, the concept of jobs immune to remote work is becoming outdated due to technological changes and the need to remove geography as a constraint to labor supply.

- Remote work strategies provide economic benefits and are expected to transform jobs, requiring human skills such as management and creativity, and necessitating new types of jobs to manage AI systems.

- All else equal, for businesses that can manage to function with a hybrid working environment plan, offering that flexibility to employees will certainly help to attract and retain neurodivergent talent.

- Organizations should implement a long-term, flexible hybrid model that respects employee autonomy, provides clarity in responsibilities, and extends supportive resources, aiming to empower employees regardless of location.

- Given the macro trends in place, it will increasingly become clear that the fiduciary responsibility of top decision makers within an organization will boil down to respecting their team members enough to trust their judgment about how they will be most productive and effective over the long term. And this approach represents a powerful strategy to attracting, retaining, and authentically including a neurodiverse team.

Chapter 13

Universal Empathy Network

"You can't understand someone until you've walked a mile in their shoes."

—Unknown

One of the most interesting people I have ever had the pleasure to know once explained to me how he conceptualized his social frustrations as an autistic ADHDer, also now known as an AuDHDer (aww-dee-aetch-dee-er):

Imagine looking up and seeing a big flock of birds flying in a V formation across the sky. And then you see this bird flying a ways off to the side and behind the flock. But it looks just like all the others in the flock. It's flying outside the formation and sort of chasing the flock, and then the whole flock turns and this one bird keeps going straight for an extra second and then pivots and turns in the new direction to chase behind the flock. Like all the other birds knew where they were going like they were all connected together by some invisible telepathic field. And that outsider bird wasn't hooked up to the field. I was that bird. I looked just like all the other birds. I was good at flying. I thought I was doing everything the same as all the rest. But I was always out there on my own trying to find a way in.

That's not the metaphor though. I guess it's a metaphor for the metaphor. But the real metaphor occurred to me when Wi-Fi networks became common with smartphones. And people would get somewhere and connect up to the Wi-Fi. I think there's something like an instinctive mind-Wi-Fi—Mi-Fi?—network connecting people together in some invisible social field. Most people have the Mi-Fi password and so they go around constantly getting all these social cues and signals about what everyone is thinking and doing and what's cool to say and what the group mood is. And that makes them all sort of part of a group mind. And my brain had a bad Mi-Fi receiver or no password or something. That's how I've always felt. And I can tell there are other people like me. But most people have access to the Mi-Fi network. And there's no customer service or genius bar or help desk. You're either on the network naturally or you're not.

It's a wonderful metaphor. But he had one critical point wrong: there is a way to gain access to the network for everyone. However, there's nothing he could do to solve the problem. He could go on building half-bridges between himself and everyone around him all day every day. But if no one else builds the other half of the bridge, it won't solve anything.

To extend his metaphor, the solution is about the network protocol for the "Mi-Fi" network. Organizations interested in embracing authentic neurodiversity inclusion as a foundational value will need to ensure that absolutely everyone has access to the Mi-Fi network. As we will see, that's all about empathy, and building mutual empathy bridges between neurotypical and neurodivergent individuals is much easier than most people think. I can attest to that from countless personal experiences in my own life and in the course of working with organizations, community groups, and schools.

Despite this reality, a deeply entrenched misconception exists today that it is impossible to develop mutual empathy with someone like my friend above. The source of this misconception can be traced to the cultural impact of a deeply established research paradigm that has shaped our understanding of autism for the past 40 years.

For a little background, in 1983, Jerry Fodor argued in his book *Modularity of Mind* that the mind is made up of specialized modules or compartments that accomplish specific types of cognitive tasks.[1] One such module was believed to be responsible for the computation of mental states, implying that the attribution of mental states to both self and others is filtered through the same cognitive module. Fodor's work dovetailed to some extent with a seminal article written five years earlier called "Does the Chimpanzee Have a Theory of Mind?" by David Premack and Guy Woodruff, which first proposed that individuals possess a theory of mind if they are able to impute mental states to themselves and others.[2]

A significant amount of research followed during the next two decades focused on showing that autistic people generally fail at tasks requiring an understanding of false beliefs, which has been presumed to be a key index for assessing theory of mind.[3]

Together, these themes cemented into place the notion that autism is more or less characterized by the absence or dysfunction of the module of mind tasked with theorizing about the mental, emotional, and episodic contents of other people's minds. Since empathy—the ability to recognize, understand, and share the thoughts and feelings of another person—is related to theory of mind, people tend to assume that autistic people are incapable of truly understanding someone else's point of view.

But minds aren't that simple.

About 10 years ago, a new theory emerged that has quickly thrown this intellectual edifice into question and produced considerable evidence that universal empathy across the entire spectrum of human neurodiversity is far from impossible.

The secret is about building bridges through shared experiences.

The Double Empathy Problem

The double-empathy problem is a fascinating emerging theory in the field of neurodiversity based on a growing body of research. It has enormous implications for authentic neuroinclusion because it implies, at root, that all people—not just neurodivergent people—struggle to understand "the other."

This is a breakthrough notion because, as noted above, it emerged to challenge the established paradigm in autism research that was predicated on the idea that autism is defined, at least in part, by a fundamental inability to engage in effective theory of mind, and that this inability makes it impossible for autistic individuals to genuinely empathize with others as a general rule.

In 2012, autism researcher Damian Milton coined the term "The Double Empathy Problem," and research by Elizabeth Sheppard and her team at the University of Nottingham, Brett Heasman at the London School of Economics, and Noah Sasson at the University of Texas at Dallas backed it up, finding that, in fact, non-autistic people struggle just as much to read the emotions and mental states of autistic people as the autistic do for the non-autistic.[4,5] At the same time, it turns out that autistic people are very good at empathizing with each other—the communication barriers go away completely.

Drilling down a bit deeper, autistic people are generally more forgiving of social faux pas and have shared experiences among each other to draw upon, including similar sensory tendencies, shared feelings of being misunderstood by most people, and challenges in obtaining employment. At the same time, neurotypical individuals are likely to mistake a lack of enthusiasm during small talk or the absence of perfect conformity with other social expectations as rudeness when engaging with autistic individuals—experiences they don't generally have when interacting with other neurotypical individuals.

In short, neurotypicals can empathize with other neurotypicals. Autistic individuals can empathize with other autistic individuals. But neither group is great at empathizing with the other. What was once thought to be a fundamental deficiency peculiar to autism can be recast as something akin to the hurdle experienced by people from different cultures trying to find common ground.

Furthermore, because this perspective is overshadowing the "mind-blind" model with a new model that explains two-way empathy barriers between neurotypicals and autistic individuals by invoking their lack of shared mental experiences, it may be fair to speculate that other neurodivergent groups (such as ADHDers and dyslexics) likely also have an easier time syncing up with others in their respective cognitive tribes.

In fact, the notion strongly matches my own lived experience and my research conducted over the past two decades in preparing for this book as I worked closely with neurodivergent individuals of all stripes engaging in community life.

The takeaway message here is that shared experiences matter. Fortunately, much can be done as a leader, ally, and organization to bridge the gaps and create a foundation of shared experiences among a neurodiverse team to promote a happier and more effective culture.

The double empathy problem centers on the premise that people with widely diverging life experiences will struggle to empathize with each other when interacting. This is likely to be exacerbated by differences in language use and comprehension as well as by what contextual elements are perceived with greatest priority in the flow of experience. Below, I provide several examples and scenarios that should (1) be helpful in building better models to explain the nature of the misunderstandings that derive from neurodiversity cross-group interaction and (2) point to what we can do to foster more effective cross-group communication experiences capable of laying a foundation of shared experience upon which we can build an empathy bridge that crosses the full spectrum of human neurodiversity.

What exactly does that mean in practice? How can we get better at meeting each other halfway to develop a basis for shared understanding? More importantly, how can we build into our organizational cultures the kind of feedback loops capable of infecting the whole with cross-tribe empathy to immunize an entire organization from communication mishaps and mutual alienation?

The good news is that there are several strategies and tactics capable of accomplishing exactly that, and I provide related tools in the online companion resource library to accompany and enhance what we discuss below. But it's important to understand what such strategies are predicated upon: the establishment of a reliable foundation of trust and psychological safety that permeates every facet of an organization along with a mutual commitment by everyone involved to create opportunities for shared experiences through perspective-taking and honest communication.

As I said earlier, accomplishing this is both essential and much easier than people generally think. I have a great deal of experience with this. It always ends the same way: with everyone realizing we aren't nearly as different from one another as cognitive biases and mental short-cuts fool us into believing.

One strategy that has been successful in building empathy bridges across neurotypes during corporate training sessions, workshops, and retreats is to facilitate perspective taking exercises involving all members of a team—neurotypical and neurodivergent alike—to help everyone gain insights into unfamiliar experiences and perspectives, and then to steer the process by degree toward an appreciation of each other's point of view.

We may start with perspectives that are equally unfamiliar to all team members, such as what it's like to live in Papua New Guinea. From there, we move on to perspective taking scenarios that have more common reference points but seen through unfamiliar eyes. We might use blindfolds and take a walk to the lunchroom to imagine life for the blind, consume potently flavored tea with different shapes on each cup to stretch our imagination toward a synesthesia perspective, or have those with no sensory overload vulnerability under normal conditions use virtual reality headsets to simulate sensory overload by sharply augmenting brightness and volume in familiar settings.

I have found that most people enjoy engaging in these exercises, which, over time, help weaken the overconfidence bias that unconsciously enslaves most of us most of the time, leaving us unaware of the silent and unquestioned subconscious presumption that our perspective is the only one worth considering.

To better illustrate the double empathy problem in situ, as it were, consider this real-life example of a misunderstanding between an autistic employee and a neurotypical employee involving the thermostat setting in an office environment. This is an actual situation that happened at an organization I worked with several years ago.

For the neurotypical person, it was already too cold in the office to the point of being genuinely uncomfortable, yet the air conditioner continued to blast out freezing air on its highest fan setting with no end in sight. "It's freezing in here," he said to the coworker one desk to his right. "This is inhuman. I need about 15 minutes of good solid heat and then let's just shut it off." His neighbor, who was wearing a thick sweater, just shook his head. "Dude, it's perfect in here. I think better when it's a little chilly."

For the autistic person across the aisle, the A/C system was loud to the point of triggering auditory sensory overload. She was near the end of her rope. When she couldn't take it anymore, she called out loud, "The A/C is on too high. It's bothering my ears."

As soon as her final syllable died away in the room's white noise, the neurotypical employee hopped to his feet, looked directly at her, pointing and nodding with a victorious grin, and marched off to the manager's office. A couple minutes later, the volume of the A/C system ratcheted up significantly as she saw him return to his desk, giving her a wink as he sat down. She nearly flew into a rage. But she knew she was already "the weird girl" to most of the rest of the office and worked hard to get herself under control and avoid a public meltdown. Still, he had clearly been in earshot when she told everyone that she was suffering from the earsplitting din in the room. But what did he do in response? He went off and somehow persuaded someone to make it even louder!

The next time he looked in her direction, she shot him a look that captured every ounce of her anger with him. She was a bit surprised by his reaction—he looked confused for an instant and then hurt. But she knew she wasn't the best at interpreting nonverbal communication, and she didn't trust him in any case. That afternoon, she filed a formal complaint with the manager about him.

On his drive home, the neurotypical employee was simmering with anger and a sense of injustice. Why did she blame him and for what? After all, he had taken up her cause, hadn't he? She said her ears were so cold that they hurt. He acknowledged her problem, even making a show of singling her out as his friend and someone he was going to stick up for, and then he immediately went off to get the A/C system flipped from Cool to Heat. And what did his kindness earn him? Blame. As if that wasn't enough, he had to spend the last 15 minutes of his day being reprimanded by an HR specialist about being sensitive to people with different needs.

The next day was my first day working on site with the company as a consultant. The timing was pure coincidence. However, it was a small team, and it didn't take me long to pick up on the tension between the two of them. She was naturally a focus of mine right from the start because she was the only employee at the company that had publicly disclosed her neurodivergent status to the organization—the degree to which she felt comfortable and able to flourish at the company was destined to inevitably play a major role guiding my process. And he had just been singled out a day earlier by his manager and the HR department as in need of coaching. Once I had talked to each of them separately for a few minutes, the full picture was crystal clear.

Around mid-morning, I invited them both to come back to the little corner office I had been assigned for the day. Neither wanted to sit. Instead, they stood at opposite ends of the room and made very little eye contact with each other. I started the conversation by talking about confirmation bias, faulty assumptions, and how tricky it can sometimes be to bridge the empathy gap. "But," I added, "sometimes all it takes is the introduction of one or two little pieces of information and everything falls into place. It's a bit like when you look at one of those paintings where all you see is a bunch of dots. And then, suddenly, the picture changes right before your eyes and all you can ever see from then on when you look at it is a dolphin or the laughing face of a clown or a rhododendron."

They were both looking at me as if I were speaking Mandarin. I sighed. "Jeremy, Erin is really, really sensitive to loud persistent noise. You may not have ever noticed this, but the A/C system here is ancient and it rumbles something awful. That's torture for Erin. But the real kicker given our current dilemma is that it gets even louder when changed to the heat mode. And Erin, I would bet my lunch that Jeremy hasn't ever heard the A/C system. When it turns on, he probably just experiences a vague sense of other noises getting softer or disappearing because it's just white noise in the subconscious background to Jeremy. Also, for both of you: ears can be bothered by either loudness or coldness."

Then I just stopped and watched them digest this information. It took about 10 seconds before the "aha" faces started to emerge. Then there was some blushing. Then a bit of laughter. I was relieved because they were both well-intentioned.

All it took to resolve was a little communication and an authentic effort to build a bridge between two perfectly reasonable people with slightly different perspectives but who both would genuinely rather live in a world that's working well for all concerned.

The Past Is Prologue

The point here is that each one of us—neurodivergent and neurotypical alike—brings a vast range of unconscious biases and assumptions into our communication with others. The double-empathy problem is a powerful framework for understanding how this fact manifests itself in an intimidating but ultimately frail barrier wall between people with different cognitive profiles.

To review, neurotypical people have just as much trouble understanding the intentions and perspectives of autistic people as autistic people have in accurately deciphering the minds of neurotypical people. Yet all communication barriers appear to fall away when members of either group interact with others in their own group.

The double-empathy problem asserts that these issues are not due to autistic cognition alone but to a breakdown in reciprocity and mutual understanding that can happen between any two people with very different ways of experiencing the world.

The scope of the theory has broad ramifications because it not only takes into account neurodiversity but the social context within which communication takes place. It is also a radical departure from how we have perceived autistic people for decades. That baggage is a separate obstacle because it has built its own scaffolding of flawed assumptions that make the barrier between us seem much more formidable than it actually is.

This contextual point is crucial and opens the door for a strategic path to authentic neurodiversity inclusion: by simply demonstrating an awareness of the double-empathy problem and its implications, organizational leaders can signal an appreciation for neurodiversity from a strength-based perspective to help build a cultural infrastructure predicated upon a commitment to universal shared responsibility for bridging gaps in communication, much as we do when we travel abroad or interact with foreigners who have traveled to visit us from distant lands.

Mama, First Contact, and Bat Psychology

The Kaluli people offer a fascinating example of how environments play critical roles in shaping how concepts are internally experienced. The concept of *mama*, for example, is not an easy one for verbal, linear thinkers to fully appreciate as it involves the internalization of a multisensory experience, as explained by anthropologist Steven Feld, with "acoustic [ways of] knowing as a centerpiece of Kaluli experience; how sounding and the sensual, bodily, experiencing of sound is a special kind of knowing, or put differently, how sonic sensibility is basic to experiential truth in the Bosavi forests."[6]

This example serves as a good reminder of just how alien another system of meaning can be.

To take it one step further, problems compound into translation errors between cultures or individuals with no shared cultural foundation when communication is attempted between them using symbology that ultimately depends, intentionally or unintentionally, upon some degree of shared cultural reference points.

The example I used in my research thesis, "The Problem of Cultural Translation," while at the London School of Economics, was NASA's now-famous Pioneer Plaque, which served as a pictorial message from mankind when sent into space aboard the Pioneer 10 space probe in 1972 (see Figure 13.1). The goal of the plaque was to offer a nonverbal communication device in the event the probe was discovered by intelligent alien life. The brainchild of Carl Sagan, the plaque's purpose was also to help alien civilizations potentially locate the plaque's makers (us) through astronomical bread crumbs that specify our home address within the Milky Way. To attempt to bridge the unknown cultural divide, the plaque contained extremely simplistic imagery. However, despite the simplicity of the symbology, it failed to escape ultimate dependence upon a degree of shared

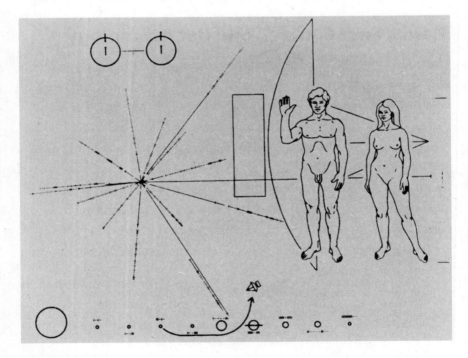

Figure 13.1
(*Source:* NASA, Public domain.)

cultural reference points—in other words, reference points not directly derivable from mathematical or astronomical facts—to be interpretable, pointing to an overwhelming likelihood of translation error if found.

For example, on the right side of the plaque, a naked man and woman appear standing in front of a spacecraft, ostensibly to display our anatomical size, shape, and features. The man is raising his right hand in an intended gesture of good will.

This could be interpreted in many unintended ways that pose real risk.

Suppose, for example, that the plaque was discovered by an alien race with a cultural history defined by psychological and physical bullying and interpersonal violence. That image of a raised hand might signal hostile rather than friendly intentions and lead to disastrous events down the road. Alternatively, perhaps the aliens see this as a submissive gesture meant to communicate our unconditional surrender. Or perhaps using just pictures was taken as cultural inferiority due to the lack of mathematical or linguistic development. Maybe humans are too barbaric to clothe themselves.

While this is all highly speculative, it demonstrates the critical point: even messages carefully crafted for universal meaning presume some level of shared knowledge that might not actually be there at all or might be present but subject to variations in interpretation with unknowable error potential. In an ironic but hardly irrelevant demonstration of this point, the vast majority of human scientific experts shown the plaque were unable to decode it!

In his seminal article "What Is It Like to Be a Bat?" published in 1974, Thomas Nagel asserts that it is pointless to attempt to truly understand the subjective perspective of some fundamentally different kind of being. The best we can do is imagine what it would be like to be ourselves inserted into the form and experiential context of that other being, which would get us no closer to being able to

257

posit that we actually understand anything at all about what it's like to be that other being from its point of view.

> Our own experience provides the basic material for our imagination, whose range is therefore limited. . . . Now we know that most bats (the Microchiroptera, to be precise) perceive the external world primarily by sonar, or echolocation, detecting the reflections, from objects within range, of their own rapid, subtly modulated, high-frequency shrieks. . . . It will not help to try to imagine that one has webbing on one's arms, which enables one to fly around at dusk and dawn catching insects in one's mouth; that one has very poor vision and perceives the surrounding world by a system of reflected high-frequency sound signals; and that one spends the day hanging upside down by one's feet in the attic. In so far as I can imagine this (which is not very far), it tells me only what it would be like for me to behave as a bat behaves. But that is not the question. I want to know what it is like for a bat to be a bat. . . . So if extrapolation from our own case is involved in the idea of what it is like to be a bat, the extrapolation must be incompletable. We cannot form more than a schematic conception of what it is like.[7]

A Sense of Proportion

Why take you on this journey through various versions of the futility of attempting to meaningfully empathize with some version of otherness where the barrier to developing a sense of shared experience and understanding is somewhere between unimaginably high and infinitely insurmountable?

I have found it to be a very effective way to introduce a sense of proportion. We are, after all, discussing the importance of attempting to meaningfully empathize with some version of neurodiversity otherness.

I am not saying the solution is to force everyone to genuinely like everyone else. Empathy is not contingent on deep friendship or mutual affection or interpersonal chemistry. It is contingent on the realization, through a few shared experiences, that we are all very much alike in terms of needs, motivations, and the desire to be heard, understood, and accepted for who we are as unique individuals. And that's more than enough common ground to serve as a basis for genuine empathy, especially among people who speak the same language and share the same goals as professional members of the same team.

You won't ever know what it's like to be a bat. But you will find it's much easier than you may think to establish a foundation of mutual respect and empathy with the neurodivergent person across the room or in the Zoom meeting window. With that foundation in place, it will be equally as easy for them to empathize with you.

It just takes a willingness to genuinely try and a little bit of shared experience.

Key Takeaways

- Problem of connection: People with the "Mi-Fi" password understand social cues and feel part of a group mind. Those without access feel disconnected. But this is not, it turns out, a law of the universe. It's a social phenomenon.

- Solution to the problem: Building bridges to make sure everyone has access to the "Mi-Fi" network. Empathy and mutual understanding are essential to connect neurotypical and neurodivergent individuals.

(continued)

(continued)

- Many people mistakenly believe autistic individuals lack the capacity for empathy due to prior research paradigms.

- A recent theory that emphasizes the mutual empathy barriers between neurotypicals and autistic individuals, akin to the hurdles experienced by people from different cultures, has emerged as a new dominant paradigm in the making.

- Shared experiences matter in promoting a happier and more effective culture within a neurodiverse team. This includes trust, psychological safety, perspective-taking, and honest communication.

- Strategies and tactics are available to establish shared understanding, trust, and cross-tribe empathy within an organization, highlighting the importance of communication and understanding differing perspectives.

- Both neurodivergent and neurotypical people bring biases into communication, creating barriers.

- The double-empathy problem explains misunderstandings between people with different cognitive profiles.

  - This is not solely due to autistic cognition but a breakdown in mutual understanding, applicable to different world experiences.

  - It is a radical departure from previous perceptions of autism and acknowledges broader social contexts.

  - Awareness of the double-empathy problem can guide strategies for neurodiversity inclusion.

- Communication errors can occur across cultures and systems, even with careful crafting, due to lack of shared reference points.

- The example of the *Pioneer 10* space probe's plaque illustrates potential misinterpretations in attempts to communicate across unknown divides.

- The inability to truly understand the experience of a fundamentally different being (e.g., a bat) highlights the limits of empathy.

- The main objective is not to force liking but to establish mutual respect and empathy, recognizing shared needs and desires.

- Building empathy bridges between and among neurotypical and neurodivergent individuals across an organization is critical to fostering sustained authentic neuroinclusion. It requires willingness and shared experience. There is no fundamental barrier to success in this endeavor.

Conclusion: Neurodiversity and the Age of Transformation

"How did you go bankrupt?" Bill asked.

"Two ways," Mike said. "Gradually and then suddenly."

—Ernest Hemingway, *The Sun Also Rises* (1926)[1]

When I was a graduate student living in Oxford in the UK, I had a few rather eccentric neighbors. One of them was a zoology professor with a passion for snails. He caught them. He bred them. He lived with them. They were his pride and joy. He would invite me over to gaze upon them so I, too, could marvel at their resilience and apparently vastly underestimated intelligence.

Another was an avid game hunter. It was his role in my life to make me forever unable to forget the putrid smell of days-old dead birds hanging outside, maturing the "traditional way" into properly gamey delicacies.

Yet another was an octogenarian Oxford Don with many notable accomplishments and a long-standing reputation as a once-in-a-generation intellect. By the time I met him, that was all "Glory Days" and well in his past, and he was now treated in academic circles with the type of veneration and respect reserved for a war hero or Nobel laureate in a nursing home: a great deal of kindness and consideration—"are you comfortable enough?"—but very few genuine opportunities for him to contribute his ideas anymore.

263

He was an intellectual titan now long past his prime, slowly sinking into the creeping tar pit of a rare cognitive degenerative disease that he branded as a "most peculiar cerebral thievery." He was also dyslexic. And he was very self-aware, readily offering up his own limitations as fair game for open discussion and a frequent topic of his own self-deprecating humor in the best-natured way. He was divorced. His kids had grown up and never seemed to visit. And I found him charming. It was like living next door to a retired dragon with an empty fire gland, growing quirkier by the day, pottering around the garden, complaining about the town council—but still a dragon!

So I made an effort to get to know him. I considered it an honor. Looking back now, I would have a very hard time if asked to name the wisest person I ever knew, but he would certainly make the very short list.

It's rare to be very smart. Rarer still to be very wise, which is a very different thing. And quite a bit rarer still to have once been a bona fide and celebrated once-in-a-generation genius, assigned the responsibility by one's peers of pushing at the frontiers of human knowledge—and to then witness one's own decline into obscurity and an ordinary existence, and yet to somehow do it with dignity and grace, growing wiser along the way.

However, that type of decline doesn't go in a straight line. And he often surprised me. Just when I would get used to pitying him, the once-in-a-generation genius would show up for tea.

One such instance was an evening in the summer of 2004. I was sitting in an Adirondack chair in the garden, watching the fireflies glow in the dusk light, working on my doctoral dissertation, bathed in the blue light of my laptop screen, when he ambled out through his back door to smoke his pipe—a John Brumfit Bent Apple—methodically navigating persistent but mild hand tremors as he packed in his precious "finest Dunhill Nightcap."

Conclusion: Neurodiversity and the Age of Transformation

This was a "thing." Most days, he would lecture me on the merits of "Brumfit and Dunhill." I would once again express my complete repulsion at the idea of any form of smoking. Then he would offer it to me with a wink and a mischievous grin. I would jerk backward in disgust. We would both smile at the ritual.

But this evening was different. He was melancholy and serious and wanted to talk about change—"Because you're so young and no matter how smart you are, you haven't lived long enough for certain ideas to come into your sphere of awareness. And I'm very old, and I don't know how much longer I have, and there's something important I want you to understand."

It was a conversation I will never forget. He wasn't quite his old self, but there was more of the once-in-a-generation genius dragon about him than I had seen in a while. Talking to him over the recent months felt a bit like trying to catch up with someone in a maze of hallways—hearing footsteps just ahead, seeing an occasional shadow from around the next corner, never quite catching a direct glimpse. But I could tell from the start that tonight would be different.

He passed away shortly thereafter.

I don't remember much of that summer. But I can recall that evening as vividly as if it were yesterday—the two of us sitting outside together in the cool evening air, his knowing grin occasionally lit by the crackling glow from his pipe.

When at last he set down his pipe and turned to face me, the words started to pour out. To this day, I'm still not entirely sure whether it was more genius than nonsense, because there was surely some of each.

"I'm worried, my dear," he started. "I'm worried because I have come to believe very strongly that the whole human experiment is going to come up against an existential challenge. And I don't think it's too far off. Probably after I've

265

gone, but certainly while you have your wits about you. This is something you will face. Your generation will be at its height in social influence and cultural capital when the world runs into an exponential function coming to a head. And history shows quite clearly that humans reliably fail when faced with exponential functions. They take so long to brew in the early going, advancing at such invisible increments across such long periods—even generations or epochs—only to explode suddenly out of nowhere into something that's already beyond our capacity to control or steer by the time we notice them at all.

"The old standard is to ask someone if they would buy your house for a daily payment over the course of a single month starting with one penny on the first day, two pence on the second, four pence on the third, and so on, until the end of the month. You will find a depressing number of people who jump at that deal without ever running the sequence through. Then you get utter disbelief when you tell them they just agreed to buy your house for almost 12 million pounds. Two weeks further, and it's 22 billion pounds. Another week, and it's 3 trillion.

"If I can help any young person understand just one thing right now, I would want it to be about this dynamic. But," he continued with a sentence I don't think I will ever forget, "we must now get in my time machine to follow this out further because the stakes this time are going to be awfully high."

I must have been wearing the expression that only a cognitive scientist can wear when in the presence of someone with a degenerative neurological condition who has just said something completely nonsensical, because he quickly flashed a reassuring smile and tamped down on the air with his hands. Then he gestured toward his car—an old and badly maintained silver Jaguar XJ with rust spots on the bumpers and a missing passenger side wing mirror.

Obediently, I rose and helped him to his feet, and we made the slow journey over to his driveway and got in the car, whereupon he pinned his necklace bifocals on the bridge of his nose, pulled out a scrap page of notes from the breast pocket of his tweed coat, studied it for a moment, glanced at his watch, and then announced, "June 28, 2004, 7:18 p.m. This is temporal experiment number one." Then he made a show of fiddling with the radio dial, turning it back and forth, turned the A/C on and off, and fixed me with an expectant grin.

At this point, I knew it was I who was failing some kind of test.

Fifteen years later, when my husband finally talked me into watching *Back to the Future*, he was confused as to why I burst out laughing when the movie got to the scene introducing the DeLorean. I considered for a moment trying to explain what was so funny but gave up and just shook my head, still giggling. What was I going to tell him? That I actually sat in a Jaguar 15 years earlier watching a stuffy old octogenarian Oxford Don, who hadn't been west of Swindon in 50 years, act out an elaborate pop culture reference in increasingly desperate detail trying to earn at least a chuckle from the young grad student who came of age in suburban Midwest America and who just happened to be probably the only person at Downers Grove South High School that couldn't tell Doc Brown from Charlie Brown?

But all I had for him then was a confused frown.

267

Conclusion: Neurodiversity and the Age of Transformation

Still, he rallied impressively. He had prepared a whole "experience" to accompany his thoughts. And he wasn't going to be derailed by the revelation, however improbable, that *he* was the resident American pop culture expert in the car that day. He had a time machine. He had notes on scrap paper. Stiff upper lip for queen and country.

"Let's you and I take a trip back about 100,000 years, shall we?" He consulted his scrap paper notes again. "Our destination? The year 109,076 BCE. And ahh yes, here we are."

He opened the driver's side window of his motionless car and made a show of surveying our surroundings. "Fire-making people. Small kinship groups. Stone tools. The potential rudiments of language. Fascinating!"

Then he rolled up the window and fiddled with the air conditioning buttons again.

"Now, let us jump forward 10,000 years." Down went the window and he theatrically surveyed the landscape once again, this time with a disappointed sigh. "Fire-making people. Small kinship groups. Stone tools. The potential rudiments of language. A bit dull."

Up went the window. Buttons and dials received another round of narrative attention. And, apparently, off we went into the time stream.

"A bigger jump forward this time."—Window down— "And behold! The year 9076 BCE. A hundred millennia since our first port of call. And my, how the world has changed!" He glanced back down at his scrap paper notes. "Complex structures. Complex language. Rudimentary pictographic writing. Mass religion. Pottery. Woven fabrics. War. Domesticated horses and dogs. Agriculture! The wheel!"

Window up. Dials. Buttons. Window down.

Conclusion: Neurodiversity and the Age of Transformation

"Another 1,000 years on, Dunne! It's 8076 BCE. Hmmm." He made a show of tapping the control panel near the radio. "No, it appears to be working fine. I suppose nothing much has changed in the past 1,000 years. Let's move on."

Again, the time machine's external access portal was sealed for temporal displacement. Again, time axis coordinates were entered into the temporal control console. Again, the time machine's external access portal was unsealed to gather data and make observations about the new period in the history of human civilization.

"Ahh . . . now here's a brave new world. We have materialized 9,000 years further into the future. The year is 924 CE. And revolutions abound."—Glance at scrap paper— "Irrigation. Ironwork. Recognizable music. Sea-faring vessels. Gunpowder. Compasses. Money. Movable type. Toilet paper!"

Window up. Buttons. Dials. Window down.

"Another century forward. It's 1024 CE, and nothing much has changed. Let's jump another millennium from our last port of call, in keeping with the exponential function, shall we?"

Window. Fiddling. Window.

"Now we can recognize the world a bit more. At least, *I* can. It's 1924. Not long after I was born, in fact. A thousand years after gunpowder and toilet paper. And just look at the world now! Airplanes. Automobiles. World wars. Electrified cities. Central banking. Cricket. Railroads. Ocean liners. Complex supply chains. Moving pictures. Telephones. Vaccines. Truly radical change in just 1,000 years, wouldn't you say? Let's take another small jump. A decade should provide some context."

Conclusion: Neurodiversity and the Age of Transformation

This time, he merely pantomimed the window and console ritual.

"Hmmm. Not much different." He looked at me pointedly now.

"How about another 90 years forward? To 2024? Obviously, the internet and e-commerce. Perhaps flying cars as well? Artificial intelligence? Robots in every home? Personal cloned-organ banks? Only 90 years into the future, and everything has changed once again. And according to the pattern we have taken on our journey so far, our next port of call—where we would presumably find yet another completely revolutionized world—would be just another 10 years hence. Ten years, Dunne!"

And then it was over. He raised his bushy eyebrows to look meaningfully at me for another moment as if to punctuate this last proclamation. Then he simply opened the door, gestured for my help getting back to his feet, and announced he was ready to retire for the evening. He suddenly looked very tired. This was the last time we ever talked at length.

Why did I include this story here?

Two reasons: first, in 2004, an octogenarian scrambled together a thought experiment just for my benefit involving a pretend time machine that took us on an imaginary adventure reaching back 111,000 years, eventually culminating in 2024. And it just so happens that 2024 was set as the publication year for my first book.

That would have been reason enough to find a place for him here even if the anecdote didn't bear directly on my argument.

However, as it turns out, his thought experiment plays a crucial role: the argument at the heart of this book would be incomplete without a closing chapter tasked with establishing, beyond any doubt in the mind of the reader, that the world now sits on the precipice of

Conclusion: Neurodiversity and the Age of Transformation

transformational change driven by the emergence of new technology that, at its root, will reveal itself to be extraordinarily relevant to our primary theme.

His insight was to point out that the seeds of this explosive period of transformational change were planted far deeper in our past than we might readily notice. And we are only now realizing that it's far too late to steer the outcome.

Just as he warned, we don't handle exponential functions very well. They sneak up on us quietly and then, here we are with no hands on the steering wheel of history. Buckle up. Figure C.1 is my attempt to depict the perspective of an Oxford Don, as related to me in 2004, on the history of human civilization from the year 109,076 BCE to 2035 CE. Exponential change driven by exponential growth in idea creation and transmission, augmented by population growth, population densification, communications technology, transportation technology, data storage and accessibility, and the self-reinforcing feedback relationships within and among those factors.

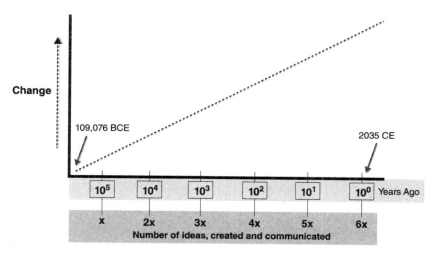

Figure C.1 My attempt to depict the perspective of an Oxford Don on the history of human civilization from the year 109,076 BCE to 2035 CE.

Conclusion: Neurodiversity and the Age of Transformation

My own added insight is that the nature of the transformation we are now embarking on will serve to powerfully elevate the crucial importance of neurodiversity inclusion as an organizational asset.

The invention of unprecented machine intelligence will carve out a very special and complementary place for human neurodivergence. AI is set to redefine how we understand our role in the world when it comes to linear thinking tasks. I would argue that the domain of linear thinking, in all its forms, will be consumed by artificial intelligence over the coming 15 years, especially as we move gradually closer toward the viability of quantum computation, which should serve to turbocharge the productivity and speed of AI research systems to unimaginable heights.

However—and this is a critical point—modes of "thinking" exist that are not derivative of the complexification of linear processing.

My experience as a Silicon Valley entrepreneur, VC advisor, technology investor, and MIT Machine Learning student has equipped me with a basic understanding of AI systems, machine learning, and neural networks. Just enough to contribute to the conversation among insiders. But an Oxford PhD in cognitive science and a lifetime working in neurodiversity has granted me legitimate claim to something approximating expertise—if there is such a thing—in human cognition.

That combination has left me somewhat skeptical about whether the current paradigm in AI systems development will ever produce something "conscious" in the sense we mean when we refer to our own feelings of self-awareness and identity. But perhaps we will reach that point. If it's possible, then it will probably be in the not-too-distant future given the exponential curve we are now traversing.

This sentiment matches the messaging we have heard over the past year from the likes of Sam Altman, Elon Musk, Ilya Sutskever (the mastermind behind ChatGPT), Marc Andreessen, and Geoffrey Hinton, the so-called godfather of modern AI systems—i.e.,

Conclusion: Neurodiversity and the Age of Transformation

the leading minds in the field admit AGI (artificial general intelligence) is a mysterious concept possibly, but not definitely, in our future at some non-immediate but relatively near point in time, with capabilities that cannot be easily predicted other than the possession of vastly superhuman linear intelligence.

It is an open question as to whether or not such a machine would, upon "waking up," suddenly acquire the capacity for lateral thought, for existential dread, for irrationally connected memories jumbled into a swirling subconscious reservoir of potential future insights. It is also an open question as to whether or not such a machine superintelligence would require some form of "embodiment"—some set of mechanisms through which to be subjected to bombardment by random or unchosen sensory data—to reach the richness of human experience, which may be a prerequisite to new modalities of thought; some mechanism that might allow it to access the equivalent of irrationally and subconsciously connecting the scent of flowers at a friend's funeral with a taxi ride through a botanical park years later, somehow ending up at a new idea for how to solve a problem at work.

At their base, all AI systems are, as Jaron Lanier has described, merely innovative forms of "social collaboration." Lanier—a prodigy mentored by Marvin Minsky, and a foundational thinker in the field of AI—notes that something like ChatGPT is an astonishingly proficient curator, but nothing more. Its creations are simply mashups of existing human expression.

Imagine such a system being trained on baroque music in the early eighteenth century—on Bach, Handel, Vivaldi, Purcell, and Corelli. Such a system would no doubt astonish us with seemingly original concertos indistinguishable from other notable pieces of the period in complexity, originality, and quality.

But it would never give us the *Moonlight Sonata*.

Conclusion: Neurodiversity and the Age of Transformation

Imagine such a system being trained on the work of naturalists in the early nineteenth century. No doubt, it would quickly compile an amazing compendium of extant and fossilized species, and possibly even arrive at general conclusions about regions and traits.

But it would never give us *On the Origin of Species*.

Obviously, no one can predict the future with perfect vision, and perhaps this dynamic will change. In any case, what we do know now is that the next decade is going to feature an explosion in applied use-cases for AI systems that drive incredible advances in most fields of research and supplant or redefine many roles in the economy. But in the absence of some hypothetical "awake" AGI that has somehow domain-hopped into a capacity for lateral reasoning and intuitive leaps of insight, AI systems will remain inescapably chained to linear reasoning.

That said, "transformational change" is set to become our grounding, where the sands begin to shift beneath our feet so fast that every step we take is in a new world. That's why I call it the "Transformation Age."

While the concept of a true "technological singularity" in history—as espoused by science fiction writers such as Vernor Vinge and futurists such as Ray Kurzweil—is still very much open for debate, it is becoming increasingly difficult to dismiss. However, even if we aren't barreling toward an epochal handoff from human to machine intelligence, we are certainly on the cusp of transformative change in the nature of how we experience life as humans due to the emergence of nonhuman intelligence and the likely future emergence of revolutionary advances in computational power.

The Transformation Age is not only set to be perhaps the period of most rapid change in human history but also perhaps the most unpredictable period in human history in terms of our ability to extrapolate from the immediate prior period to generate basic assumptions about the near future.

Conclusion: Neurodiversity and the Age of Transformation

The notion of the "Singularity" is drawn from a conceptual parallel with how we view black holes in cosmology. Singularities are special in physics because they conceal everything about the reality that lies beyond their event horizons. In other words, there is a point up to which we can observe reality and make predictions according to the laws of physics.

Beyond that point, it's a mystery.

As an executive or organizational leader, what do you do to plan for a period where the ground is shifting beneath your feet in a fundamental sense every step of the way, and long-range strategic planning is subject to the type of confidence coefficient physicists admit to when hypothesizing about the interior of black holes?

I argue that cognitive diversity will be one of the essential resources common to organizations that survive and thrive in that future. Imagine trying to respond to emerging dynamics driven by this accelerating curve while being hamstrung by groupthink, having no voices in the room used to living comfortably outside the box, engaging in decision-making processes dominated by concerns about social status in a hierarchy.

This is the moment to embrace authentic neurodiversity inclusion as a core organizational value. It isn't the whole solution to anything. But it is part of the solution to nearly everything.

■ ■ ■

In this book, we have discussed the reasons for adopting a proactive strategic appreciation for authentic neurodiversity inclusion. Neurodivergent people should be valued every bit as much as a part of the human condition as neurotypicals.

In the Transformation Age, we will need neurodivergent problem solvers to complement neurotypical cognition and AI-driven machine intelligence more than ever. This view, which I offered during a fireside chat at The Next Web conference and in a recent *MIT Sloan Management Review* article, is gaining momentum in cognitive science and technology circles.[2] In recent years, interest in neurodiversity-at-work pilot programs has grown. But the larger business world is badly lagging behind the curve in aligning organizational values with authentic neurodiversity inclusion, especially with respect to how that inclusion may represent a significant strategic asset in navigating the landscape of inevitable long-term transformational change ahead of us. For any given organization, this is good news: it means a competitive advantage is still accessible; there remains an opportunity to be proactive and join the early movers in a human resources revolution that is gradually gaining an air of inevitability at its core.

We have discussed the advantages of this revolution in terms of innovation, creativity, cognitive diversity, groupthink immunity, and the economics of a labor shortage context. We have also discussed how embracing this paradigm is not a trade-off but an asset and how that asset is ultimately cost-effective as an investment.

We have further discussed the ground-level ideas involved in navigating the process of embracing authentic neuroinclusion as an organization—how to implement new talent-acquisition strategies, changes that should be made in the interview process, how to build a thriving organizational culture that values cognitive diversity, how to understand where lines should be drawn in terms of flexible office protocols, how to accommodate necessary infrastructure concepts, including sensory differences, to align with the principles of universal design, and how to articulate and implement organizational goals—as well as how to measure progress toward them—in service of all of these objectives.

However, none of that means a thing without the active participation of organizations and their leaders. And a very good case can be made that without taking this simple step, resistant organizations may be increasingly at risk of ruin.

Conclusion: Neurodiversity and the Age of Transformation

Neurodivergence broadly correlates with uncommon cognitive strategies, including evidence of lower vulnerability to the risks posed by cognitive biases and the groupthink dynamic, particularly among autistic people. While support needs may vary among and within the neurodivergent population, there is also evidence of increased prevalence of nonlinear thinking, generally increased access to non-traditional solution pathways, creative problem solving, and other unique approaches to perceiving and thinking about the surrounding world and its challenges and opportunities.

A recent article in *The Military Times* revealed that there are already autistic leaders in senior positions in the intelligence community, and how matters of national security are too important and challenging to leave only to people who see the world in typical ways.[3] Autistic workers, for example, have been shown to detect sensitive geospatial imagery patterns with significantly higher precision rates. In this book, we reviewed several studies that also showed that ADHDers displayed increased originality of thought driven by flashes of intuitive insight, with a wider range of cognitive access to semantic choices. Dyslexic people also have shown a higher likelihood for associative and systems thinking, as well as creativity.

As we blaze ever faster toward a world inextricably entwined with the incorporation of artificial intelligence, these properties—lateral thinking, intuitive insight, inductive leaps of creativity, resistance to manipulation or social pressure—will become increasingly important because they represent pathways of thought capable of being complementary to those produced by AI systems, which are inescapably chained to linear progressions of reason.

No matter how advanced, the paradigm of artificial intelligence that is ascending to dominance during the current period is bound, at its core, to linear progressions—to lightspeed processes that ultimately involve merely answering yes or no to billions or even trillions of inputs as data pathways are navigated toward a result that fits some predetermined objective.

You can't model such a system to include lateral leaps of creative thought. It's just not possible. Given what we now understand about the fundamental processes underlying AI, you can't get out of Flatland by simply building an infinite number of two-dimensional ladders infinitely fast. They will move faster and more competently within the boundaries of linear rationality than any human is capable of. But they will always be bound within the confines of that map.

Perhaps over time such systems will get better at simulating something that approximates this type of process—after studying enough instances of creative genius at work among human beings through historical examples. But there is, at present, no reason to believe that such a goal even exists among those creating such systems. And even if there was, the result still wouldn't be the actual instance of lateral thinking. It would merely be a lateral-thinking simulation performed through a linear progression.

Such a process is not capable of extrapolating Beethoven or Mozart from Bach and Handel. As they say in Maine, you can't get there from here.

As every organization falls down the gravity well of history into the warm embrace of an eternity of increasing reliance on increasingly powerful AI systems—the ultimate Red Queen's Race—it may well be that the only source of sustained differentiating edge—of tapping into the N+1 axis that extends perpendicularly out of Flatland— lies in building an organizational culture fundamentally committed to the proactive and authentic inclusion of different kinds of minds.

Appendix: Tools to Inspire Authentic Neurodiversity Inclusion & Belonging

Online resource library of tools that reinforce the strategies in this book can be accessed with your book purchase. Please go to www.theneurodiversityedge.com for instructions about how you can access a variety of applied templates, resources, and tools, including the following:

- Sample summary neurodiversity organizational audit report

- Exercises to bridge communication and foster empathy across neurotypes

- Expanded glossary and jargon-free neurodiversity summary resource for staff and managers

- Sample strategic planning template based on the Pyramid of Neuroinclusion framework

- Customizable template to track authentic neuroinclusion organizational goals

- Expanded online access to additional perspectives and illustrations of the experiences of both neurodivergent people and organizational leaders/managers

- Example of an organizational sensory kit and protocols

- Example of a strength-based onboarding template

- Assistive technology and support options

Sample Neurodiversity-Friendly Organizational Culture Checklist

Download updates at www.theneurodiversityedge.com.

Codification:

☐ Have you adopted a Neurodiversity Inclusion Value Statement?

☐ Is Neurodiversity explicitly named in inclusivity and diversity policies?

☐ Does your organization have anti-bullying and anti-harassment policies that explicitly cover neurodivergent people?

☐ Do you offer flexible work arrangements, such as remote only, remote first, or hybrid?

☐ Does your organization include an optional disclosure during the job application process?

☐ Do job posting procedures focus on the requirements of the role with a streamlined application process stripped of unnecessary and superfluous steps?

☐ Do policies allow jobseekers the opportunity for adjustments to customize their strategy to focus on strengths when applying for employment or internship opportunities? For example, are applicants allowed to submit a project portfolio to demonstrate unique/individualized skill sets?

- ☐ Does your organization offer alternative interview processes that are not biased toward traditional communication and social skills?

- ☐ Do you have a structured internal process to ensure that qualified neurodivergent employees who may be less inclined to regularly socialize with upper management are not unfairly overlooked for leadership roles and opportunities for advancement?

- ☐ Does the organization explicitly support managers with decision-making authority to focus on work results while allowing for flexibility in how employees or interns engage in daily workflow to achieve results?

- ☐ Do your HR policies allow for and support the use of items such as noise-canceling headphones, sunglasses, weighted blankets, and fragrance sprays to maximize productivity and help employees cope with sensory issues?

- ☐ Does your office have a dedicated quiet space where neurodivergent employees can take breaks?

- ☐ If there is a dress code or uniform, do you allow for accommodations for neurodivergent employees to wear alternative attire that is sensory friendly?

- ☐ Do you have an evaluation framework that leads with a strength-based paradigm?

- ☐ Has the organization adopted specific, clear, realistic, understandable, memorable, measurable, aligned, timebound, easily communicated, and simple (SCRUM MATES) Neuroinclusion goals?

- ☐ Do you include human cognitive diversity in your organizational strategic planning when thinking about AI integration?

Conduct:

- ☐ Is transparent communication encouraged, valued, and rewarded?

- ☐ When speaking about diversity, does the senior leadership in your organization include neurodiversity?

Sample Neurodiversity-Friendly Organizational Culture Checklist

☐ Do you conduct trainings and workshops for staff across the entire organization to promote a neurodiversity-friendly organizational culture?

☐ Has your organization hired an external firm or consultant with neurodiversity expertise to conduct an audit to uncover implicit biases that could/would make it disproportionately challenging for neurodivergent individuals to be hired and succeed in long-term employment?

☐ Are employees treated with dignity and respect if/when they behave in ways that appear atypical even though such employees are known to produce quality work? For instance, when an employee inaudibly moves lips while writing on a whiteboard, draws pictures in the air while brainstorming, requests a standing desk, likes to wear earbuds, storyboards notes, fidgets with hair or taps a foot during meetings, and/or prefers to work late at night rather than attend a party.

☐ Do you promote an organizational culture with daily habits that are psychologically safe for neurodivergent individuals (where discriminatory jokes, bullying, and gossip based on differences are not permitted and allyship is encouraged)?

☐ Are alternative communication preferences acknowledged and respected (i.e., text communication rather than phone calls)?

☐ Do you observe anyone in the office comfortably wearing noise canceling headphones, adjusting LED lighting, or using a fidget spinner?

☐ Does your organization support access to coaches, buddies, and/or navigators?

☐ Does your organization reward people who take intellectual risks by articulating new ways of thinking or dissenting opinions?

Sample Neurodiversity-Friendly Organizational Culture Checklist

☐ Do individuals feel valued where redistribution of tasks based on strengths occurs and teams are comprised of complementary skills?

☐ Are expectations communicated clearly and transparently without the need for guesswork?

☐ For any products, services, or marketing campaigns involving neurodiversity, are neurodivergent people with lived experience included in meaningful roles?

☐ Do managers, leaders, and peers openly listen in good faith and with empathy to different points of view?

☐ Are any neurodivergent individuals represented on your leadership team and/or board of directors?

☐ Are employee strengths, interests, and passions discussed when determining performance goals?

☐ Do leaders and managers communicate positive stories about neurodivergent people with a focus on strengths to their teams?

Sample Neurodiversity-Friendly Organizational Culture Checklist

Glossary of Terms

Allistic: Allistic refers to non-autistic people.

Asperger's Syndrome: After 2013, Asperger's syndrome is no longer a separate diagnosis according to *The Diagnostic and Statistical Manual of Mental Disorders* (DSM-5) as it has been reclassified within the broader autism spectrum disorder (ASD) umbrella. Some people who were diagnosed with Asperger's syndrome before this change still use this term. It was thought of in similar terms to what is now classified as Support Level 1 Autism with mild to low support needs.

Aspie: Self-advocates who were diagnosed with Asperger's syndrome when it was still a separate category from autism spectrum disorders or those who otherwise identify this way sometimes call themselves or each other Aspie.

Attention Deficit Hyperactivity Disorder (ADHD): ADHD, one of the most common learning differences, is usually diagnosed in childhood but lasts through adulthood. ADHDers experience attentional differences and may be impulsive and hyperactive but also highly creative. ADHDers can sometimes hyperfocus on projects and tasks that are of particular interest to them. ADHDers often experience challenges with organization and completing routine tasks (such as paying bills on time, household chores, or returning phone calls). There are three distinct types of ADHD: 1) Hyperactive-impulsive; 2) Inattentive; and 3) Combined type.

Au: Shorthand for Autistic identity. Some autistic people have Au after their name on social media.

AuDHD: The way some people refer to themselves who are both autistic and ADHDers.

Autism/autism: Autism with a capital A refers to Autism as an identity. Autism with the lower case a can be interpreted as the diagnosis.

Autism Spectrum Disorders (ASD): Autism spectrum disorders (sometimes called autism spectrum conditions) is a lifelong developmental difference based on neurological differences and traits that start in childhood. The ASD profile shows differences in social communication and interaction, restricted or passionate interests, and repetitive behaviors. Many autistic people experience sensory overload.

Autistic person: Term used to describe Autism as part of personhood.

Broad Autism Phenotype (BAP): The broad autism phenotype, also called broader autism phenotype, describes a range of traits that resemble autism but are considered subclinical, or not enough to qualify for a diagnosis of autism spectrum disorder.

Butterfly Symbol: The neurodiversity butterfly symbol originated from an ADHD Facebook group but is recognized as a powerful symbol by most groups that fall under the neurodiversity umbrella. Autistic people recognize the butterfly symbol especially when paired with the infinity symbol. A blue butterfly is very often used to represent dyslexia, and a rainbow-colored or multi-colored butterfly is routinely used to represent neurodiversity more generally.

Developmental Language Disorder (DLD): Developmental Language Disorder (DLD) begins in early childhood and is characterized by difficulties with communication, which may manifest as struggles with receptive and/or expressive language. Previously DLD was also referred to as Specific Language Impairment.

Dyscalculia: Dyscalculia is a unique cognitive typology that affects number-based information and math.

Dyslexia: Dyslexia is a unique cognitive typology that affects how one reads, writes, and spells. Developmental dyslexia is the most common learning difference and is believed to affect as many as 17% of the population.

Dyslexic Thinking: An approach to problem solving, assessing information, and learning often used by people with dyslexia that involves pattern recognition, spatial reasoning, lateral thinking, and interpersonal communication. LinkedIn officially recognizes #DyslexicThinking as a skill.

Dyspraxia: Dyspraxia is a cognitive typology under the neurodiversity umbrella that affects physical coordination.

Hyperlexia: Hyperlexia is a unique cognitive typology where reading skills and abilities are advanced far beyond chronological age. "Hyper" refers to "better than," and "lexia" refers to the written word. Hyperlexic children may quickly decode words but may not comprehend the meaning entirely.

Identity-first Language: Identity-first language—preferred by many neurodivergent people—places the focus on the typology as central to one's identity. Someone wants to be seen not as a person with autism but rather as an autistic person.

Infinity Symbol: The rainbow infinity symbol—used to represent neurodiversity—describes the idea that people experience and interact with the world around them in many different ways; there is no one "right" way of thinking, learning, and behaving, and differences are not viewed as deficits.

Lateral Thinking: Lateral thinking is strongly associated with creativity and novel problem solving. It is synonymous with nonlinear thinking, thinking creatively, or thinking "outside the box" to solve a problem. Edward de Bono first described lateral thinking as the capacity to solve problems with unique methods where solutions cannot be arrived via deductive or logical thinking processes. Most often, logical thinking is used to solve problems in a direct, straightforward way (also known as vertical or linear thinking).

Neurodistinct: Neurodistinct is an alternative way of describing a neurodivergent person.

Neurodivergent: A person who identifies with one or more unique cognitive typologies that fit under the neurodiversity umbrella.

Neurodiverse: A group of people who include both neurotypical and neurodivergent individuals.

Neurodiversification: The method proposed in this book which involves taking a strength-based approach to neurodiversity, and applying it to human resources, management, and commerce. The core principle focuses on diversifying the workforce to include the broadest range of cognitive abilities and perspectives.

Neurodiversity: "Neurodiversity" is an umbrella term that represents all the unique ways that each brain processes information and the argument that unique cognitive typologies that fall under neurodivergence are just as valuable as neurotypical.

Neuroinclusion: The authentic inclusion of all cognitive typologies, including neurodivergent people, where people find a sense of genuine belonging without being forced to be like someone else.

Neurotypical: The presumed majority neurotype or cognitive typology where someone is not neurodivergent.

Nonverbal Learning Disability (NVLD): Nonverbal learning disorder is a learning difference that may manifest as challenges with motor, visual-spatial, and social skills. People with this unique cognitive typology may be very articulate and may write well but still struggle with implicit social cues and abstract concepts. NVLD social and communication differences sometimes look similar to autism even though the two typologies are distinct.

Person-first Language: Person-first language focuses on the person before the typology, such as "person with autism."

Pyramid of Neuroinclusion: The Pyramid of Neuroinclusion is an actionable framework introduced in this book that shows how authentic neuroinclusion depends on many factors, but psychological safety and transparent communication are paramount. All factors introduced by the framework are important to achieve the goal of neuroinclusion, but deep progress at the DNA level of the organization cannot be achieved without psychological safety.

Sensory overload: Sensory overload happens when input from one or more of the five senses (such as vision, sound, smell, touch, and taste) is greater than what the brain is able to process and creates an experience of overwhelm and varying ranges of discomfort.

Sensory Processing Disorder: Sensory processing disorder (SPD) affects how sensory information is processed. It may inhibit the ability to filter out sensory information which can lead to the feeling of being overstimulated in some environments. There may be sensitivities in one or several sensory modalities, including the subjective experience of sound, what is seen, tactile sensations, smell, and taste.

Synesthesia: Synesthesia is when the brain routes sensory information through multiple unrelated senses, causing one to experience more than one sense simultaneously. Some examples include tasting words, linking colors to numbers and letters, seeing music as color, or ideas as shapes.

Systems Thinking: Systems thinking allows for an understanding of the complexity of a problem by analyzing the whole system and its relationship to component parts. Systems thinking is connected with big-picture thinking, creativity, and strategic awareness.

Tourette's Syndrome (TS): Tourette's syndrome is a typology where people tend to experience tics or suddenly occurring and repeated twitches, vocal sounds, or movements. An example is involuntary blinking.

Twice Exceptional (2e): Intellectually gifted people who also fit within one or more unique cognitive typologies under the neurodiversity umbrella. 2e learners process information in distinct ways and may fit the profile of dyslexia, ADHD, autism, synesthesia, and/or other cognitive typologies. They may show strengths in creativity, lateral thinking, data analysis, original thinking, or hyperfocus.

Universal Design: Universal Design principles are based on the premise that environments, including education and work, should be designed in such a way to benefit the widest range of people.

Variable Attention Stimulus Trait (VAST): VAST is a recently introduced term to describe ADHD within a strength-based framework. Instead of focusing on ADHD in terms of deficits in attention, VAST focuses on the variability and differences of attention.

Notes

Introduction

1. Abbott, Edwin A. 1884. *Flatland: A Romance of Many Dimensions*. London: Seeley & Co.
2. Zen Business Research Report, 2023. "New ZenBusiness Research Finds Class of 2023 Sees Neurodiversity as an Asset in Leadership & is Primed to be the Most Entrepreneurial." https://www.businesswire.com/news/home/20230614082058/en/New-ZenBusiness-Research-Finds-Class-of-2023-Sees-Neurodiversity-as-an-Asset-in-Leadership-is-Primed-to-be-the-Most-Entrepreneurial
3. Tallo July Report, 2021. "Workplace neurodiversity is important to Gen Zers." https://www.hrdive.com/news/gen-z-hiring-recruiting-neuro diversity/604453/
4. Institute of Leadership & Management. n.d. "Half of All Leaders and Managers Would Not Employ a Neurodivergent Person." Retrieved March 8, 2023. https://www.institutelm.com/resourceLibrary/half-of-all-leaders-and-managers-would-not-employ-a-neurodivergent-person.html.
5. Boston Consulting Group, 2018. "How Diverse Leadership Teams Boost Innovation". https://www.bcg.com/publications/2018/how-diverse-leadership-teams-boost-innovation
6. CDC. n.d. "Data & Statistics on Autism Spectrum Disorder." Last reviewed April 4, 2023. https://www.cdc.gov/ncbddd/autism/data.html.

Chapter 1: A Tale of Two Worlds

1. Dong, Shihao, Tao Lin, James C. Nieh, and Ken Tan. 2023. "Social Signal Learning of the Waggle Dance in Honey Bees." *Science* 379, no. 6636 (2023): 1015–1018.

2. Taylor, Helen, Bryce Fernandes, and Sarah Wraight. 2022. "The Evolution of Complementary Cognition: Humans Cooperatively Adapt and Evolve through a System of Collective Cognitive Search." *Cambridge Archaeological Journal* 32, no. 1 (2022): 61–77.

3. Payne, Adam, and Dana Kaminstein. 2021. "How a Values-Based Approach Advances DEI." *MIT Sloan Management Review*, February 24, 2021. https://sloanreview.mit.edu/article/how-a-values-based-approach-advances-dei/.

4. White H.A., and P. Shah. 2016. "Scope of Semantic Activation and Innovative Thinking in College Students with ADHD." *Creativity Research Journal* 28 (2016): 275–282. https://doi.org/10.1080/10400419.2016.1195655.

5. White, H.A. 2018. "Thinking "Outside the Box": Unconstrained Creative Generation in Adults with Attention Deficit Hyperactivity Disorder". *The Journal of Creative Behavior*. 54. 10.1002/jocb.382.

6. Majeed NM, Hartanto A, Tan JJX. 2021. "Developmental dyslexia and creativity: A meta-analysis." *Dyslexia*. May: 27(2),187–203. doi: 10.1002/dys.1677. Epub 2021 Feb 14. PMID: 33586314.

7. Cancer, Alice, Serena Manzoli, and Alessandro Antonietti. 2016. "The Alleged Link between Creativity and Dyslexia: Identifying the Specific Process in Which Dyslexic Students Excel." *Cogent Psychology* 3 no. 1 (2016). Article 1190309. https://doi.org/10.1080/23311908.2016.1190309

8. Shah A, Frith U. "Why do autistic individuals show superior performance on the block design task?" *J Child Psychol Psychiatry*. 1993 Nov;34(8): 1351-64. doi: 10.1111/j.1469-7610.1993.tb02095.x. PMID: 8294523.

9. Shah, A., and U. Frith. 1983. "An Islet of Ability in Autistic Children: A Research Note." *Journal of Child Psychology and Psychiatry* 24 (1983): 613–620. https://doi.org/10.1111/j.1469-7610.1983.tb00137.x.

10. Best, C., Arora, S., Porter, F. et al. 2015. "The Relationship Between Sub-threshold Autistic Traits, Ambiguous Figure Perception and Divergent Thinking." *J Autism Dev Disord* 45, 4064–4073(2015). https://doi.org/10.1007/s10803-015-2518-2

11. Lunke, K. and Meier, B. 2018. "Creativity and involvement in art in different types of synaesthesia." *British Journal of Psychology*, Vol 110, Issue 4, pp. 727–744. https://bpspsychub.onlinelibrary.wiley.com/doi/full/10.1111/bjop.12363

Chapter 2: The Perils of Groupthink

1. Galileo Galilei. 1632. Dialogue Concerning the Two Chief World Systems.

2. Kenton, W. n.d. "What Is Groupthink? Definition, Characteristics, and Causes," Investopedia, updated December 5, 2022. https://www.investopedia.com/terms/g/groupthink.asp.

3. Sunstein, Cass R., and Reid Hastie. 2014. *Wiser: Getting Beyond Groupthink to Make Groups Smarter*. Boston: Harvard Business Review Press.

4. Sunstein, Cass R., and Reid Hastie. 2014. *Wiser: Getting Beyond Groupthink to Make Groups Smarter*. Boston: Harvard Business Review Press.

5. Sunstein, Cass R., and Reid Hastie. 2014. *Wiser: Getting Beyond Groupthink to Make Groups Smarter*. Boston: Harvard Business Review Press.

6. Asch, Solomon E. 1956. "Studies of Group Influence: I. An Experimental Analysis of Conformity." *Psychological Monographs: General and Applied* 75, no. 416 (1956): 1–70.

7. Izuma K, Matsumoto K, Camerer CF, Adolphs R. 2011. "Insensitivity to social reputation in autism." *Proc Natl Acad Sci U S A*. 2011 Oct 18;108(42):17302-7. doi: 10.1073/pnas.1107038108. Epub 2011 Oct 10. PMID: 21987799; PMCID: PMC3198313.

8. Farmer, G.D., S. Baron-Cohen, and W.J. Skylark. 2017. "People with Autism Spectrum Conditions Make More Consistent Decisions." *Psychological Science* 28, no. 8: 1067 -1076. https://doi.org/10.1177/09567976 17694867.

9. Kuzmanovic B, Rigoux L, Vogeley K. 2019. "Brief Report: Reduced Optimism Bias in Self-Referential Belief Updating in High-Functioning Autism." *J Autism Dev Disord*. Jul;49(7):2990–2998. doi: 10.1007/s10803-016-2940-0. PMID: 27757736.

10. Yafai, A.F., Verrier, D. and Reidt, L. 2014. "Social conformity and autism spectrum disorder: a child-friendly take on a classic study." *Autism*, 18 (8). http://shura.shu.ac.uk/7450/3/Verrier_Autism_and_Conformity.pdf

11. Vaughan, Diane. 1997. *The Challenger Launch Decision: Risky Technology, Culture, and Deviance at NASA*. University of Chicago Press.

Chapter 3: The Economics of Neurodiversity Inclusion

1. Verne, Jules. 1875. *The Mysterious Island*. Authorized Edition. New York: Scribner, Armstrong, & Co.

2. Federal Open Market Committee. 2022. "Press Conference Following the Federal Open Market Committee Meeting," December 14, 2022. https://www.federalreserve.gov/mediacenter/files/FOMCpresconf20221214.pdf.

3. BlackRock Investment Institute. 2022. "Demographics Limit U.S. Growth Outlook." October 2022. https://www.blackrock.com/corporate/insights/blackrock-investment-institute/economic-insights/2022/10/demographics-limit-us-growth.

4. US Census Bureau. 2019. "By 2030, All Baby Boomers Will Be Age 65 or Older." December 17, 2019. https://www.census.gov/library/stories/2019/12/by-2030-all-baby-boomers-will-be-age-65-or-older.html.

5. Collinson, Catherine, Patti Rowey, and Heidi Cho. 2021. "Living in the COVID-19 Pandemic: The Health, Finances, and Retirement Prospects of Four Generations." Transamerica Center for Retirement Studies, August 2021. https://transamericacenter.org/docs/default-source/retirement-survey-of-workers/tcrs2021_sr_four-generations-living-in-a-pandemic.pdf.

6. Global Workplace Analytics. n.d. https://globalworkplaceanalytics.com/how-many-people-could-work-from-home.

Chapter 4: The Hitchhiker's Guide to Cognitive Diversity

1. Rao, Anand S., and Gerard Verweij. 2017. "Sizing the Prize: What's the Real Value of AI for Your Business and How Can You Capitalise?" PwC. https://pwc.to/349x8w5.
2. Dunne, Maureen N. 2008. "Visual and Verbal Thinking." PhD. diss., University of Oxford, 2008, p.46.
3. Dunne, Maureen N. 2008. "Visual and Verbal Thinking." PhD. diss., University of Oxford, 2008, p.46.
4. Fleming, Jory. 2021. *How to Be Human: An Autistic Man's Guide to Life*. New York: Simon & Schuster.
5. Jones, Alexander Raymond. 2023. "Ptolemy." Encyclopedia Britannica. https://www.britannica.com/biography/Ptolemy.

Chapter 5: From Why to How

1. Peterson, Joel. 2008. "Company culture." Stanford University Graduate School of Business Lecture.

Chapter 6: Thinking Outside Check-the-Box

1. Emerson, Ralph Waldo. 1917. "Social Aims," Letters and Social Aims (vol. 8 of The Complete Works of Ralph Waldo Emerson), p. 96
2. "Comparing Steel and Iron." Wasatch Steel, 2023. https://www.wasatch steel.com/comparing-steel-iron/#:~:text=Element%20vs%20 Alloy&text=In%20general%2C%20due%20to%20its,better%20 tension%20and%20compression%20properties.
3. Page, S.E., and D.A. Thomas. 2016. "Diversity Trumps Expertise: Why Teams with Members from Different Backgrounds Make Better Decisions." *Harvard Business Review* 94 no. 1: 60–67. https://doi .org/10.1007/ s11784-016-9264-4.

4. Dixon-Fyle, Sundiatu, Kevin Dolan, Dame Vivian Hunt, and Sara Prince. 2020. "Diversity Wins: How Inclusion Matters." McKinsey & Company. May 19, 2020. https://www.mckinsey.com/featured-insights/diversity-and-inclusion/diversity-wins-how-inclusion-matters/.

5. Payne, Adam, and Dana Kaminstein. 2021. "How a Values-Based Approach Advances DEI." *MIT Sloan Management Review*, February 24, 2021.https://sloanreview.mit.edu/article/how-a-values-based-approach-advances-dei/.

6. The Valuable 500. 2022. "The Valuable Truth Report 2022." https://www.thevaluable500.com/wp-content/uploads/2022/05/The-Valuable-Truth-2022.pdf.

7. Dixon-Fyle, Sundiatu, Kevin Dolan, Dame Vivian Hunt, and Sara Prince. 2020. "Diversity Wins: How Inclusion Matters." McKinsey & Company. May 19, 2020. https://www.mckinsey.com/featured-insights/diversity-and-inclusion/diversity-wins-how-inclusion-matters/.

Chapter 7: Neurodiversification Versus Culture Fit

1. Grant, Adam. 2017. "Hire for Culture Fit or ADD?," Stanford eCorner presentation, 2017.

2. West, Thomas G. 2020. *In the Mind's Eye: Visual Thinkers, Gifted People with Dyslexia and Other Learning Difficulties, Computer Images and the Ironies of Creativity*. Amherst, NY: Prometheus Books.

3. Webb, Stephen. 2002. *If the Universe Is Teeming with Aliens . . . WHERE IS EVERYBODY?: Seventy-Five Solutions to the Fermi Paradox and the Problem of Extraterrestrial Life*. 2nd ed. Cham, Switzerland: Springer International.

4. Weinbaum, Cortney. 2023. "In National Security, Autism Is in the Closet. Here's Why." *Military Times*, July 17, 2023, https://www.militarytimes.com/opinion/2023/07/17/in-national-security-autism-is-in-the-closet-heres-why/.

Chapter 8: Tricks Minds Play

1. Adams, Douglas. 1992. *Mostly Harmless*. Chapter 9. Harmony Books.

2. Haselton, Martie G., Daniel Nettle, and Paul W. Andrews. 2015. "The Evolution of Cognitive Bias." *In The Handbook of Evolutionary Psychology*, ed. David M. Buss. https://doi.org/10.1002/9780470939376.ch25.

3. Lord, C.G., L. Ross, and M.R. Lepper. 1979. "Biased Assimilation and Attitude Polarization: The Effects of Prior Theories on Subsequently Considered Evidence." *Journal of Personality and Social Psychology* 37, no. 11 (1979): 2098 -2109. https://doi.org/10.1037/0022-3514.37.11.2098.

4. Fyock J, Stangor C. 1994. The role of memory biases in stereotype maintenance. *Br J Soc Psychol*. 1994 Sep;33 (Pt 3):331–43. doi: 10.1111/j.2044-8309.1994.tbnotes029.x. PMID: 7953221.

5. Tversky and Kahneman. 1974. "Judgment under Uncertainty: Heuristics and Biases: Biases in judgments reveal some heuristics of thinking under uncertainty. *Science*, Vol 185, Issue 4157, pp. 1124–1131. https://www.science.org/doi/10.1126/science.185.4157.1124

6. Frye, William B. 2005. "A Qualitative Analysis of Sensationalism in Media." Master's thesis, West Virginia University.

7. Ross, Lee 1977. "The Intuitive Psychologist and His Shortcomings: Distortions in the Attribution Process". In Berkowitz, Leonard (ed.). *Advances in Experimental Social Psychology*. Vol. 10. pp. 173–220. New York: Academic Press. doi:10.1016/S0065-2601(08)60357-3. ISBN 9780120152100.

8. Thorndike, E.L. 1920. "A constant error in psychological ratings". *Journal of Applied Psychology*. 4 (1): 25–29. doi:10.1037/h0071663.

9. Nisbett, R.E., and T.D. Wilson. 1977. "The Halo Effect: Evidence for Unconscious Alteration of Judgments." *Journal of Personality and Social Psychology* 35, no. 4: 250–256.

10. Fu F, C.E. Tarnita, N.A. Christakis, L. Wang, D.G. Rand, and M.A. Nowak. 2012. "Evolution of In-Group Favoritism." *Scientific Reports* 2, no. 460 (2012). https://doi.org/10.1038/srep00460.

11. Tversky and Kahneman. 1974. "Judgment under Uncertainty: Heuristics and Biases: Biases in judgments reveal some heuristics of thinking under uncertainty." *Science*, Vol 185, Issue 4157, pp. 1124–1131. https://www.science.org/doi/10.1126/science.185.4157.1124.

Chapter 9: Building a Sturdy Foundation

1. Edmondson, Amy C. 2018. *The Fearless Organization*. New York, NY: John Wiley & Sons.
2. Humphrey, N., & Hebron, J. 2015. "Bullying of children and adolescents with autism spectrum conditions: a state of the field review." *International Journal of Inclusive Education*, 19(8), 845–862. https://doi.org/10.1080/13603116.2014.981602
3. Schwedel, Andrew, James Root, James Allen, John Hazan, Eric Almquist, Thomas Devlin, and Karen Harris. 2022. "The Working Future: More Human, Not Less." https://www.bain.com/contentassets/d620202718c146359acb05c02d9060db/bain-report_the-working-future.pdf.
4. Duhigg, Charles. 2016. "What Google Learned from Its Quest to Build the Perfect Team." *New York Times*, February 28, 2016. https://www.nytimes.com/2016/02/28/magazine/what-google-learned-from-its-quest-to-build-the-perfect-team.html.
5. Clark, Timothy R. 2020. *The Four Stages of Psychological Safety: Defining the Path to Inclusion and Innovation*. San Francisco: Berrett-Koehler.

Chapter 10: Recruiting for Cognitive Diversity

1. Grant, Adam. 2023. *Think Again: The Power of Knowing What You Don't Know*. New York, NY: Penguin.
2. Willis, C, Powell-Rudy, T., Kelsie, C., and Prasad, J. 2021. "Examining the Use of Game-Based Assessments for Hiring Autistic Job Seekers," *Journal of Intelligence*, Vol 9, Issue 4.
3. Alemany and Vermeulen. 2023. "Disability as a Source of Competitive Advantage." *Harvard Business Review*.

Chapter 11: Accommodating Humans

1. Brown, Brené. 2022. *The Gifts of Imperfection: Let Go of Who You Think You're Supposed to Be and Embrace Who You Are.* Center City, PA: Hazelden Information & Educational Services.

2. Seven principles of universal design: 2022 Report, The Center for Universal Design, NC State University. https://design.ncsu.edu/wp-content/uploads/2022/11/principles-of-universal-design.pdf

3. Machell, Millicent. 2023. "Employees with Invisible Disabilities Left to Source Workplace Support Alone." *HR Magazine*, May 9, 2023. https://www.hrmagazine.co.uk/content/news/employees-with-invisible-disabilities-left-to-source-workplace-support-alone/.

4. Deloitte Insights. 2022. "A Rising Tide Lifts All Boats: Creating a Better Work Environment for All by Embracing Neurodiversity." Deloitte Center for Integrated Research, 2022. https://www2.deloitte.com/content/dam/insights/articles/us164891_cir-career-paths-and-critical-success-factors-for-neurodivergent-workforce/DI_CIR_Career-paths-and-critical-success-factors-for-neurodivergent-workforce.pdf.

Chapter 12: Workplace Flexibility

1. Various replies to question posted by pwwrecruiting, "Work from Home vs in Office," Reddit, r/Jobs, May 4, 2022, www.reddit.com/r/jobs/comments/ui5t95/work_from_home_vs_in_office/

2. Global Workplace Analytics. n.d. https://globalworkplaceanalytics.com/how-many-people-could-work-from-home.

3. Glaser, L. 2020. "Zoom, Microsoft Teams, and Slack Have Exploded Due to the COVID-19 Pandemic. Can They Hold onto This Frowth?" GLG Insights.https://glginsights.com/articles/zoom-microsoft-teams-and-slack-have-exploded-due-to-the-covid-19-pandemic-can-they-hold-onto-this-growth/

4. McKinsey Global Institute Report. 2017. Jobs lost, jobs gained: Workforce transitions in a time of automation. mgi-jobs-lost-jobs-gained-executive-summary-december-6-2017.pdf (mckinsey.com)

5. Schiffer, Zoë. 2021. "Apple Employees Push Back Against Returning to the Office in Internal Letter." *The Verge*, June 4, 2021. https://www.thev erge.com/2021/6/4/22491629/apple-employees-push-back-return-office-internal-letter-tim-cook.

6. Knight, Rebecca. 2023. "Swipe Your Badge or Get Fired? Employers and Workers Face a Reckoning over Returning to the Office," Insider, June 8, 2023. https://www.businessinsider.com/fight-return-to-office-mandates-remote-work-amazon-apple-2023-3.

7. ADP Research Institute. 2022. "People at Work 2022: A Global Work-force View." Retrieved May 21, 2023. https://www.adpri.org/research/people-at-work-2022-a-global-workforce-view/.

8. GlobalData. 2022. "Automotive Autonomous Vehicles Market and Trend Analysis by Technology, Key Companies and Forecast, 2021–2036." February 14, 2022.

Chapter 13: Universal Empathy Network

1. Fodor, Jerry A. 1983. *The Modularity of Mind: An Essay on Faculty Psychology*. Cambridge, MA: MIT Press.

2. Premack, David, and Guy Woodruff. 1978. "Does the Chimpanzee Have a Theory of Mind?" *Behavioral and Brain Sciences* 1, no. 4 (1978): 515–526. https://doi.org/10.1017/S0140525X00076512.

3. Baron-Cohen, S., A. M. Leslie, & U. Frith. 1985. "Does the autistic child have a 'theory of mind'?" *Cognition*, 21(1), 37–46. https://doi.org/10.1016/0010-0277(85)90022-8.

4. Milton, Damian. 2012. "On the Ontological Status of Autism: The 'Double Empathy Problem.'" *Disability and Society* 27, no. 6 (2022):883–687. Https://doi.org/10.1080/09687599.2012.710008.

5. Sheppard, E., Pillai, D., Wong, G.TL. et al. 2016. "How Easy Is It to Read the Minds of People with Autism Spectrum Disorder?". *J Autism Dev Disord* 46: 1247–1254. https://doi.org/10.1007/s10803-015-2662–8.

6. Feld, Steven. 1982. *Sound and Sentiment: Birds, Weeping, Poetics, and Song in Kaluli Expression*. University of Pennsylvania Press, Philadelphia.

7. Nagel, Thomas. 1974. "What Is It Like to Be a Bat?" *Philosophical Review* 83 (Oct): 435–450.

Conclusion

1. Hemingway, Ernest. 1926. *The Sun Also Rises*. 135. New York: Scribner.
2. Dunne, Maureen. 2023. "Building the Neurodiversity Talent Pipeline for the Future of Work." *MIT Sloan Management Review*. November 28, 2023. https://sloanreview.mit.edu/article/building-the-neurodiversity-talent-pipeline-for-the-future-of-work/.
3. Weinbaum, Cortney. 2023. "In National Security, Autism Is in the Closet. Here's why." *Military Times*, July 17, 2023, https://www.militarytimes.com/opinion/2023/07/17/in-national-security-autism-is-in-the-closet-heres-why/.

Bibliography

Abbott, Edwin A. 1884. *Flatland: A Romance of Many Dimensions*. London: Seeley & Co.

Adams, Douglas. 1992. *Mostly Harmless*. Chapter 9. Harmony Books.

Abi Tyas Tunggal, "What Is the Cost of a Data Breach in 2023?" UpGuard, updated August 7, 2023. https://www.upguard.com/blog/cost-of-data-breach.

ADP Research Institute. 2022. "People at Work 2022: A Global Workforce View." Retrieved May 21, 2023. https://www.adpri.org/research/people-at-work-2022-a-global-workforce-view/.

Alemany and Vermeulen. 2023. "Disability as a Source of Competitive Advantage." *Harvard Business Review*.

Alvarez, Pablo. 2022. "What Does the Global Decline of the Fertility Rate Look Like?" World Economic Forum, June 17, 2022. https://www.weforum.org/agenda/2022/06/global-decline-of-fertility-rates-visualised/.

Asch, Solomon E. 1956. "Studies of Group Influence: I. An Experimental Analysis of Conformity." *Psychological Monographs: General and Applied*, vol. 75, no. 416 (1956): 1–70.

Austin, Robert D., and Gary P. Pisano. 2017. "Neurodiversity as a Competitive Advantage." *Harvard Business Review* (May–June 2017). https://hbr.org/2017/05/neurodiversity-as-a-competitive-advantage.

Ball, Philip. 2016. "The Tyranny of Simple Explanations." *The Atlantic*, August 11, 2016. https://www.theatlantic.com/science/archive/2016/08/occams-razor/495332/.

Baron-Cohen, S., A. M. Leslie, & U. Frith. 1985. "Does the autistic child have a 'theory of mind'?" *Cognition*, 21(1), 37–46. https://doi.org/10.1016/0010-0277(85)90022-8

Best, C., Arora, S., Porter, F. et al. "The Relationship Between Subthreshold Autistic Traits, Ambiguous Figure Perception and Divergent Thinking." . *J Autism Dev Disord* 45, 4064–4073(2015). https://doi.org/10.1007/s10803-015-2518-2

BlackRock Investment Institute. 2022. "Demographics Limit U.S. Growth Outlook." October 2022. https://www.blackrock.com/corporate/insights/blackrock-investment-institute/economic-insights/2022/10/demographics-limit-us-growth.

Boston Consulting Group. 2018. "How Diverse Leadership Teams Boost Innovation". https://www.bcg.com/publications/2018/how-diverse-leadership-teams-boost-innovation

Bower, Marvin. 1966. *The Will to Manage: Corporate Success Through Programmed Management*. New York: McGraw-Hill.

Brown, Brené. 2022. *The Gifts of Imperfection: Let Go of Who You Think You're Supposed to Be and Embrace Who You Are*. Center City, PA: Hazelden Information & Educational Services.

Cameron, Kim S., and Jane E. Dutton. 2003. "The Power of Values: How to Create a Culture That Drives Performance." *Harvard Business Review*. hbr.org/2003/03/the-power-of-values.

Cancer, Alice, Serena Manzoli, and Alessandro Antonietti. 2016. "The Alleged Link Between Creativity and Dyslexia: Identifying the Specific Process in Which Dyslexic Students Excel." *Cogent Psychology* 3 no. 1 (2016). Article 1190309. https://doi.org/10.1080/23311908.2016.1190309.

CDC. n.d. "Data & Statistics on Autism Spectrum Disorder." Last reviewed April 4, 2023. https://www.cdc.gov/ncbddd/autism/data.html.

The Center for Neurodiversity & Employment Innovation, Werth Institute for Entrepreneurship and Innovation, University of Connecticut. (n.d.). https://entrepreneurship.uconn.edu/neurodiversitycenter-2/.

Clark, Timothy R. 2020. *The Four Stages of Psychological Safety: Defining the Path to Inclusion and Innovation*. San Francisco: Berrett-Koehler.

Collinson, Catherine, Patti Rowey, and Heidi Cho. 2021. "Living in the COVID-19 Pandemic: The Health, Finances, and Retirement Prospects of Four Generations." Transamerica Center for Retirement Studies, August 2021.

https://transamericacenter.org/docs/default-source/retirement-survey-of-workers/tcrs2021_sr_four-generations-living-in-a-pandemic.pdf.

Deloitte Insights. 2022. "A Rising Tide Lifts All Boats: Creating a Better Work Environment for All by Embracing Neurodiversity." Deloitte Center for Integrated Research, 2022. https://www2.deloitte.com/content/dam/insights/articles/us164891_cir-career-paths-and-critical-success-factors-for-neurodivergent-workforce/DI_CIR_Career-paths-and-critical-success-factors-for-neurodivergent-workforce.pdf.

Dixon-Fyle, Sundiatu, Kevin Dolan, Dame Vivian Hunt, and Sara Prince. 2020. "Diversity Wins: How Inclusion Matters." McKinsey & Company. May 19, 2020. https://www.mckinsey.com/featured-insights/diversity-and-inclusion/diversity-wins-how-inclusion-matters/.

Dong, Shihao, Tao Lin, James C. Nieh, and Ken Tan. 2023. "Social Signal Learning of the Waggle Dance in Honey Bees." *Science* 379, no. 6636 (2023): 1015–1018.

Duhigg, Charles. 2016. "What Google Learned from Its Quest to Build the Perfect Team." *New York Times*, February 28, 2016. https://www.nytimes.com/2016/02/28/magazine/what-google-learned-from-its-quest-to-build-the-perfect-team.html.

Dunne, Maureen, and Cathy Schwallie Farmer. 2020. "Neurodiversity: An Organizational Asset." *American Diversity Report*, October 18, 2020. https://americandiversityreport.com/neurodiversity-an-organizational-asset-by-maureen-dunne-cathy-schwallie-farmer/.

Dunne, Maureen. 2023. "Building the Neurodiversity Talent Pipeline for the Future of Work." *MIT Sloan Management Review*. November 28, 2023. https://sloanreview.mit.edu/article/building-the-neurodiversity-talent-pipeline-for-the-future-of-work/.

Dunne, Maureen. 2023. "Embracing neurodiversity in the AI-powered workplace: A new paradigm for success," Maddyness. https://www.maddyness.com/uk/2023/10/06/embracing-neurodiversity-in-the-ai-powered-workplace-a-new-paradigm-for-success/.

Dunne, Maureen N. 2022. "What Workplace Best Suits Neurodiverse Employees?" People *Management Magazine*. https://www.peoplemanagement.co.uk/article/1804949/workplace-model-best-suits-neurodiverse-employees.

Dunne, Maureen N. 2008. "Visual and Verbal Thinking." PhD. diss., University of Oxford.

Edmondson, Amy C. 2018. The Fearless Organization. New York, NY: John Wiley & Sons.

Emerson, Ralph Waldo. 1917. "Social Aims," Letters and Social Aims (vol. 8 of The Complete Works of Ralph Waldo Emerson), p. 96.

Ernst & Young. 2018. "The value of dyslexia."

Farmer, G.D., S. Baron-Cohen, and W.J. Skylark. 2017. "People with Autism Spectrum Conditions Make More Consistent Decisions." *Psychological Science* 28, no. 8: 1067–1076. https://doi.org/10.1177/0956797617694867.

Federal Open Market Committee. 2022. "Press Conference Following the Federal Open Market Committee Meeting," December 14, 2022. https://www.federalreserve.gov/mediacenter/files/FOMCpresconf20221214.pdf.

Feld, Steven. 1982. *Sound and Sentiment: Birds, Weeping, Poetics, and Song in Kaluli Expression*. University of Pennsylvania Press, Philadelphia.

Fleming, Jory. 2021. *How to Be Human: An Autistic Man's Guide to Life*. New York: Simon & Schuster.

Fodor, Jerry A. 1983. *The Modularity of Mind: An Essay on Faculty Psychology*. Cambridge, MA: MIT Press.

Friedman, Thomas L., and Anna J. Nathan. 1985. *Fiasco: The American Military Adventure in Cuba, 1961*. New York: Simon & Schuster.

Frye, William B. 2005. "A Qualitative Analysis of Sensationalism in Media." Master's thesis, West Virginia University.

Fu F, C.E. Tarnita, N.A. Christakis, L. Wang, D.G. Rand, and M.A. Nowak. 2012. "Evolution of In-Group Favoritism." *Scientific Reports* 2, no. 460 (2012). https://doi.org/10.1038/srep00460.

Fyock J, Stangor C. 1994. The role of memory biases in stereotype maintenance. Br J Soc Psychol. 1994 Sep;33 (Pt 3):331–43. doi: 10.1111/j.2044-8309.1994.tbnotes029.x. PMID: 7953221.

Galileo Galilei. 1632. *Dialogue Concerning the Two Chief World Systems*.

Galinsky, A.D., and G.B. Moskowitz. 2000. "The Nature of In-group Bias: Enhanced Interpersonal Empathy in Perceived Groups." *Journal of Personality and Social Psychology* 78, no. 6: 1019–1031.

Glaser, L. 2020. "Zoom, Microsoft Teams, and Slack Have Exploded Due to the COVID-19 Pandemic. Can They Hold onto This Frowth?" GLG Insights. https://glginsights.com/articles/zoom-microsoft-teams-and-slack-have-exploded-due-to-the-covid-19-pandemic-can-they-hold-onto-this-growth/

GlobalData. 2022. "Automotive Autonomous Vehicles Market and Trend Analysis by Technology, Key Companies and Forecast, 2021–2036." February 14, 2022.

Global Workplace Analytics. n.d. https://globalworkplaceanalytics.com/how-many-people-could-work-from-home.

Grandin, Temple. 2006. *Thinking in Pictures: And Other Reports From My Life With Autism*. New York, Vintage Books.

Grant, Adam. 2023. *Think Again: The Power of Knowing What You Don't Know*. New York, NY: Penguin.

Grant, Adam. 2017. "Hire for Culture Fit or ADD?," Stanford eCorner presentation, 2017.

Griffiths, A.J., Giannantonio, C.M., Hurley-Hanson, A.E., & Cardinal, D. 2016. Autism in the Workplace: Assessing the transition needs of young adults with Autism Spectrum Disorder. *Journal of Business and Management,* 22(1), 5-22.

Haselton, Martie G., Daniel Nettle, and Paul W. Andrews. 2015. "The Evolution of Cognitive Bias." In *The Handbook of Evolutionary Psychology*, ed. David M. Buss (Hoboken, NJ: Wiley, 2015). https://doi.org/10.1002/9780470939376.ch25.

Hemingway, Ernest. 1926. *The Sun Also Rises*. 135. New York: Scribner.

Hoque, Faisal. 2023. *Reinvent: Navigating Business Transformation in a Hyperdigital Era*. New York: Fast Company Press.

Humphrey, Neil, and Judith Hebron. 2014. "Bullying of Children and Adolescents with Autism Spectrum Conditions: A 'State of the Field' Review." *International Journal of Inclusive Education* 19, no. 8 (2014): 845–862. https://doi.org/10.1080/13603116.2014.981602.

Institute of Leadership & Management. n.d. "Half of All Leaders and Managers Would Not Employ a Neurodivergent Person." Retrieved March 8, 2023. https://www.institutelm.com/resourceLibrary/half-of-all-leaders-and-managers-would-not-employ-a-neurodivergent-person.html.

Izuma, K, Matsumoto K, Camerer CF, Adolphs, R. 2011. "Insensitivity to social reputation in autism." *Proc Natl Acad Sci U S A.* (2011) Oct 18; 108(42):17302-7.doi: 10.1073/pnas.1107038108. Epub 2011 Oct 10.PMID: 21987799; PMCID: PMC3198313.

Jones, Alexander Raymond. 2023. "Ptolemy." Encyclopedia Britannica. https://www.britannica.com/biography/Ptolemy.

Kenton, W. n.d. "What Is Groupthink? Definition, Characteristics, and Causes," Investopedia, updated December 5, 2022. https://www.investopedia.com/terms/g/groupthink.asp.

Knight, Rebecca. 2023. "Swipe Your Badge or Get Fired? Employers and Workers Face a Reckoning over Returning to the Office," Insider, June 8, 2023. https://www.businessinsider.com/fight-return-to-office-mandates-remote-work-amazon-apple-2023-3.

Kuzmanovic B, Rigoux L, Vogeley K. 2019. "Brief Report: Reduced Optimism Bias in Self-Referential Belief Updating in High-Functioning Autism." *J Autism Dev Disord.* Jul;49(7):2990–2998. doi: 10.1007/s10803-016-2940-0.PMID: 27757736.

Ledgin, Norm. 2000. *Diagnosing Jefferson: Evidence of a Condition That Guided His Beliefs, Behavior, and Personal Associations.* Arlington, TX: Future Horizons.

Lord, C. G., Ross, L., and Lepper, M. R. 1979. "Biased Assimilation and Attitude Polarization: The Effects of Prior Theories on Subsequently Considered Evidence." *Journal of Personality and Social Psychology* 37, no. 11 (1979): 2098–2109. https://doi.org/10.1037/0022-3514.37.11.2098.

Lorenzo, Rocío, Nicole Voigt, Miki Tsusaka, MattKrentz, and Katie Abouzahr. 2018."How Diverse Leadership Teams Boost Innovation," BCG, January 23, 2018. https://www.bcg.com/publications/2018/how-diverse-leadership-teams-boost-innovation.

Lunke, K. and Meier, B. 2018. "Creativity and involvement in art in different types of synaesthesia." *British Journal of Psychology*, Vol 110, Issue 4, pp. 727–744. https://bpspsychub.onlinelibrary.wiley.com/doi/full/10.1111/bjop.12363.

Machell, Millicent. 2023. "Employees with Invisible Disabilities Left to Source Workplace Support Alone." *HR Magazine*, May 9, 2023. https://www

.hrmagazine.co.uk/content/news/employees-with-invisible-disabilities-left-to-source-workplace-support-alone/.

Majeed NM, Hartanto A, Tan JJX. "Developmental dyslexia and creativity: A meta-analysis." *Dyslexia*. 2021 May;27(2):187-203. doi: 10.1002/dys.1677. Epub 2021 Feb 14. PMID: 33586314.

Milton, Damian. 2012. "On the Ontological Status of Autism: The 'Double Empathy Problem.'" *Disability and Society* 27, no. 6 (2022): 883–687. https://doi.org/10.1080/09687599.2012.710008.

Milton, Damian, Emine Gurbuz, and Beatriz López. 2022. "The 'Double Empathy Problem': Ten Years On." *Autism* 26, no. 8 (2022): 1901–1903. https://doi.org/10.1177/13623613221129123.

Mitchell, Peter, Elizabeth Sheppard, and Sarah Cassidy, 2021. "Autism and the Double Empathy Problem: Implications for Development and Mental Health," *British Journal of Developmental Psychology* 39, no. 1 (January 4, 2021): 1–18. https://doi.org/10.1111/bjdp.12350.

Nagel, Thomas. 1974. "What Is It Like to Be a Bat?" *Philosophical Review* 83 (Oct): 435–450.

Nisbett, R.E., and T.D. Wilson. 1977. "The Halo Effect: Evidence for Unconscious Alteration of Judgments." *Journal of Personality and Social Psychology* 35, no. 4: 250–256.

Page, S.E., and D.A. Thomas. 2016. "Diversity Trumps Expertise: Why Teams with Members from Different Backgrounds Make Better Decisions." *Harvard Business Review* 94, no. 1, 60–67. https://doi.org/10.1007/s11784-016-9264-4.

Payne, Adam, and Dana Kaminstein. 2021. "How a Values-Based Approach Advances DEI." *MIT Sloan Management Review*, February 24, 2021. https://sloanreview.mit.edu/article/how-a-values-based-approach-advances-dei/.

Peterson, Joel. 2008. "Company culture." Stanford University Graduate School of Business Lecture.

Premack, David, and Guy Woodruff. 1978. "Does the Chimpanzee Have a Theory of Mind?" *Behavioral and Brain Sciences* 1, no. 4 (1978): 515–526. https://doi.org/10.1017/S0140525X00076512.

Rao, Anand S., and Gerard Verweij. 2017. "Sizing the Prize: What's the Real Value of AI for Your Business and How Can You Capitalise?" PwC. https://pwc.to/349x8w5.

Ross, Lee (1977). "The Intuitive Psychologist and His Shortcomings: Distortions in the Attribution Process". In Berkowitz, Leonard (ed.). *Advances in Experimental Social Psychology*. Vol. 10. pp. 173–220. doi:10.1016/S0065-2601(08)60357-3. ISBN 9780120152100.

Schiffer, Zoë. 2021. "Apple Employees Push Back against Returning to the Office in Internal Letter." *The Verge*, June 4, 2021. https://www.theverge.com/2021/6/4/22491629/apple-employees-push-back-return-office-internal-letter-tim-cook.

Schwedel, Andrew, James Root, James Allen, John Hazan, Eric Almquist, Thomas Devlin, and Karen Harris. 2022. "The Working Future: More Human, Not Less." https://www.bain.com/contentassets/d620202718c146359acb05c02d9060db/bain-report_the-working-future.pdf.

Seven principles of universal design: 2022 Report, The Center for Universal Design, NC State University. https://design.ncsu.edu/wp-content/uploads/2022/11/principles-of-universal-design.pdf.

Shah, A., and U. Frith. 1983. "An Islet of Ability in Autistic Children: A Research Note." *Journal of Child Psychology and Psychiatry* 24 (1983): 613–620. https://doi.org/10.1111/j.1469-7610.1983.tb00137.x.

Shah, A., and U. Frith. 1993. "Why Do Autistic Individuals Show Superior Performance on the Block Design Task?" *Journal of Child Psychology and Psychiatry* 34, no.8 (Nov. 1993): 1351–1364. https://doi.org/10.1111/j.1469-7610.1993.tb02095.x.

Sheppard, E., D., Pillai, G.TL., Wong, et al. 2016. "How Easy Is It to Read the Minds of People with Autism Spectrum Disorder?". *J Autism Dev Disord* 46: 1247–1254. https://doi.org/10.1007/s10803-015-2662-8

Sunstein, Cass R., and Reid Hastie. 2014. *Wiser: Getting Beyond Groupthink to Make Groups Smarter*. Boston: Harvard Business Review Press.

Sutherland, Rory. 2020. *Alchemy: The Dark Art and Curious Science of Creating Magic in Brands, Business, and Life*. New York: Simon & Schuster.

Szechy, Kathryn A. and Turk, Pamela D. and O'Donnell, Lisa A. 2023. "Autism and Employment Challenges: The Double Empathy Problem and Perceptions of an Autistic Employee in the Workplace." *Autism in Adulthood*, https://doi.org/10.1089/aut.2023.0046.

Tallo July Report, 2021. "Workplace neurodiversity is important to Gen Zers." https://www.hrdive.com/news/gen-z-hiring-recruiting-neurodiversity/604453/.

Taylor, Helen, Bryce Fernandes, and Sarah Wraight. 2022. "The Evolution of Complementary Cognition: Humans Cooperatively Adapt and Evolve through a System of Collective Cognitive Search." *Cambridge Archaeological Journal* 32, no. 1 (2022): 61–77.

Thorndike, E.L. (1920). "A constant error in psychological ratings". *Journal of Applied Psychology*. 4 (1): 25–29. doi:10.1037/h0071663.

Taylor, Chloe. 2019. Billionaire Richard Branson: Dyslexia helped me to become successful. https://www.cnbc.com/amp/2019/10/07/billionaire-richard-branson-dyslexia-helped-me-to-become-successful.html.

Trading Economics. n.d. "United States Unemployment Rate." June 2023 data, 1948–2022 historical (citing the US Bureau of Labor Statistics). Accessed July 15, 2023. https://tradingeconomics.com/united-states/unemployment-rate.

Tversky and Kahneman. 1974. "Judgment under Uncertainty: Heuristics and Biases: Biases in judgments reveal some heuristics of thinking under uncertainty. Science, Vol 185, Issue 4157, pp. 1124–1131. https://www.science.org/doi/10.1126/science.185.4157.1124.

U.S. Bureau of Labor Statistics. Employment Situation Summary. U.S. Bureau of Labor Statistics website. December 8, 2023. https://www.bls.gov/news.release/empsit.nr0.htm.

US Census Bureau. 2019. "By 2030, All Baby Boomers Will Be Age 65 or Older." December 17, 2019. https://www.census.gov/library/stories/2019/12/by-2030-all-baby-boomers-will-be-age-65-or-older.html.

The Valuable 500. 2022. "The Valuable Truth Report 2022." https://www.thevaluable500.com/wp-content/uploads/2022/05/The-Valuable-Truth-2022.pdf.

Vaughan, Diane. 1997. *The Challenger Launch Decision: Risky Technology, Culture, and Deviance at NASA*. University of Chicago Press.

Waldmeir, Patti. 2020. "Overlooked workers gain appeal in challenging times". Financial Times. https://www.ft.com/content/ea9ca374-6780-11ea-800d-da70cff6e4d3

Wasatch Steel, 2023. "Comparing Steel and Iron." https://www.wasatch-steel.com/comparing-steel-iron/#:~:text=Element%20vs%20Alloy&text=In%20general%2C%20due%20to%20its,better%20tension%20and%20compression%20properties.

Webb, Stephen. 2002. *If the Universe Is Teeming with Aliens . . . WHERE IS EVERYBODY?: Seventy-Five Solutions to the Fermi Paradox and the Problem of Extraterrestrial Life*. 2nd ed. Cham, Switzerland: Springer International.

Weinbaum, Cortney. 2023. "In National Security, Autism Is in the Closet. Here's Why." *Military Times*, July 17, 2023, https://www.militarytimes.com/opinion/2023/07/17/in-national-security-autism-is-in-the-closet-heres-why/.

Weissman, Sara. 2023. "Recognizing an 'Untapped Resource.'" *Inside Higher Ed*, June 6, 2023. https://www.insidehighered.com/news/students/diversity/2023/06/06/illinois-lawmakers-urge-neurodiversity-inclusion-higher-ed.

West, Thomas G. 2020. *In the Mind's Eye: Visual Thinkers, Gifted People with Dyslexia and Other Learning Difficulties, Computer Images and the Ironies of Creativity*. Amherst, NY: Prometheus Books.

White, H.A. 2018. "Thinking "Outside the Box": Unconstrained Creative Generation in Adults with Attention Deficit Hyperactivity Disorder". *The Journal of Creative Behavior*. 54. 10.1002/jocb.382.

White H.A., and P. Shah. 2016. "Scope of Semantic Activation and Innovative Thinking in College Students with ADHD." *Creativity Research Journal* 28 (2016): 275–282. https://doi.org/10.1080/10400419.2016.1195655.

Whiting, Kate. 2022. "How to Create a Workplace That Supports Neurodiversity." World Economic Forum. April 1, 2022. https://www.weforum.org/agenda/2022/04/neurodiversity-work-inclusion-autism/

Willis, C, Powell-Rudy, T., Kelsie, C., and Prasad, J. 2021. Examining the Use of Game-Based Assessments for Hiring Autistic Job Seekers, *Journal of Intelligence*, Vol 9, Issue 4.

World Economic Forum. 2022. "Global Decline of Fertility Rates Visualized." June 10, 2022, Retrieved April 22, 2023. https://www.weforum.org/agenda/2022/06/global-decline-of-fertility-rates-visualised/.

Yafai, A.F., Verrier, D. and Reidt, L. 2014. "Social conformity and autism spectrum disorder: a child-friendly take on a classic study." *Autism*, 18 (8). http://shura.shu.ac.uk/7450/3/Verrier_Autism_and_Conformity.pdf

Zen Business Research Report, 2023. "New ZenBusiness Research Finds Class of 2023 Sees Neurodiversity as an Asset in Leadership & is Primed to be the Most Entrepreneurial." https://www.businesswire.com/news/home/20230614082058/en/New-ZenBusiness-Research-Finds-Class-of-2023-Sees-Neurodiversity-as-an-Asset-in-Leadership-is-Primed-to-be-the-Most-Entrepreneurial.

Index

316

Index

318

Index

319

Index

320

Index

323

Index

324

Index